Trees in Indian Art
Mythology and Folklore

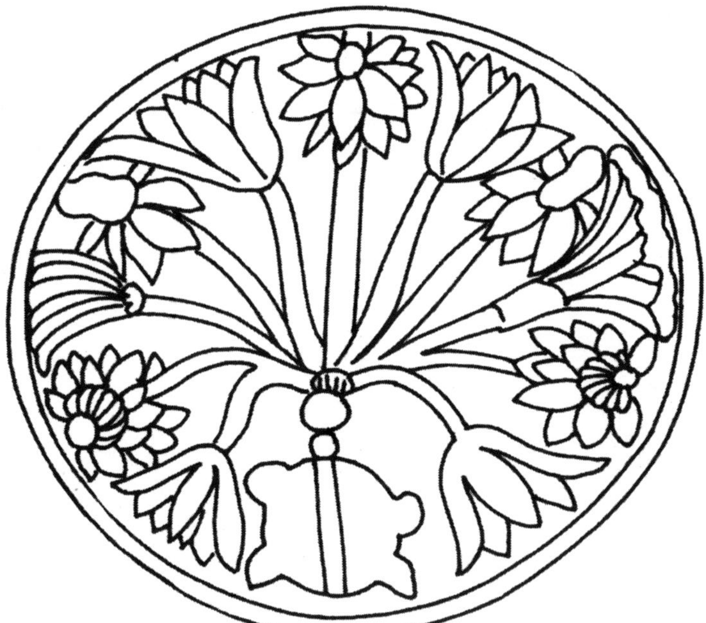

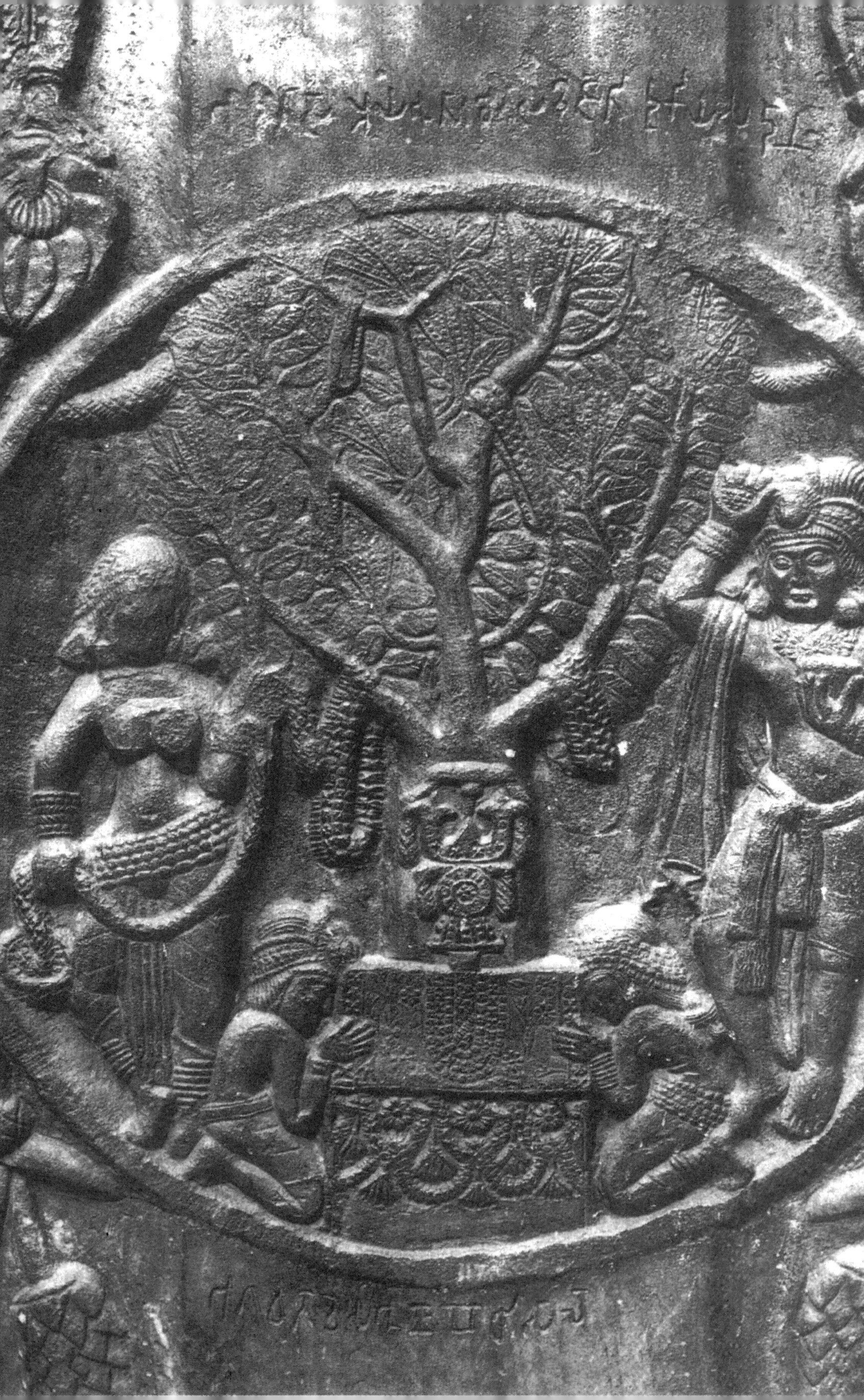

Trees in Indian Art Mythology and Folklore

Bansi Lal Malla

Aryan Books International
New Delhi

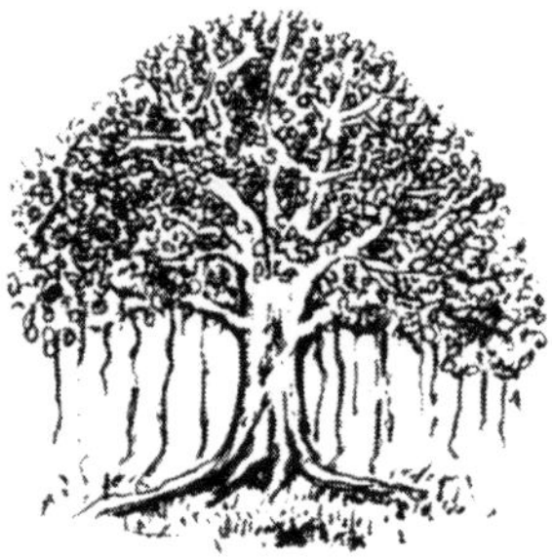

TREES IN INDIAN ART MYTHOLOGY AND FOLKLORE

ISBN: 978-81-7305-179-1

First Published: 2000

Reprinted: **2023**

Published by:
Aryan Books International
Pooja Apartments, 4B, Ansari Road, New Delhi-110 002 (India)
Tel.: 23287589, 23255799; Fax: 91-11-23270385
E-mail: aryanbooks@gmail.com
www.aryanbooks.com

Printed in India

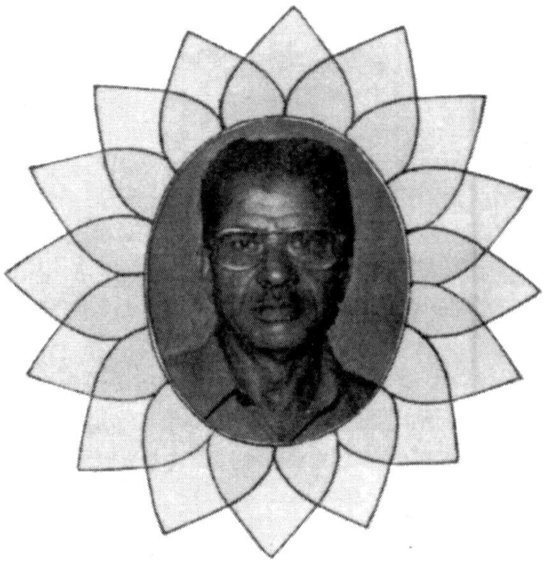

न जायते म्रियते वा कदाचि-
न्नायं भूत्वा भविता वा न भूयः।
अजो नित्यः शाश्वतोऽयं पुराणो
न हन्यते हन्यमाने शरीरे।।

(Gītā II.20)

"The Soul is never born nor dies; nor does it become only after being born. For it is unborn, eternal, everlasting and ancient; even though the body is slain, the Soul is not."

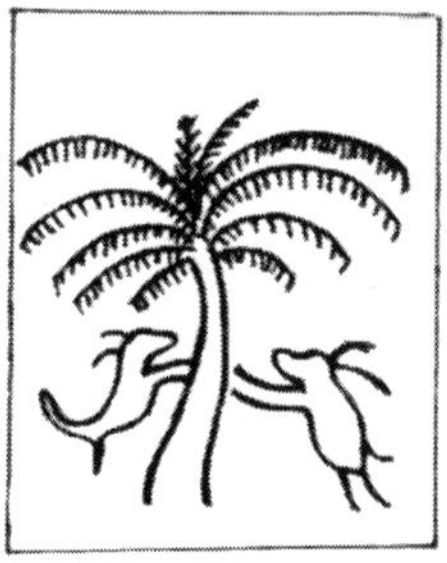

FOREWORD

When learning about Art in India one is struck by the extraordinary feat of traditional thought. The Indian Vision is both simple and complex. Simple words are used so that everybody can understand the Nature of Art and the Art of Nature. At a higher level, it becomes cosmology instead of simple explanation. There is also a deep anthropology which is not apparent to the eye, but only to the "eye" of experience.

All religions view the Universe as God's artifact. God is the supreme Artist. In Islam, one of the many names of Allah is *Musawwer*, the Artist. In Hinduism, God is the originator of every kind of Art. Viṣṇu has a thousand (infinite) names of which many refer to the works of Art. He is the divine architect. He is the designer of all. He is the divine craftsman who, with all the pleasing skill, like a smith, blasted and smelted the Universe together. He is the divine inspirer. He is the poet. He is the Word. He is the bestower of forms. He is the giver of happiness. He is the best. He is the sweet. He is the beautiful. He who smiles like flower. He who has lotus eyes. He who holds conch. Śiva has also a thousand names. He is the cosmic dancer. God's epithet as the supreme Artist found the greatest emotional stimulus among the saint poets of India. Kabir, for instance, used conventional similes to describe God as the Weaver, the Potter, the Painter, the Originator of music, the Bird that sings within the body.

Many traditional societies have no term for Art, no separate word for artist. All men and women sing and dance. Majority of them can paint and carve. The priest may have the privilege for producing paintings and songs in ceremonies. Or members of a clan may hold such status. But this does not mean that they can do it better than others. A very striking and important example is of the Pithora painters of western India. They have no formal training. Have no word for paintings. The painter is called *lakhera*, "writer". Painting is called *likhana*, "writing". It is executed on the walls by a group of ten or twelve painters. What is painted is the creation story, said to be originally "written" by God Pithora. The installation of Pithora involves painting, singing, dancing, and worship. The priest identifies the painted figures. He goes into a trance and, taking up the sword, moves from one end of the painting to the other. He accounts for each form, as he identifies them one by one. Animal sacrifice follows the painting ceremony. Once the ritual is completed, it is believed, God Pithora stays on the walls of the house where he has been installed, and its inhabitants live with him for ever.

The thrust is clear. Artistic activity is directly associated with God. God is the First Artist. Man imitates God's primordial works of Art.

The God's work is the natural world, visible to the human eye. The upanisadic sages have described it as the Cosmic Tree rooted in Brahman, the Ultimate, the Absolute. It is the "three-quartered Brahman" whose branches are space, wind, fire, water, earth, and the like. On the symbolic representation of the Cosmic Tree, it has been said: "This Tree is the Great World Mother, the Goddess of Nature who nourishes all Life with the milk of her breast". Following the metaphor of Cosmic Tree, it shows: Sacred is the proper context of both Art and Nature. Man is inseparable from Nature. He is not merely an artefact, he plays with God. Displays his aesthetic sensibility to God's Beauty. As part of Nature, he is grounded in the spiritual. What he does, as an artist, is "cosmography", a *kairological* Art on which all the arts hang.

This world view will not communicate to blind eyes and deaf ears what the "modern" man really is now, anthropologically speaking, "man makes himself". Art is his invention. But all men are not artist. Art is grounded in the physical rather than the spiritual. Anthropologists of Art make ethnic distinctions. Primitive Art is the Art of primitive peoples. Historians of Art stress on the time-frame. They are locked up, these days, in dating the Rock Art. They cannot "see" the Eternal Fig Tree, cannot "listen" to the unifying resonance between man and Tree. On the one hand, there are what are usually described as the "Art–critics" who build up a world of flattery, value the notion of "private Arts". On the other hand there are historians who claim privilege-right to evaluate Art in its own term. The first degenerates into naive romanticism, whereas the second slides into evolutionism. There is another kind of analysis which takes beyond the two extremes, and indeed it does stand out as rare.

Trees in Indian Art, by Bansi Lal Malla, tells the complete story of Art. The author is a young historian of Art whose work can best be described as a mixture of history and anthropology. He is concerned to, what he calls, "the holistic survey of all the aspects of Tree-worship in India, more importantly the scientific importance of tree worship, the medicinal values of trees and their bounties to mankind in general". He draws interesting parallels using the textual code of the primal vision of the World Tree. Adopting an interdisciplinary approach, he builds up a viable theory for the history of Art. The fascinating richness of this book lies in the "mythology" of Art which provides a conceptual explanation of the nature of Art. Much in Malla's writings appears matured thought, certain things remain unresolved. It needs to be mentioned that without understanding the *logos* of the myth there shall be no true understanding of the Art.

With this work, I think, not only historians of Art but anthropologists of religion will be in a position to follow the fascinating thought-trails in Art and Nature. It is superfluous to say that the tradition of Art belongs to the Vedic age. For, the Veda is not a point in space and a point in time. It cannot be individualized. Tradition is timeless; it is also fresh.

IGNCA, New Delhi **Baidyanath Saraswati**

CONTENTS

Foreword vii
Preface xiii
List of Illustrations xix

1. Primal Vision of the [World] Tree 1
2. Tree Worship in Pre-Vedic Era 11
3. Tree Worship in Metahistorical Texts 23
4. Tree Worship in Bio-cultural Contexts 49

    I. Trees and Ethno-religious Aṭtitudes 51
    II. Fertility Cult 59
    III. Ecological Awareness 74
    IV. Medicinal Trees (*Rogī Taru*) 83

5. Tree Motifs in Indian Art 93

    I. Tree in Sculptural Art 95
    II. *Kalpavṛkṣa* (Wish-fulfilling Tree) and *Kalpalatā* (Wish-fulfilling Creeper) 104
    III. Tree in Coins 109

6. Art is Religion, Religion Art 113

Appendices 121
Bibliography 131
Index 139

PREFACE

A few Art historians on Indian art had commented that Indian artists were using trees, plants and flowers as decorative motifs only. This contained an implicit reflection on the artisan's knowledge or awareness about the species of the flora and their properties. For a student of Indian Art history, this statement was rather vague and therefore to some extent questioning. It raised relevant questions: Was there a cult of tree-worship in ancient India? What were the promptings from such a worship? Was there any socio-religious significance of the entire kingdom of trees establishing the impact it made on the spectrum of the religious art of India? And, a pursuit for detailed information and facts set the present author on this project of compiling and analysing relevant data through all the known sources of history–art, archaeology, mythology, literature and folklore.

No doubt, man since his evolution on the earth could not detach himself from the broad influences exerted on him by the environmental elements. That nature broadly assisted him in living a much more comfortable and healthy life was what he learnt from the interaction he had with nature. It was only from his surroundings that he got food to eat, medicines to counter the baneful effects of diseases and shelter from inclement weather and last but not the least fuel to warm himself and also to cook food for its better relish. It was only by these five utilitarian purposes of trees (*pañca-yajña*) that man was led to probe into the mysteries latent in them; maybe the beauty of their flowers had also excited his imagination. As he held them in great reverence, he embarked upon the task of protecting the trees from any ravages. This action on the part of man unwittingly resulted in the ecological preservation necessary for a healthy and natural interaction between environment and man. That trees were sacred and abodes of various gods led to a point where man dared not fell them or inflict hurt on them. Such trees were designated as *Brahmā-taru*. Some trees were given out to sustain life by the sap present in them (*jīvana-vṛkṣa*). Then, there were trees having medicinal value thereby earning man's tremendous reverence (*rogī taru*). Even the Buddhists and Jains recognised divine concept of the trees. The notion of *caitya vṛkṣa*, *bodhi* trees, *kevala vṛkṣa, jñāna vṛkṣa* gained popularity among the Buddhists and Jains. In Brahmanical religion *vaṭa* (*Shorea-robusta*) was identified with Śiva, *aśvattha* (*Ficus religiosa*) with Viṣṇu, lotus with Sūrya and nine leaves of nine trees (*navapatrikā*) were associated with nine different aspects of Durgā. As a presiding deity over vegetation, Rudra is believed to have manifested himself in different types of lands and sources of water. He is *kṣetrāṇāṁpati*, the lord of cultivable land, appears in fertile as well as unfertile lands, and even in marshy, rocky and lands with pebbles and sands. Obviously, he is the maker of fertility in lands and responsible for productivity or unproductivity. Among the Greeks, the oak or beech was the emblem of Jupiter, the laurel of Apollo, and the olive of Minera. The myrtle was sacred to Aphrodite, and the apple was associated with Juno.

That man had concern for trees and plants dates back to the Harappan culture. There are evidences available from Indus valley civilization sites establishing the fact of people's interest in tree goddess (*vṛkṣkā*) and *Aśvattha adhisthāri devatā*. Besides secular literature, the early Indian texts, *Vedas*, *Brāhmaṇas*, *Āraṇyakas*, *Upaniṣads*, *Sūtras*, *Smṛtis*, *Mahākāvyas*, *Purāṇas*, Buddhist and Jain literature glorified trees and plants and prescribed some of these to be symbolic of gods and goddesses. Such trees and plants were represented in various ways and were delineated throughout the ages. A few books have been written and a number of articles have been contributed on this subject but it appears that till date a critical estimate with logical and scientific evaluation has not been taken up by any scholar.

The subject however, appears to have been a popular one with the scholars of Indian art and religion. One of the earliest attempts was made in a serious work entitled *Tree and Serpent Worship* by J. Fergusson in 1868. Another book on the subject was written by G.P. Majumdar in 1935 entitled *Upavana Vinoda* (a Sanskrit treatise of Arbori-horticulture). The next book on the subject, *The Cult of Trees and Tree Worship in Buddhist-Hindu Sculptures* was published by M.S. Randhawa in the year 1958. A praiseworthy book was edited by S. Sengupta in 1965 entitled *Tree Symbol Worship in India*. E.O. James in 1966 discussed certain aspects of tree worship in his book *Tree of Life—An Archaeological Study*. In 1971 two more important books were written on the subject. One among these entitled *Plant Myths and Traditions in India* was written by S.M. Gupta. The other work *Phallic Tree Worship Cults Arborum* is anonymous. Yet another good book *Tree Worship in Ancient India* was authored by B.C. Sinha in the year 1979. In the same year U.N. Roy produced an interesting book on the subject *Śālabhañjikā in Art, Philosophy and Literature*. In the year 1992, K.G. Senadeera published his book *Buddhist Symbolism of Wish-fulfillment*. The latest publications on the subject are *Plants in Indian Temple Art* (1996) by Shakti M. Gupta and *Conserving the Sacred for Biodiversity Management* (1998) edited by P.S. Ramakrishnan, K.G. Saxena and U.M Chandrashekara.

In addition to these works, many articles by a number of scholars have been contributed on the subject. One of the earliest articles was contributed by A.K. Coomaraswamy, who came out with a paper "The tree of Jesse and Indian parallels or sources", published in the *Art Bulletin* (1929). The same author published his second article in the year 1938 on "The Inverted Tree" in the *Quarterly Journal of the Mythical Society*. K.R. Pisharoti brought out an article in 1935 on "Dohada or the woman and tree motifs etc.", which was published in the *Journal of Indian Society of Oriental Art*. In the same journal an interesting paper on "*Kalpavṛkṣa*: The wish-fulfilling tree", was published by V.S. Agrawala in 1943. Again in the said journal in the same year H. Saraswati produced an article on "The world tree." After a gap of a few years, G. Roth in 1957 published a paper on "The woman and tree motif", in the *Journal of the Asiatic Society, Letters and Sciences*. In the year 1971-72, S. Kramrisch published an article on "Śarīravṛkṣa, the body tree", in the *Journal of the Indian Society of Oriental Art*. T.K. Biswas and P.K. Debnath came forward with an important article on "*Aśoka* (*Saraca Indica Linn*): A cultural and scientific evaluation" in the *Indian Journal of History of Science*, which was published in 1972. The same authors published another article entitled "*Aśvattha* (*Ficus religiosa Linn*): A cultural and medicinal observation." in *Vishveshavaranand Indological Journal* in the year 1974. In the year 1985 T.K. Biswas produced another article on "Culakoka Devata and the related issue of fertility cult" in the *Bhāratī*. It was in the year 1974 that H.C. Patyal published his article on "The significance of the *Aegle Marmelos* (*bilva*) in the Veda" in the *Vishveshvaranand Indological Journal*.

Despite the wealth of material contained in these published works and articles, the author feels that the study of tree worship in India still needs a comprehensive and critical estimate. Each book and each article appears confined in range and compass thus allowing but a partial view of the total subject. Almost no work has dilated on the socio-religious relevance of tree worship, the role of trees in maintaining an ecological balance and also the problem of pollution and atmospheric changes as were instinctively understood by our ancestors. There is hardly a book available dealing with these aspects of tree worship in India and also from artistic point of view. The present work therefore stands out as it attempts to make a holistic survey of all the aspects of tree worship in India more importantly the scientific importance of tree worship, the medicinal values of trees and their bounties to mankind in general. In doing so, the present work has been divided into the following chapters.

The first chapter records the primal vision of the (world) tree — the meaning and the function of the *axis mundi*, the concept of cosmic tree and cosmic space.

The second chapter deals with the notion of tree worship in pre-Vedic period as is evidenced from the Indus valley and its extended cultural zones. It includes the information regarding tree goddesses, *Aśvattha-adhiṣthātri devatās* and cult of fertility at length. The study of trees and vegetals as evident on the art of Indus valley is also made in this chapter.

In the third chapter literary references to tree worship in ancient India are recorded. These include references from the *Vedas, Brāhmaṇa, Āraṇyaka, Smṛiti, Sūtra, Mahākāvyas*, Buddhist literature and the *Purāṇas*, along with certain non-religious texts.

The fourth chapter studies the bio-cultural contexts of the tree worship in India including the study of the origin and evolution of cultivation (the fertility-cult); women and tree motifs (*caitya-vṛkṣa, śālabhañjikā, dohada*, etc.); medicinal trees (*rogī-taru*); identification, cultivation and protection (notion of ecological balances); and pollution alongwith atmospheric changes *vis-a-vis*, deforestation, afforestation, etc.

The discussion about the tree worship and its reflection on the early Indian art has been rendered in the fifth chapter on the basis of examples culled from various sources. It includes the study of tree and vegetal motifs on the art of Indus valley, Mauryan ring stones and gateways of *stupas* at Bharhut, Bodhgaya, Sanchi, Amaravati, Nagarjunakonda, etc. The relation of trees with Buddhist gods and goddesses, Jain Tīrthāṅkaras and with the Brahmanical gods and goddesses from 1st century AD to 1200 AD has also been discussed at length.

The concluding sixth chapter gives a resume of the entire study.

The present work has its roots in an Indian Council of Historical Research project "Tree Worship in Ancient India," awarded to the author under the ICHR post-doctoral fellowship programme from 1990 to1993. The project report that was submitted to the ICHR has been modified and added with some additional information and chapters before sending it to the press. The author acknowledges the constant assistance and cooperation received from the authorities of ICHR during the fellowship period. The work was a challenging one and there had been dearth of comprehensive books.

In all humility the author accepts the good done unto him by many of his friends, guides and scholars. He has no hesitation to admit that the present work would not have been possible without their valued suggestions. He is highly indebted to his preceptors Dr. (Mrs.) Kapila Vatsyayan, Academic Director, Indira Gandhi National Centre for the Arts (IGNCA); Shri M.C. Joshi, Member Secretary, IGNCA; Prof. B.N. Saraswati, UNESCO Professor, IGNCA, New Delhi; Dr. T.K. Biswas, Joint Director, Bharat Kala Bhawan, BHU, Varanasi for their immense help, guidance and perpetual encouragement that helped him a lot in giving final shape to this volume. Dr. Biswas has been a great source of inspiration to him for taking up this challenging project. He specially thanks Prof. Saraswati for writing the thought-provoking "foreword" to the book. He is equally beholden to Shri O.P. Tandon, former Officer on Special Duty, Banaras Hindu University, Varanasi for his careful and meticulous scrutiny of the manuscript and valuable suggestions.

The author extends his heartfelt thanks to the following for their advice, suggestions and cooperation: Shri M.A. Dhaky, Director (Emeritus), AIIS, Gurgaon; Shri Krishna Deva, former Director, ASI, New Delhi; Shri B.M. Pande, former Director, ASI, New Delhi; Prof. M.L. Koul, Govt. College for Women, Srinagar (now at Jammu due to migration); Shri J.S. Yadav, Deputy Director (Library), AIIS, Gurgaon; Shri R. Sharma, Archivist, AIIS, Gurgaon; Shri S.B. Singh, Bharat Kala Bhavan, Varanasi; Shri P.T. Deshpande, Artist, IGNCA, New Delhi; Shri R.S. Taragi, Assistant Artist, IGNCA, New Delhi.

During the course of investigation many institutes extended valuable help and cooperation to the author. He is indeed indebted to the following Institutions: Indira Gandhi National Centre for the Arts, New Delhi; American Institute of Indian Studies, Varanasi; Archaeological Survey of India, New Delhi; National Museum, New Delhi; Indian Museum, Calcutta; Patna Museum, Patna; Bharat Kala Bhavan, Varanasi; Madras Museum, Chennai; Central Museum, Indore; Central Museum, Gwalior; Govt.

Museum, Mathura; Central Museum, Allahabad; State Museum, Lucknow; State Museum, Bhanpura; State Museum, Bharatpur; Rajputana Museum, Ajmer; Nalanda Museum, Nalanda; Government Museum, Mathura; Site Museum, Mathura; Site Museum, Sirpur.

The author is beholden to Shri Vikas Arya of the Aryan Books International, New Delhi for bringing out the book so well in so short a time.

Lastly, the author is deeply indebted to his revered mother Smt. Sheela Devi and elder brother Shri C.K. Malla. Without their blessings, this work would not have been possible. The book has been presented as a token of respect to his father late Shri Triloki Nath Malla, who left for heavenly abode on 31st December, 1994, leaving behind everlasting memories.

New Delhi **Bansi Lal Malla**

LIST OF ILLUSTRATIONS

Figures

1. Tree Spirit in association with worshippers and animal; seal; Harappa; National Museum, New Delhi; 2000 BC.
2. Goddess giving birth to the vegetation; seal; Harappa; National Museum, New Delhi; 3000 BC.
3. Horned human figure seated in a yogic stance; Mohenjo-daro; National Museum, New Delhi; 3000 BC.
4. Tree Spirit in association with a tiger; seal; Mohenjo-daro; National Museum, New Delhi; 3000 BC.
5. A half-woman and half-buffalo figure with horns of divinity in association with tiger and śamī tree; Mohenjo-daro; National Museum, New Delhi; 3000 BC.
6. Korku men worshipping the carved wooden board under a sacred tree; at Baba Garden in Pachmarhi town (Madhya Pradesh).
7. Representation of male and female; pot; Daimabad (Maharashtra); Chalcolithic Period.
8. "Opulent" Mother Goddess; Gold Plaque; Lauriya (Distt. Champaran); Pre-Asokan; (courtesy: Desai 1975).
9. Ring stone representing "Opulent" Mother Goddess; Murtaziganj (Patna); Patna Museum; 3rd century BC.
10. Headless nude goddess; terracotta; Bhita, Maharashtra; (courtesy: Desai 1975).
11. Nude goddess in Uttānapad pose; stone; Alampur, Andhra Pradesh; 8th century AD.
12. Goddess Pālaghaṭa in a Warli marriage painting from Ganjad, Maharashtra; mural painting; (courtesy: Dalmia 1988).
13. Pāñcacūḍa Goddess; Terracotta; Tamluk; Ashmolean Museum, Oxford; 2nd century BC.
14. Pūrṇaghaṭa from Bhimbetka (M.P.) rock shelter; Early historic period.

15. Pūrṇaghaṭa; Amaravati; 3rd century AD.
16. Goddess Śrī touching her own breasts; Bharhut; Indian Museum, Calcutta; 2nd century BC.

Plates

1. Stone disc depicting Mother goddess attended by priests with palm trees, birds and animals; Murtaziganj (Patna); Patna Museum; 3rd century BC.
2. Bull capital (detail); Rampurva; Rashtrapati Bhavan, New Delhi; 3rd century BC.
3. Padma and utpala creepers issuing from mouth of a man; Bharhut Stupa Great railing, crossbar medallion; sandstone; Indian Museum, Calcutta; 2nd century BC.
4. Padma and utpala creepers issuing from the man's navel (other details are same as in Pl. 3).
5. Kalpalatā emanating from elephant's mouth on a coping stone (other details are same as in Pl. 3).
6. Kalpalatā yielding jewellery etc. (other details are same as in Pl. 3).
7. Bodhi tree of Viśvabhu on a pillar (other details are same as in Pl. 3).
8. Jetavana Jātaka (other details are same as above).
9. Udumbara, Bodhi tree of Kanakmuni (other details are same as above).
10. Architectural fragment depicting huge aśvattha tree, Jaggayapetta (Guntur A.P.); white marble; Madras Museum; 2nd century BC.
11. Elephants paying homage to Bodhi tree; Pillar: (for details cf. Pl. 3).
12. Patali tree, Bodhi tree of Buddha Vipasyin; Pillar; (cf. Pl. 3 for other details).
13. Nāga King Erapata worshipping Bodhi tree; Bharhut Stupa, Great railing, South gate, Corner pillar; Sandstone, Indian Museum, Calcutta; 2nd century BC.
14. Tree within railing; Besnagar (M.P.), Railing Pillar; Sandstone; Central Museum, Gwalior; 2nd century BC.
15. Kalpavṛkṣa; Besnagar; Sandstone; Indian Museum, Calcutta, 2nd century BC.
16. Culakoka Devatā; Pillar; (cf. Pl. 13 for other details).
17. Yakṣi Candra bust; north gate; (cf. Pl. 13 for other details).
18. Kalpavṛkṣa with female figure; Chausa (Sahabad-Bihar); Bronze; Patna Museum; 1st century BC.

19. Lady playing a harp under a tree; Gopalpur (Mathura); Red sandstone; Government Museum, Mathura; 1st century BC.
20. Jātaka Scene (?) on crossbar; Mathura; Red sandstone; Patna Museum; 1st century BC.
21. Bodhi trees of seven Manusi Buddhas; Sanchi, (M.P.), Stupa I, Eastern Gateway, west side, superstructure; Buff sandstone; 1st century BC.
22. Sporting ladies under aśoka tree, back view; Kota (Mathura); Red sandstone; Government Museum, Mathura; 1st century AD.
23. Buddha seated under aśvattha tree; Katra Keshav Deo (Mathura); Red sandstone; Government Museum, Mathura; 1st century AD.
24. Buddha's enlightenment; Amaravati (A.P.), Rail post; Limestone; Indian Museum, Calcutta, 2nd century AD.
25. Lintel showing worship of Śivaliṅga under tree; Mathura (Bhuteśara); Red sandstone; Mathura Museum; 2nd century AD.
26. Aśoka tree on the back view of Caturvyuha-Viṣṇu; Saptasamudri Kuan (Mathura); Buff sandstone; Government Museum, Mathura; 2nd century AD.
27. Clay seal depicting a tree on its obverse above a line with designs on both sides at its upper half; India; clay; Government Museum (Mathura); 4th century AD.
28. Fan-palm capital; Pawaya (Gwalior, M.P.); Buff sandstone; Central Museum, Gwalior; 4th-5th century AD.
29. Śālabhañjikā; Kopa (Basti, U.P.); Terracotta; Municipal Museum, Allahabad; 5th century AD.
30. Two Vyuhalas and stylised lotuses issuing out from the mouth of a pitcher (ghaṭa); Tala (Bilaspur, M.P.); Jethani temple, Main entrance on south, east pillar, lower detail; stone; 6th century (late) AD.
31. A panel carved with some story; Malhar (Bilaspur, M.P.); Buff sandstone; Site Museum, Mathura; 5th-6th century AD.
32. Nara and Nārāyaṇa under trees; Deogarh (Lalitpur, U.P.), Dasāvatara temple, East Jaṅgha, Rathikabimba; Red sandstone; ca. AD 500-25.
33. Mock coronation of child Kṛṣṇa; Badami (Bijapur-Karnataka), Cave 3; sandstone; ca. AD 500-78.
34. Ambika standing under a mango tree; Sirpur (Raipur, M.P.); Buff sandstone; Site Museum (Sirpur); 6th century AD.
35. Buddha seated under a tree in bhadrāsaṇa; Kanheri (Bombay-Maharashtra), cave 90; 6th century AD.

36. Jaina couple seated under a tree; Sahet Mahet (Gonda, U.P.); State Museum, Lucknow; 5th century AD.
37. Mahāvira seated under a tree; Rajgir (Nalanda); Sonabhandar cave; Sandstone; 4th-7th century AD.
38. Uma-Maheśvara under tree; Bhanpura (Mandasore, M.P.); State Museum (Bhanpura); 8th century AD.
39. Indra seated under a Kalpavṛkṣa; Ellora (Aurangabad, Maharashtra), cave 32; ca. AD 810-80.
40. Buddha seated in bhumisparśa mudrā under an aśvattha tree; Tetrawan (Patna); Black basalt; Indian Museum, Calcutta; 9th century AD.
41. Ganeśa seated in lilāsaṇa under a mango tree; Nalanda (site 3); Basalt; Nalanda Museum; 9th-10th century AD.
42. Ādināthā under a nyagrodha tree; Jaghina (Bharatpur, Rajasthan); Buff sandstone; State Museum, Bharatpur; ca. AD 900.
43. Gomateśvara entwined with aśoka creepers; Sravanabelgola (Chikamagalur, Karnataka); Granite; ca. AD 983.
44. Daksinamurti Śiva seated under a tree; Madras; Granite, Tanjore Art Gallery; 10th century AD.
45. Pārsvanātha under a tree, India; Buff sandstone; Bharat Kala Bhavan, Varanasi; 11th century AD.
46. Kalpavṛkṣa; Modi (Mandasore, M.P.); Sandstone; Central Museum, Indore; 11th century AD.
47. Kṛṣṇa tied to a mortar; Amritpur (Chikmagalur, Karnataka); Amriteśvara temple; Soapstone; ca. AD 1196.
48. Lakṣmī-Nārāyaṇa on Garuḍa under a tree; Halebid (Hassan, Karnataka); Basalt; National Museum; 12th century AD.
49. Kṛṣṇa going to punish serpent king; Arsikera (Hassan, Karnataka); Iśvara temple; Soapstone; ca. AD 1220.
50. Panel depicting Mātṛkas with trees; Deo Baloda (Durg, M.P.); Śiva temple; Buff sandstone; late 13th century AD.
51. Vāsupūjya under a Kalpavṛkṣa; Khambat (Cambay) (Kheda, Gujarat); Marble; Private Collection; 13th century AD.
52. Indra; Javagal (Chikmagalur, Karnataka); Lakṣmīnarasiṁhā temple, Soapstone; 13th century AD.
53. Ṛsabhadeva seated in dhyāna mudrā under a stylised nyagrodha tree; Tantoti (Ajmer, Rajasthan); Black stone; Rajputana Museum, Ajmer; 13th-14th century AD.

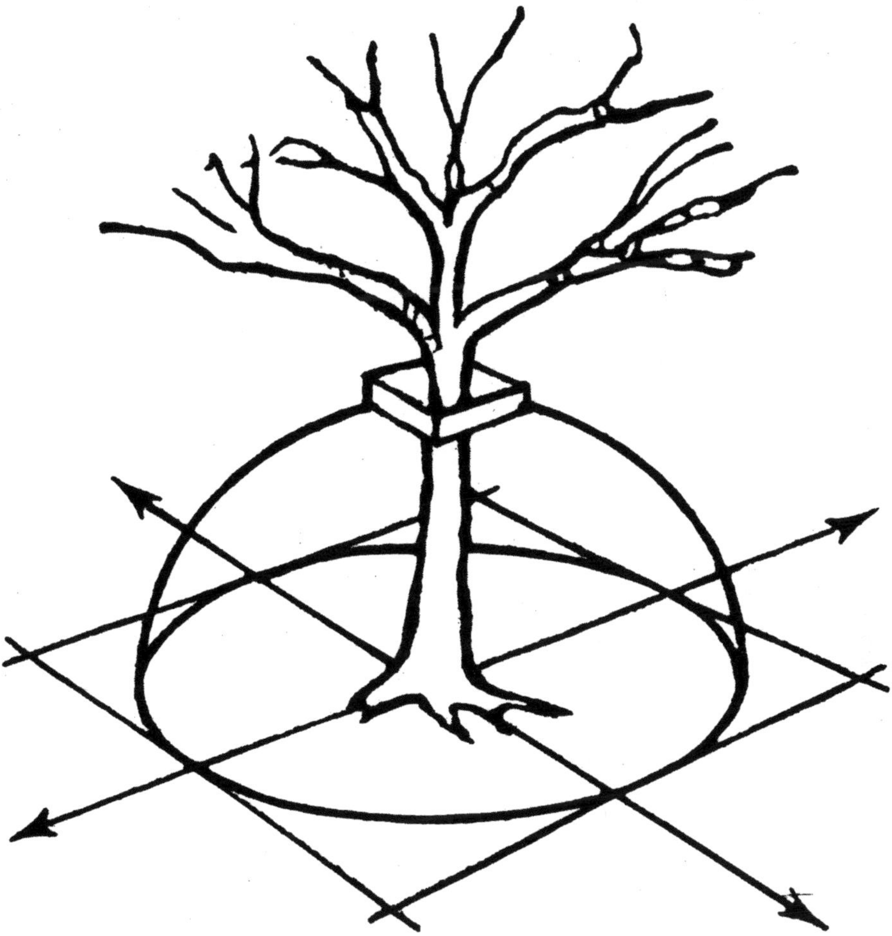

1 PRIMAL VISION OF THE [WORLD] TREE

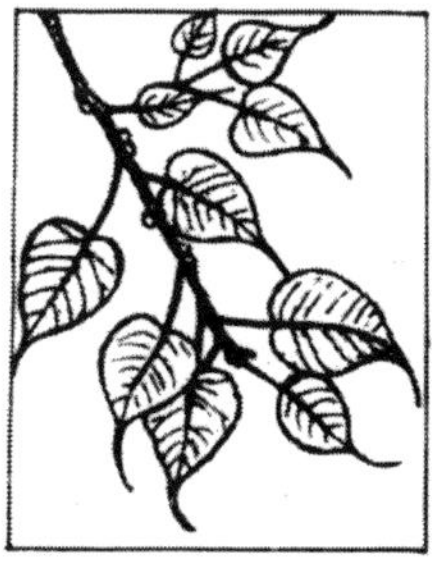

Axis Mundi

Tree represents a power in the eyes of primordial man. It evokes verticality. It achieves communication, between the three levels of the cosmos: subterranean space, earth and sky. It provides one with an access to the invisible. In many cultures the universe is portrayed as multilayered, the layers kept distinct and in place by a world tree running through the exact centre (*axis mundi*) of the cosmos. The *axis mundi* symbolises the communication between cosmic regions; and the extension of an organised and habitable world existed around it. The meaning and the function of the *axis mundi* rests not in abstract and geometrical concepts alone but in every day gesture that can effect the transcendence. The symbolism of the centre of the world may also be expressed through a sacred mountain, a sacred place, a ladder, a vine, a rope, a pillar and a bridge — all of which serve as an *axis mundi* connecting heaven and earth on various cosmic realms of being. There is a tendency to replicate the image of the *axis mundi* in multiple forms. Such is the case with the cross — the cosmic tree of Christianity. In many cultures a particular species or a single tree is designated as cosmic : the fig tree in India; the oak of the Celts and the Gauls; the oak of Zeus at Dodona, of the Capitoline Jupiter, of Abraham at Sichem and at Hebron; the ash of the Greeks in Hesiod; the date palm of the Mesopotamians; the Siberian birch; the Chinese *Chien-mu* tree; and the cedar of Lebanon[1]. In India the fig tree is also regarded as the 'tree of the human psyche' due to its archetypal character[2].

In cultures that conceive of the universe as multiple realms of heavens, hells and strata for various kinds of beings, the *axis mundi* is their point where all realms intersect and where the most direct contact with the sacred is obtained. In the Vedic rites "the sacrificer makes himself a ladder and a bridge to reach the celestial world" (*Taittirīya Saṁhitā* 6.6.4.2). Before he can ascend to the upper world, the sacrificer must first propose and consecrate the sacrificial stack, the *yūpa*. This is fashioned from a tree likened to the cosmic tree. After a *yūpa* is made, it is installed as cosmic pillar, upholding as connecting all realms of being : "List thyself up, O Lord of the Forest, into the summit of the earth!" (*Ṛgveda* 3.8.3). The idea is made explicit in the *Śatapatha Brāhmaṇa* (3.7.1.4) : "With thy summit thou dost hold up the heavens, why the branches thou fillest the air, with thy foot thou steadiest the earth". While ascending the stake, he may extend his arms, just as a bird stretches out wings and exclaim, "I have attained to heaven to the Gods : I have become immortal!" (*Taittirīya Saṁhitā* 1.7.9.). Similarly, the cultures in North America, Oceania, Africa and ancient Egypt all possess myths concerning ascent to heaven along a cosmic ladder.

Indian tradition offers many variations of the cosmic tree. The *Ṛgveda* (IX.5.107) mentions the cosmos as the tree of a thousand branches (*Sahasravalśa Vanaspati*). The *aśvattha* was made the basis of a profound metaphysical doctrine. The thousand branches of the "Eternal Cosmic tree" represent the innumerable universe and systems of world order and the human mind cannot bring them into any computation[3]. Its roots grasp deeply into the mysterious earth, its trunk was often used as the main pillar of primitive dwellings, and its branches sway, like the birds, in the realm of the air, the sky, the celestial. This form of the tree is the image of a connection between heaven and earth, and its structure has a marked symbolic content. There was also much meaning in the conception of Brāhmaṇa as the Tree and Brāhmaṇa as the Forest (*Brahmā tad vanaṁ, Brahmā sa vṛkṣa āsa*)[4]. Here the tree is three-quartered Brāhmaṇ whose branches are space, wind, fire, water, earth and the like. It is regarded as a manifestation of Brahmā in the universe. In the *Bhagavadgītā*, the *aśvattha* tree described as having its roots above and branches below, is the same as the cosmic tree of thousand branches. It is described in the *Kaṭhopaniṣad* (cf. s.16) as the eternal tree with its roots upward and its branches downward, which is the pure immortal Brāhmaṇa, in which all these worlds are situated and beyond which there is nothing else[5]. This tree is also believed as rising from the navel of Varuṇa or of Nārāyaṇa as he floats in the waters of the universe.

The Old World has used the symbol of cosmic tree to describe the world-ground, the world-producer : A Scandinavian creation story tells of a cosmic tree called yggdrasill with branches that reach the heaven and cover the whole world and roots that run under the earth and support it. The ancient Babylonians know the black kisnaku tree that grows at Eridu, the centre of the world. It shines like lapis lazuli - meaning that it shines like the night sky - and spreads its branches out towards the cosmic Ocean that surrounds and supports that world. The Chinese mythology tells of a miraculous tree that grows at the centre of the universe and that unites the nine springs and nine heavens. In other words it marks that point at which the various cosmic levels intersect[6]. Salishan Indians of North America hold that their deity made three worlds, one above the other : the sky world, the earth and the underworld. All are connected by a single tree that passes through the middle of each. Similarly, the Vasyugan Ostiak (khanty) also believe that the cosmic tree's branches touched the sky and its roots extended to the underworld. The ancient Egyptians believed that the sky was a huge tree that overarched the earth. The stars were fruits or leaves on the tree and the gods perched on its boughs. This tree separated the ocean from the sky, the upper world from the lower world. In the Maya World, the silk-cotton tree is presented as *axis-mundi*, with roots down into the lower world and trunk and branches passed through different layers of the heavens[7]. The Zuni in their story of creation blends the cosmic tree, the trees of four corners, and the tree of life as sacred elements brings Zuni to their present world and that serves as important parts of their religious beliefs. The ancient Sumerians of Eridu tell of a wondrous tree[8] with its roots of white crystal stretched towards the deep, its seat the central place of the earth, its foliage the couch of the primeval mother.

The cosmic tree is regarded as the great world Mother, the Goddess of Nature, who nourishes all life. Even to reach metaphysical level the Mother - symbol is most appropriate : "The tree is, in fact, rooted in the unmanifest darkness of the Parabrahman, which is usually symbolised as 'above'. Though in fact it is no less truly 'beneath' as well. From the transcending rooting-place it sends down its trunk of manifestation through the worlds, and on that trunk are seven main branches each of which splits into countless branches and twigs. Nevertheless the trunk itself is one, for it is the Tree of the Mother, the great Mūla-*Prakṛti*, the substance of the universe. The sap that runs in its veins is the very Life of all beings and on its Branches hang the stars themselves"[9].

Many traditions believe that the cosmic tree stands for the sacrality of the world, its creation, continuation and fertility. In Indian context it also represents genealogical tree (*Vaṁśa vṛkṣa*). Its roots represent the first known family ancestors (*Bijapuruṣa*); branches represent generations (*Pidhi*) and leaves represent the siblings. In many cases the world tree is a tree of life and immortality as well. In the *Vedas,* Varuṇa lifted up the celestial tree and by squeezing its fruits between two stones obtained *soma* or *amṛta,* the drink of immortality. On certain occasions in India the *aśvattha* is called as 'tree of life' or the 'tree of creation' or the 'tree of knowledge'. The

Babylonians believed that the trees guarded the eastern entry to the heaven : the 'tree of truth' and the 'tree of life'. Similarly, the narrative in the Bible centres around the planting of the 'tree of life' and 'knowledge' in the garden of Eden. Hebraic teachings and Islamic traditions describe the 'tree of life' with its roots in heaven and its branches overarching the earth. Zoroastrianism teaches that 'tree of all seeds', or the 'tree of all healing', which grows in the cosmic sea, Vouruvasha, is responsible for life on earth. In Jewish tradition the 'tree of life' was a date-palm, while in the Norse mythology 'tree of life' is a huge ash tree, called yggdrasill. In Japanese stories the 'tree of life' is described having a trunk and branches of gold, root of silver and fruits of gems. In some stories they are the peach, the plum,, and the pine.

The celestial tree was also a 'tree of life' in ancient Egypt. Out of this tree emerge divine arms, some of which bear gifts while others pour out the water of life from an Uru. Its fruits kept the gods and the souls of the dead in eternal youth and wisdom. Such a conception seems to have been a part of Indian folk cult also. The notion of *Kalpavṛkṣa* (wish-fulfilling tree) in the Hindu mythology is a jewel which was produced at the time of the churning of the Ocean, and later on became the tree par excellence of the royal garden of Lord Indra. It has the capacity to fulfil all the desires of mankind (Details in chapter 5).

The Cosmic tree transfixes the levels of the world and makes communication and passage among them possible. There is a connection between the tree-image of the cosmos and the sun which also embraces the entire universe. The sun directs his beams down towards earth and keeps his roots in heaven. The ancient Egyptians believed that the sun was born from the tree every day while the celestial tree disappeared each morning, thus making the periods of night and day. The year was also symbolised by 365 trees representing the days of their calendar year[10]. In the Baltic religious traditions the saules koks, the 'Tree of the Sun' stood at the centre of the world. It is unique and inaccessible. It may be described as made of precious metal, gold, or silver. A supernatural orb descends through its branches, perhaps associated with Saule, the sun, the source of life.

Cosmic Space

The cosmic space is also defined by trees in addition to the centre of the earth and the sacred tree with its branches defining the world of the man and the gods. Many American Indians add trees and their associated colours, birds or other animals, and gods, to each of the four cardinal directions. The number four perhaps symbolizes the totality of space and time. The Maya, the Aztec and the Indian cultures[11] believe that five sacred trees (the four corners of the world and the centre) were responsible for the organization of the universe. They allotted particular times of the year or entire year in some cases, to serve under the dominion of each direction.

It is believed that in the most archaic stage of religious life the sacred places were small-scale reproductions of the world in toto achieved by forming a landscape of stones, water and trees. The tree-altar-stone pattern characterized sacred places throughout India and East Asia. Often a vertical post or pillar representing the *axis-mundi* was added, presumably as a stylised tree meant to enhance the sacred power already present in the microcosmic landscape. It seems that over the course of time the elements of such a landscape were reduced to the single most important element: the tree or sacred pillar.

Vanaspati

The forest as a whole appears as a deity under the name of *Āryaṇyāni*. For the ancient sages none was more important, or full of power, than Vanaspati, the Lord of the Forest (*Ṛgveda* 10, 146). In Vedic literature, the vegetable world is roughly divided between *oṣadhi* or *virudha* 'plants' and *vana* or *vṛkṣa* 'trees'. According to the Vedic beliefs and myths, all plants and trees are sacred as they possess the gifts of immortality, health and general prosperity.[12] Their nourishing and nurturing have made them infinitely precious, as wondrous as the mother with her life-giving milk. "Plants, O ye Mothers, I hail you as Goddesses" (*Yajurveda* IV.2.6). The spring, the rock and the tree are regarded as visible manifestations of the divine spirit. However, the plant, tree and forest deities play a very significant part in the religion of *Ṛgveda* and in *Atharvaveda*. It seems from these texts that the people of Vedic period were lovers of nature. In the *Ṛgveda, aprisūktas, vanaspatis* are found to be invoked. The same text refers to *oṣadhis* as 'mothers' and 'goddesses' and are invoked chiefly with waters and mountains.[13] Interestingly, there is also a reference to *caitya-vṛkṣas* in the *Atharvaveda-Pariśiṣṭa* (LXXI). The post-Vedic literature of Hindu, Buddhist and Jain thought is imbued with reverence, love and compassion for nature and also with concepts of not only the unity of life but also the unity of what is *cetan* (living) and what is *acetana* (non-living). The

Svetāśvatara Upaniṣad captures the essence of this integration and unity, when it describes nature in following terms:

> The God who is in fire, who is in water, who pervades the whole universe, who is in medicines, who is in vegetation, we salute that God.

In Indian culture forests constitute a very important part, and are considered the abode of gods. Most of the ancient books, like *Vedas, Purāṇas, Brāhmaṇas* and *Āraṇyakas* were written by *Ṛṣis* living in forests. One finds reference to three main types of *vana* of ancient times, i.e. *Mahāvana, Tapovana* and *Śrīvana.*

Mahāvana was devoid of human habitation and the human interference was therefore negligible. Such forests were dense, virgin and natural covering large mountainous and low lying areas. Lord *Śiva* is believed to be the presiding deity of this forest.

Tapovana was the forest where sages did *tapas* (penance and meditation)[14]; our *Upaniṣads* and *Āraṇyakas* were written in these forests. Most of the *tapovanas* are extinct now. One of such forests is near Haridwar even today. These forests were usually full of plants and trees which gave edible and medicinal leaves, roots, fruits, shades and soothing climate.

Śrīvanas were the local (village or town) forests and were managed by village and town *pañcāyatas*. They were full of various kinds of trees, depending on soil, climate and other environmental conditions and local needs. Thus, the concept of social forestry was known to Indians even in that hoary past. Generally, five species of trees (banyan, *pipal*, *aśoka, bela* and *harda*) were must in a *śrīvana*. The name *Pañcavaṭī* is probably derived from these five trees, and every village has a *Pañcavaṭī* even if it did not have a *śṛīvana*. The trees were not necessarily the same as mentioned above nor was the number of trees fixed. They differed from region to region and sometimes from place to place and people to people.

NOTES AND REFERENCES

1. Eliade, Mircea (Ed.), *Encyclopaedia of Religions*, Vol. 4, 8-11 New York, London, 1987, p. 158.
   For the ancient Mexicans, the world was built on a cross—the crossroads joining east to west and south to north. Thus the cross became a symbol of world unity. Maya civilization have given us many models of the cross.

In manuscripts, the centre and the four cardinal points are sometimes marked by stylized trees with a bird (*Ibid.*).

2. Saraswati, B.N., "The Logos and the Mythos of the Sacred Grove", *Conserving the Sacred for Biodiversity Management*, edited by P.S. Ramakrishnan, K.G. Saxena and U.M. Chandrashekara, New Delhi, 1998, pp. 31-46.
3. Agrawala, V.S., *Ancient Indian Folk Cults*, Varanasi, 1970, pp. 116-17.
4. *Ibid.*
5. Saletore, R., *Encyclopaedia of Indian Culture*, Vol. I, New Delhi, p. 142.
6. Eliade, Mircea (Ed.), *op.cit.*, Vol. 15, p. 244.
7. Cf. fn.2 above.
8. *Ibid.*
9. *Ibid.* cf., Prem, Sri Krishna, *The Yoga of the Kathopanishad*, Ahmedabad, 1982, p. 217.
10. Eliade, Mircea (Ed.), *op.cit.*, Vol. 15, p. 28.
11. *Ibid.*
12. Cf. Patyal, H.C., "The significance of the Aegle Mardelos (Bilva) in the Veda", *Vishveshvaranand Indological Journal*, Vol. XII, Nos. I & II, 1974, p. 261.
13. Grisworld, H.D., *The Religion of the Ṛgveda*, London, Edinburg, Glasgow, New York, Toronto, Melbourne, Cape-Town, Bombay, 1923, pp. 306-7.
14. The ancient Germans also worshipped their gods in groves and woods.

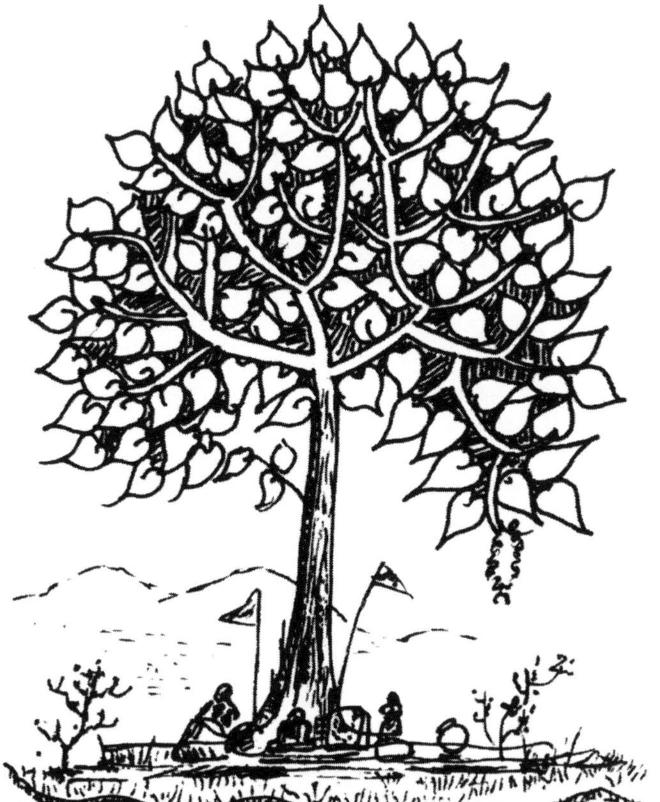

2 TREE WORSHIP IN PRE-VEDIC ERA

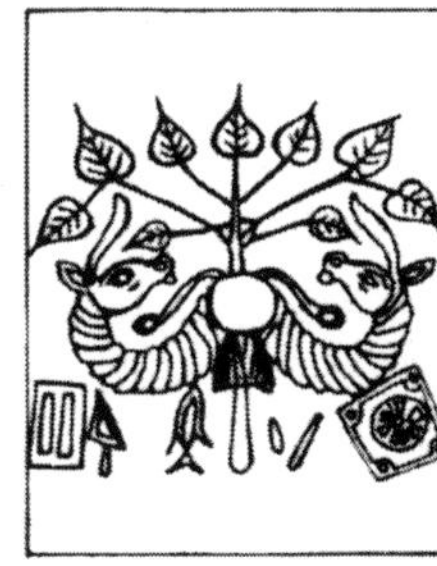

Tree worship is a living faith in Indian society. The worship of trees is often witnessed not only in rural areas but in urban too. There arises, therefore, a question as to why Indians worship trees and from which time the tradition of the tree worship started? These questions compel us to peep into the distant past. In the prehistoric period the role played by trees is very difficult to establish, although there are references to their presence on some rock paintings,[1] and also on some potteries.[2] The nature of depictions in the prehistoric paintings and other artifacts of the period does not allow us to conclude that the trees were worshipped. But, there are some scholars who believe that the indigenous Indians worshipped a few trees and had given them auspicious status. Excavations and explorations of the Indus valley sites and contemporary sites in other parts of India yielded some artifacts which bear definite signs of tree worship during the chalcolithic period in India. According to Pandey (1993: 225-26), even the traces of tree worship are found in the historic rock paintings. Special mention may be made of the figure of *Vanadeva* found at Adamgarh and of the fertility symbol at Abchand in Sagar district. The figure of *Vanadeva* is shown in the anthropomorphic form, having a lotus crown on his head. In one hand he holds a bud; in the other hand is shown an arrow. The whole body of the deity is covered with flowers. The idea of fertility is depicted by the female organ, from which emerge a number of branches with flowers at the end. At Kharwai, most probably a *kalpavṛkṣa* is drawn inside the railing and two peacocks are standing at its left.

Marshall was one of the earliest scholars who came forward with his thought provoking book *Mohenjo-daro and the Indus Civilization* in 1931. To him, in Mohenjo-daro and Harappa, two forms of tree worship were in practice. In one form, the tree itself is worshipped in its natural form[3] and in the other, tree spirit is personified and endowed with human shape and human attributes (Fig. 1). He also reported several seals and sealings indicating the presence of tree cult in pre-Vedic India. In one of these most important seals (Fig. 1), the epiphany of the deity is the tree and is portrayed in a half-realistic, half-conventional way. The tree appears to be the *pipal* (*Ficus religiosa*) as is evident from its leaves and the said tree is still an object of universal worship throughout India.[4] The same seal is dealt also by Sastri[5] at length in a critical manner. Similarly, on the other seals,[6] the tree appears conventionalized into the form of an arch surrounded by leaves in which the deity is framed, as if standing in a shrine. In another case, the nude deity appearing between the branches is very small and roughly portrayed. It may be mentioned here that in the days gone by, it used to be possibly a custom for women to walk naked around a *pipal* tree in order to gain fertility.[7]

Mackay (1937-38) was the next scholar who treated the subject in a concise way in his book *Further Excavations at Mohenjo-daro* (Vols. I & II). The tree in the seal (Fig. 1) according to Mackay, is undoubtedly a *pipal*. He further identifies another tree on a clay amulet, as a *neem* (*Margosa*) from the way the leaves hang downwards.[8]

Dikshit (1939) in his book *Prehistoric Civilization of the Indus Valley* referred to the worship of *pipal* tree in the Indus valley. In this regard, he draws attention to a few seals of religious significance including the unique *pipal* tree and the seated god.[9] According to him, with the upper classes, the worship of mother-goddess, the goddess of fertility and crops, must have been the central point round which other religious practices and beliefs were interwoven. A deity is seen represented by an interesting seal from Harappa in which a tree is shown as issuing out of her womb (Fig. 2), and the two rampant tigers stand guard on the mystery of birth. P. Jayakar has defined this seal (Fig. 2) in a nice way:

> From her womb a plant springs, straight and lithe, with its fine leaves uprising and auspicious. The earth is the great *yoni*. The woman's body in the Indus valley seal is the earthbound root, the fecundating source. The arms of the inverted figure are stretched to touch the knees as in the *yogāsanas*. The rampant tigers, guardians of initiation, protect the mysteries and the immense magic creation. The tigers are separated from the Earth Mother by the Indus valley script, a *mantra* or *dhāriṇī* or protection.[10]

In a pictorial theme found over a wide expanse of Africa and Asia, the goddess rises between two branches of a tree in the centre of circle. Incidentally, reference may be made of the representation of a goddess, which is found in more than one tablets as standing in the bifurcated branch of a *pipal* tree, and she has been identified as a mother-goddess. In this

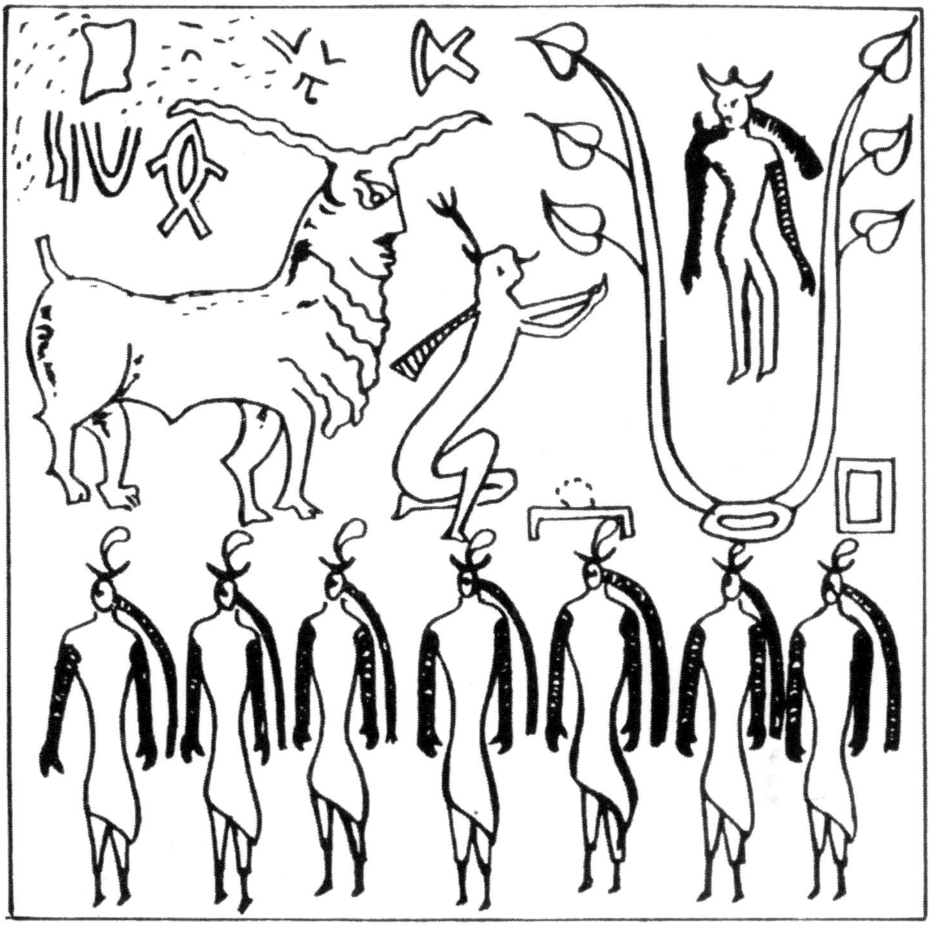

Fig. 1. *Tree Spirit in association with worshippers and animal;* seal; Harappa; National Museum, New Delhi

case, the worshipper appears to have brought a goat with a view to sacrifice it while a number of people in a row are seen standing in the lower register as if taking part in the said sacrifice[11] (Fig.1). These seven ministrant godlings have been identified by John Marshall, Mackay and other scholars as human attendants wearing short tunic-like jackets cut aslant at the lower border. According to both the scholars, the tree deity, the worshipper and the seven attendants are all females. But Sastri contradicts and believes that they are all male. He further adds that the *pipal* god was the supreme

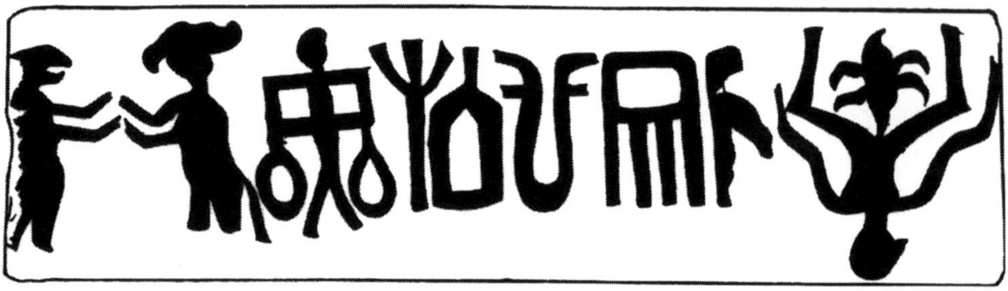

Fig. 2. *Goddess giving birth to the vegetation;* seal; Harappa; National Museum, New Delhi

deity of the Indus valley and the buffalo-headed god was only next to him in rank. Under the command of this supreme deity there was a host of smaller deities and semi-divine beings, some being anthropomorphic, some theriomorphic and others syncretic.[12] The present seal is a graphic representation of the legendary scene where the *pipal* deity figures prominently. The circular socket at the base of the tree is the seed vessel or basin from which the tree is issuing.

Sastri (1957) in his outstanding book *New Light on the Indus Civilization*, Vol. I, did little more justice with the subject than other scholars. He is of the opinion that like the Sumerians, the Indus people, too, had a tree legend. The *pipal* and acacia, probably *śamī*, were held sacred, one being the tree of knowledge (*brahmā-taru*) and the other the tree of life (*jīvana-taru*). Besides the tree spirit, the tree of life was guarded by a human-head composite animal, a three-headed chimera and probably by the divine bull or the buffalo. He has reported two Mohenjo-daro seals,[13] on which the game of 'Vaulting over the sacred bull' by priests is depicted. In one of these seals is shown the ceremony being performed in front of acacia, the tree of life, under the benign patronage of the buffalo-headed god. These seals have been dated in the first quarter of 3000 BC.[4]

The god under reference (Fig. 3) is carved on a square steatite seal. As seen on this Mohenjo-daro seal, the head-dress of the god looks a stylized copy of the *pipal* tree, flanked by two unicorn heads. In this, the buffalo horns represent the two conventionalised unicorn heads, and the headgear, the fan-shaped crest imitates the form of the foliage of the *pipal* tree. Thus, the pipal tree and the unicorn are symbols of the *pipal* God.[15] Sastri believes that Mother Goddess was not the supreme deity of the Indus valley but

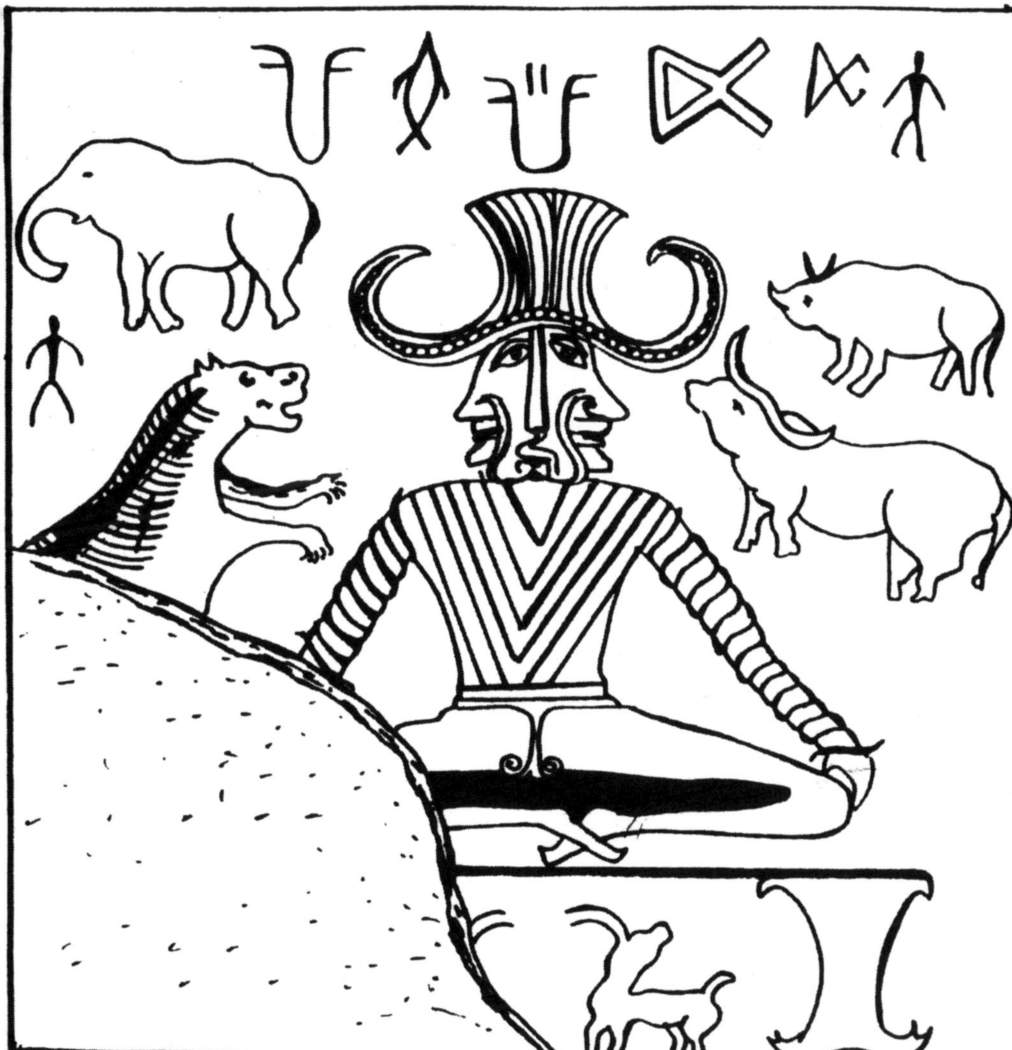

Fig. 3. *Horned human figure seated in a yogic stance;* Mohenjo-daro; National Museum, New Delhi

it was male god supposed to be the presiding spirit of the divine tree of knowledge that enjoyed this honour.[16]

Probably many religious beliefs and traditions of the Indus people were inherited by the Vedic Aryans. It may reasonably be deduced that the *pipal*

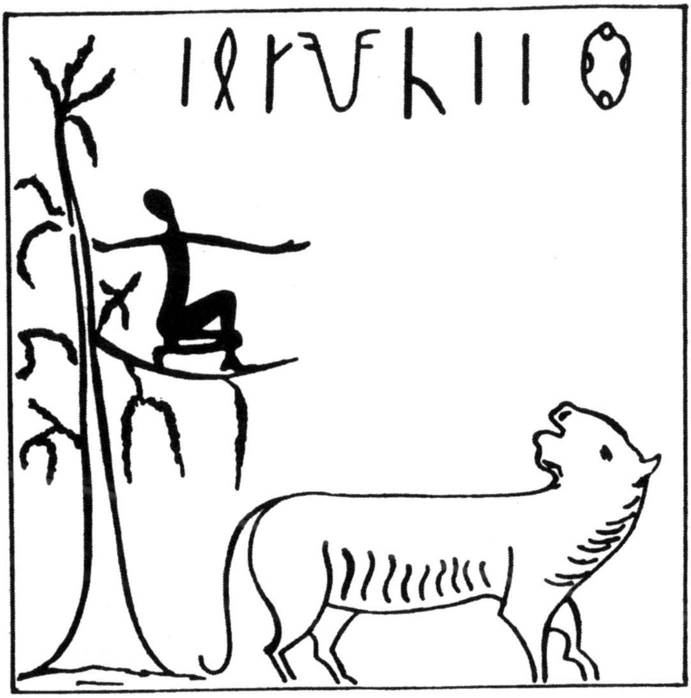

Fig. 4. *Tree Spirit in association with a tiger;* seal; Mohenjo-daro; National Museum, New Delhi

god of the Indus people held similar position even in the remote pre-Vedic age. His association with the *pipal* tree would lead us to believe that he was the creator god, the prototype of the Vedic *Prajāpati* (later Brahmā) and was held in high esteem. Besides, we are aware that the tree legend in the Indus valley is similar to Sumerian legend. It looks that there was a constant struggle on the part of the demons to take possession of the divine "Tree of life" for downing its branches on their heads whereby they could defy death and become invisible.[17] A reference may be made of a seal (Fig. 4) depicting tree spirit in mysterious dialogue with the tiger. The spirit, an *apsarā*, sits erect, her body held in perfect yogic equipoise, on the branch of a *neem* or *śamī* tree. The tiger stands below the tree without movement, in a still moment of listening. The long linear body of the tree spirit looks as a part of the tree and its branches, and has no separate volume or substance. In another seal (Fig. 5) from Mohenjo-daro, the tree woman has undergone transformation and metamorphosis. In this case the linear body form has given place to a rounded woman's body. She is now shown as half-woman, half-buffalo, with the horns of divinity. The body of the buffalo woman bends forward, one arm stretched to touch and claim the tiger. The horns of the tiger are formed of the leaves of *śamī* tree. His chest and pawn are inscribed with leaf patterns.

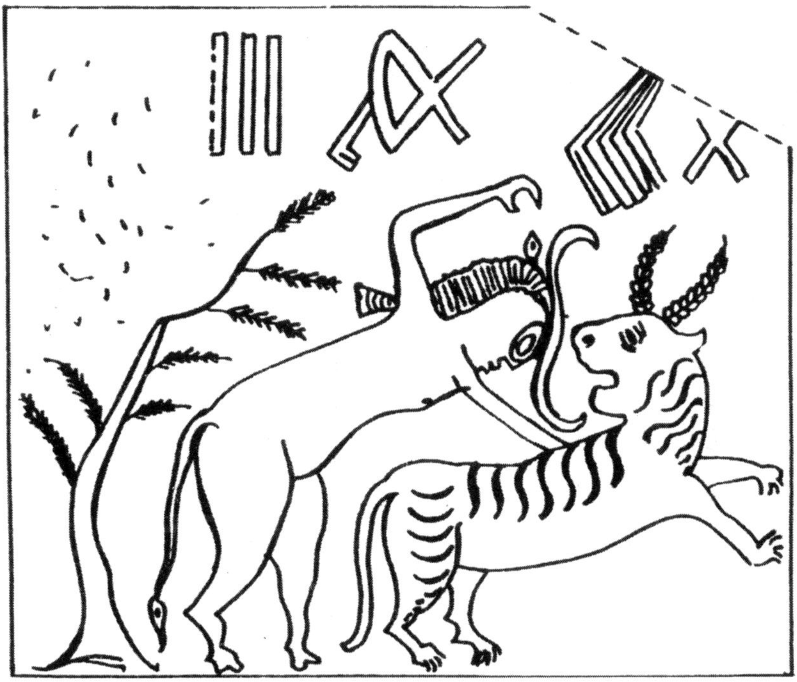

Fig. 5. *A half-woman and half-buffalo figure with horns of divinity in association with tiger and śamī tree*; Mohenjo-daro; National Museum, New Delhi

Lothal also produced five Indus seals, one of which is engraved with a unicorn. This animal as we know from the Mohenjo-daro seal, was sacred to *pipal* god and as such it shows that the people living at Lothal had preserved to some extent the dying religious traditions of their homeland.[18] It will not be out of place to mention here that unlike the other two sites of Rangpur and Rupar, Lothal was occupied throughout its life by the Harappans and by no other people.

The trees which can be definitely identified are the date palm, the *pipal* and the acacia, and it is really interesting to see them depicted on the seals and sealings. According to Sankalia, the acacia and the *pipal* are frequently depicted on terracotta and faience sealings. The best representation of a date palm is on a seal from Ḥarappa. This is shown vertically presenting the whole tree with palm leaves. It is worked and shown realistically with regard to the *pipal* tree. While the general form of the leaf can be made out from paintings on pottery, on the seal, the leaves are depicted perhaps too realistically. Thus, Mackay's earlier statement that the *pipal* tree does not appear on Mohenjo-daro pottery needs reconsideration.[19]

The prehistoric and proto-historic man in Indus valley must have had acquaintance with a number of trees. The archaeological examples as discussed above reveal that a few trees were opted for representation on the seals and sealings. These few trees include the *pipal*, the *neem*, the acacia, the *śamī* and the date palm. Therefore, the question arises, why only these trees were depicted? In the absence of other corroborative evidences it is to be believed that most likely the proto-historic people discovered usefulness of these trees in various manners. In order to save these trees from being cut by the wood hunters, these trees were associated with certain religious beliefs. Perhaps it was believed that, gods dwell in the tree (*Vṛkṣa Devatā* or *Vṛkṣa Devi*), therefore, their divine character was depicted in a befitting manner, sometime trees as such and sometime, trees personified. The sacrifices offered to the trees or the divine emergence of the trees from the body of a female goddess or the branches of the trees attached to the headgears of the divinities are some of the interesting examples which persuade one to believe that the notion of tree worship was already there in the minds of the pre-Vedic people. There are hundreds of references in the Vedic and post-Vedic literature where the glorification of the trees was noted. The archaeological evidences of the same were recorded as early as in the period of the Mauryas (4th century BC onwards) and thereafter. The tree worship remained a living faith among the Indians throughout the ages.

NOTES AND REFERENCES

1. Neumayer, E., *Prehistoric Indian Rock Paintings*, New Delhi, 1983, pp. 32-34, 41-42.
2. Ghosh, A. (Ed.), *An Encyclopaedia of Indian Archaeology*, New Delhi, 1989, p. 228.
3. Marshall, John (Ed.), *Mohenjo-daro and the Indus Civilization*, Vol. I, London, 1931, p. 65; cf. Plates XII, Figs. 16, 20, 21, 25 & 26.
4. *Ibid.*, pp. 63-65.
5. Sastri, K.N., *New Light on the Indus Civilization*, Vol. I, Delhi, 1957, pp. 15-18.
6. Incidentally, a reference may be added here that in Mesopotamia, the deities standing under arched tree coverlets were believed to be the underworld

deities. Thus Allatu, the queen of the nether world is shown under the cover of a bent tree (cf. Ward, H.H., *The Seal Cylinders of Western Asia*, p. 53).

7. According to Hewitt, Mariamma, the great mother-goddess of south India, was a tree goddess. The practice of marrying brides to a tree, he traced to matriarchal conditions, when true marriage was not recognized. According to Crooke, the idea behind these marriages is to bring the bride and bridegroom into close association with the fertility of nature. [See Marshall, John (Ed.), *op.cit.*, Vol. I, p. 66; cf. Hewitt in *Journal of Royal Asiatic Society*, 1899, pp. 338-39].
8. Mackay, E.J.H., *Further Excavations at Mohenjo-daro,* Vol. I, New Delhi, 1938, p. 341, pl. XC, 23b, 24b. According to Mackay, *neem* tree is regarded as sacred in most parts of India. Its leaves are supposed to repel snakes and they are eaten to cure various ailments. It is also the dwelling place of deities, especially the godlings of disease; and twigs of *neem* are much favoured as tooth brushes by the Indians of the villages who fray out one end.
9. Dixit, K.N., *Prehistoric Civilization of the Indus Valley*, Madras, 1939, pp. 33-34, 40-44.
10. Jayakar, P., *Earthen Drum: An Introduction to the Ritual Arts of Rural India*, New Delhi, 1980, p. 48.
11. The sanctity of the *pipal* tree has descended to the present day, but its association with the mother-goddess has not continued to the same extent. The sacrifice of animals, particularly of goats, is the most characteristic feature of the worship of Śakti, and this appears to have been one of the most significant survivals from the Indus religion.
12. Sastri, K.N., *op.cit.*, pp. 18-19.
13. *Ibid.*, pp. 2-3.
14. In a note appended to the Annual Report of Archaeological Survey of India for the year 1934-35, Dr. C.C. Fabri tried to show that these sacred sports were borrowed by the Indus people from Minoan Crete where they were periodically held in honour of the mother-goddess who was symbolised by the sacred tree, the divine dove and the double axe (cf. *ibid.*).
15. *Ibid.*, pp. 8-9.
16. *Ibid.*, p. 15.
17. *Ibid.*, p. 39.
18. *Ibid.*, p. 4.
19. Sankalia, H.D., *Pre-Historic Art in India*, New Delhi, Bombay, Bangalore, Calcutta, Kanpur, 1978, p. 16.

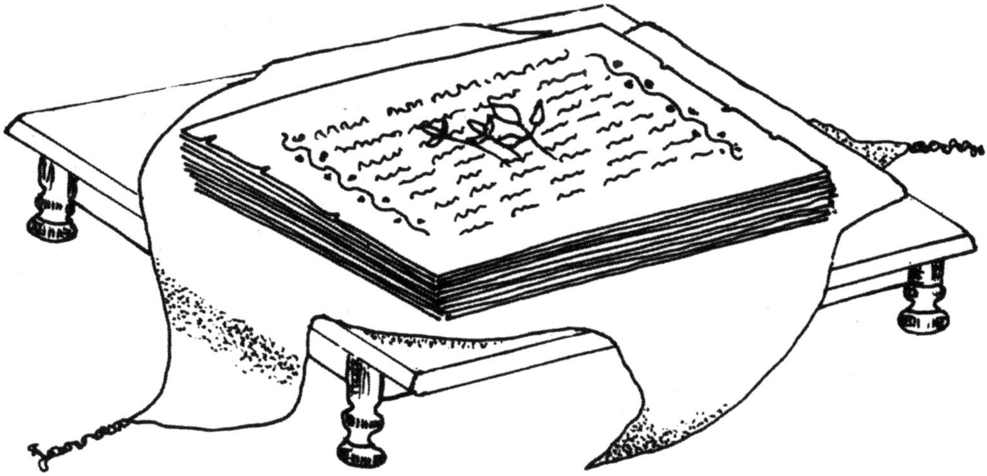

3 TREE WORSHIP IN METAHISTORICAL TEXTS

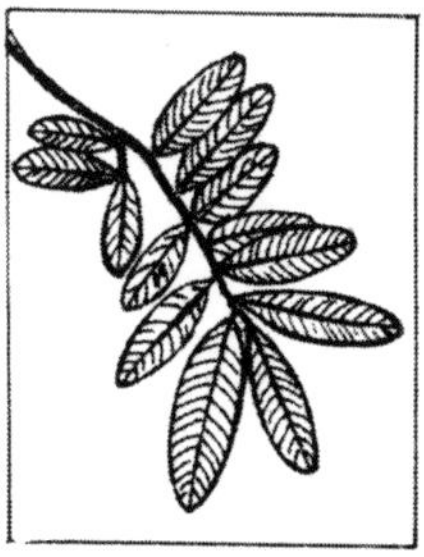

The Indian philosophy, thought, values and ethics have always had reverence for all that exists in nature, so much so that it evolved the concept that all that is alive, from plants to human species, belongs to a single family (*Vasudhaiva Kuṭuṁbakam*). They have originated from a common source and are interdependent. This cultural dictum was accepted by almost all religions (i.e. Hindus, Buddhists, Jains) which existed in India since ancient times. Even religions like Christianity and Islam have been influenced by these values in India. All civilizations have made use of tree symbol as fundamental expression of life, growth, fertility, procreation and so on.

A number of trees and plants have been held sacred and venerated since the Vedic times, which include the *soma (Sarcostemma acidum), pipal* (*Ficus religiosa*), *śamī* (*Prosopis ceneraria*), banyan (*Ficus indicus*), *udumbara* (*Ficus glomerata*), *bilva* (*Aegle marmelos*), *khadira* (*Acacia catechu*), *neem* (*Azadirachta indica*), *tulsi* (*ocimum sanctum*), *palaṣa* or *plakṣa* (*Butea frondusa*) and the lotus (*nelumbo nucifera*).

Soma

The *soma* plant and its juice were considered to have divine powers and the tree occupies an important place in the galaxy of Vedic gods, which include incarnation of *soma*, the revered Vedic god of the *soma* juice deity of the moon, and Lord of the stars and vegetation.[1] The *Ṛgveda* (9.91, 1) has referred to the high antiquity of *soma* worship as follows. "*By thy guidance, O brilliant (Soma), our courageous fathers have obtained treasures among the Gods.*" The whole of the ninth *Maṇḍala* (book) of *Ṛgveda* and six hymns in other *Maṇḍalas*, are presented in the praise of this plant. There is a belief that the tree abode of *soma* is regarded as heaven and is the Lord of that place. He was brought down from heaven by an eagle and is born as the Lord of the plants; this is further testified by the belief.[2] At a place in the said text (*Ṛgveda* IX. 5.9) *soma* is identified with Prajāpati, the Lord of beings, where the bard after summoning nature's artisan, Tvstṛ, then proceeds to identify both Indra and Soma, called Indu and Prajāpati with Soma, called Pavamana. The legendary *soma* plant also has connection with water. The *Ṛgveda* (12: 1-2) describes it both as a spring or stream and as a paradisiacal plant that promises life, fertility and regeneration. Therefore, *soma* has been praised as the creator and Lord of all that we perceive. *Soma* drink was also used in Vedic sacrificial rites in honour of Lord Indra.[3] The plant brought from the Himalaya was regarded of its kind and was very much sought for by the sacrificers (*ṚV.* IX.82, 3).[4] In the *Atharvaveda* (6, 136) a herb to be used medicinally is spoken of as a 'goddess born on the goddess earth.'

In the *Brāhmaṇas*, the plants are connected with *soma*, being styled *Saumya*. Irrespective of his being Lord of plants, Soma is often, like other leading gods, called a king.[5] It seems that the word *soma* is used indiscriminately in the Vedic texts, both as a god and as a plant. According to *Śatapatha Brāhmaṇa*, the sacrifice of *soma* is equivalent to the sacrifice of *puruṣa/prajāpati:* "For when the gods in the beginning seized (slew) a victim then as it was drawn upwards, its sacrificial essence flowed downwards, and from it sprang the tree" (*Sat. Br.* 3.8.2.17).

Here, the eternal exchange is clearly stated, which is the movement upwards and downwards. Without such exchange there can be no world.[6] There is also mention of seven other holy trees in the *Taittirīya Brāhmaṇa* (1.1.3).

During the Vedic period the trees became the sacrificial stake or even the royal column venerated at the entrance to all the towns and villages. No sacrifice could be completed without wood. It seems that Hindus were quite conscious about the significance of tree in their daily life. According to H.T. Colebrooks, a Brāhmaṇa rising from sleep, is enjoined, under the penalty of losing the benefits of all rites performed by him, to rub his teeth with a twig of the fig tree pronouncing to himself this prayer:

> Attend, Lord of the forests. *Soma,* king of herbs and plants has approached the; mayest thou and he cleanse my mouth with glory and good auspices, that I may eat abundant food.

The following prayer is also used on this occasion:

> Lord of the forest, grant me life, strength, glory, splendour, offspring, cattle, abundant wealth, virtue, knowledge and intelligence.[7]

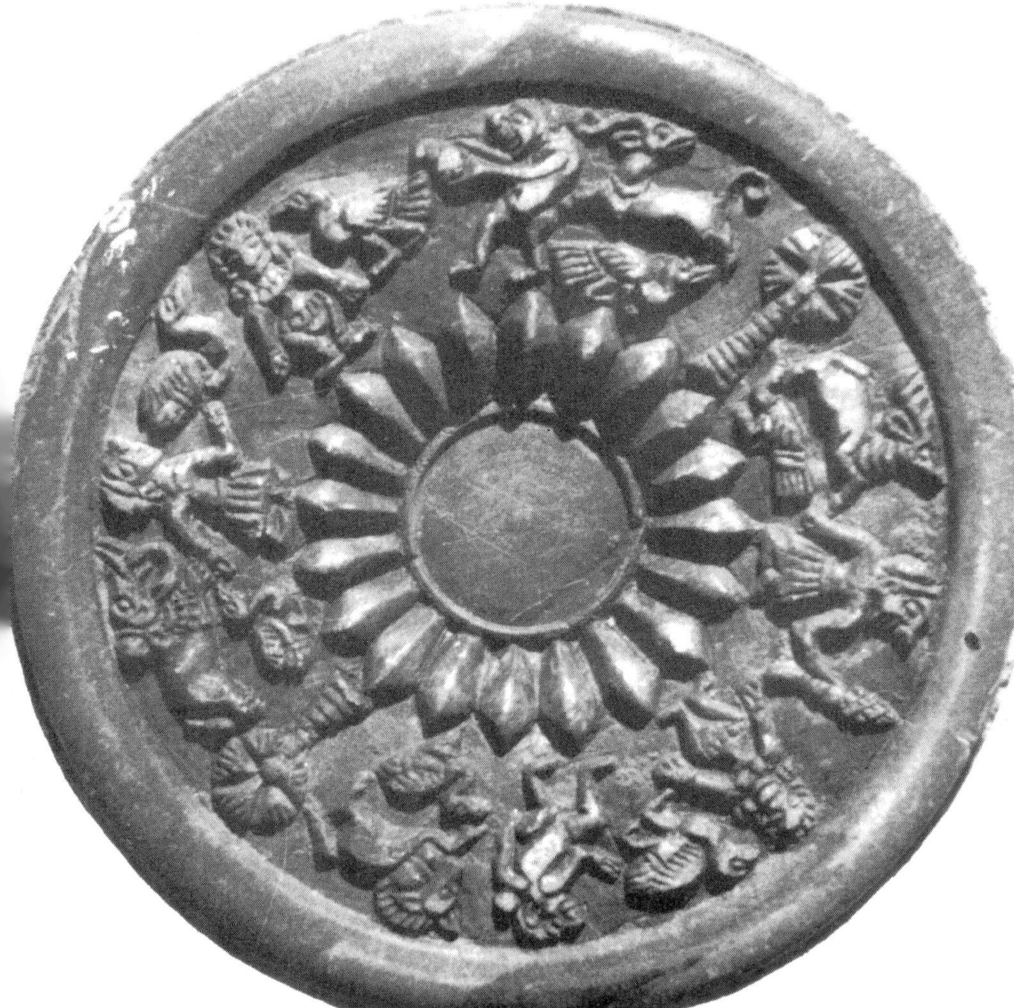

Pl. 1. Stone disc depicting Mother goddess attended by priests with palm trees, birds and animals; Murtaziganj (Patna); Patna Museum; 3rd century BC.

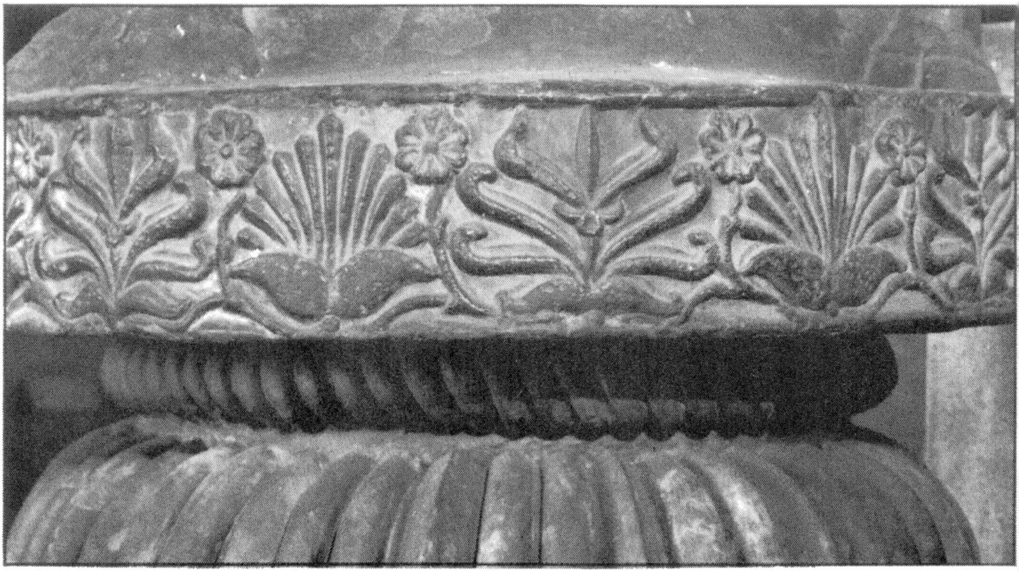

Pl. 2. Bull capital (detail); Rampurva; Rashtrapati Bhavan, New Delhi; 3rd century B

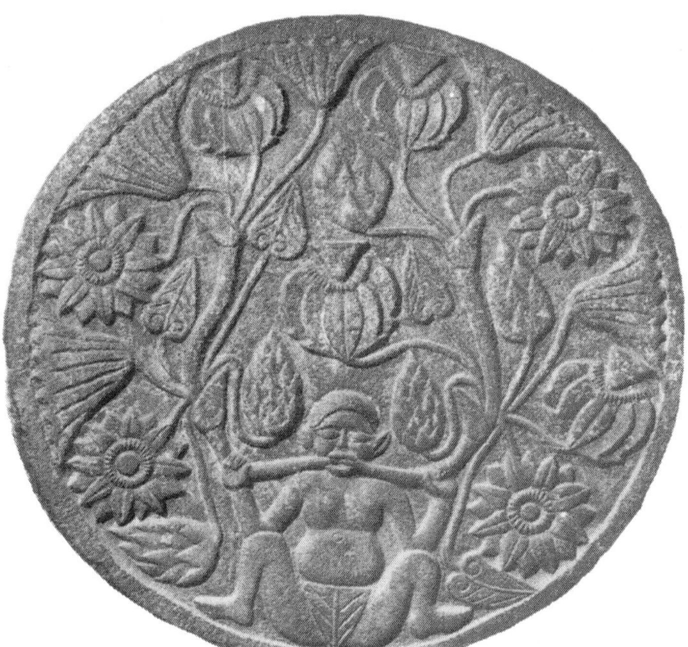

Pl. 3. Padma and utpala creepers issuing from mouth of a man; Bharhut Stupa Great railing, crossbar medallion; sandstone; Indian Museum, Calcutta; 2nd century BC.

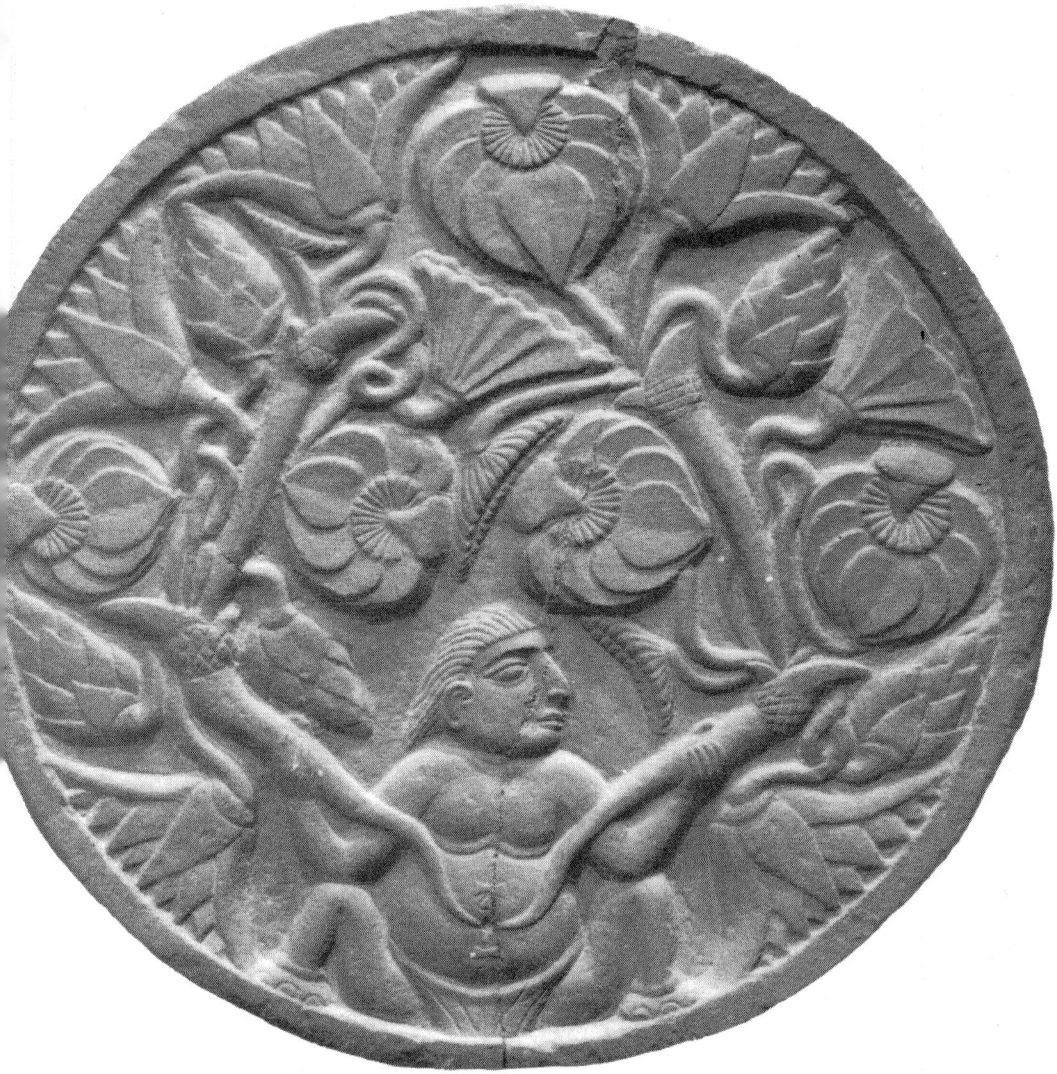

Pl. 4. Padma and utpala creepers issuing from the man's navel (other details are same as in Pl. 3).

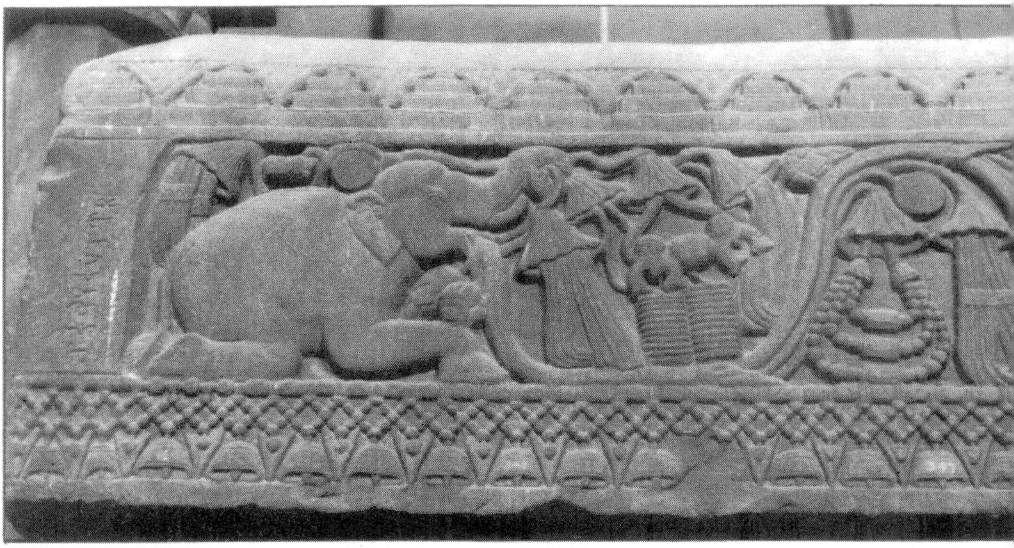

Pl. 5. Kalpalatā emanating from elephant's mouth on a coping stone (other details are same as in Pl. 3).

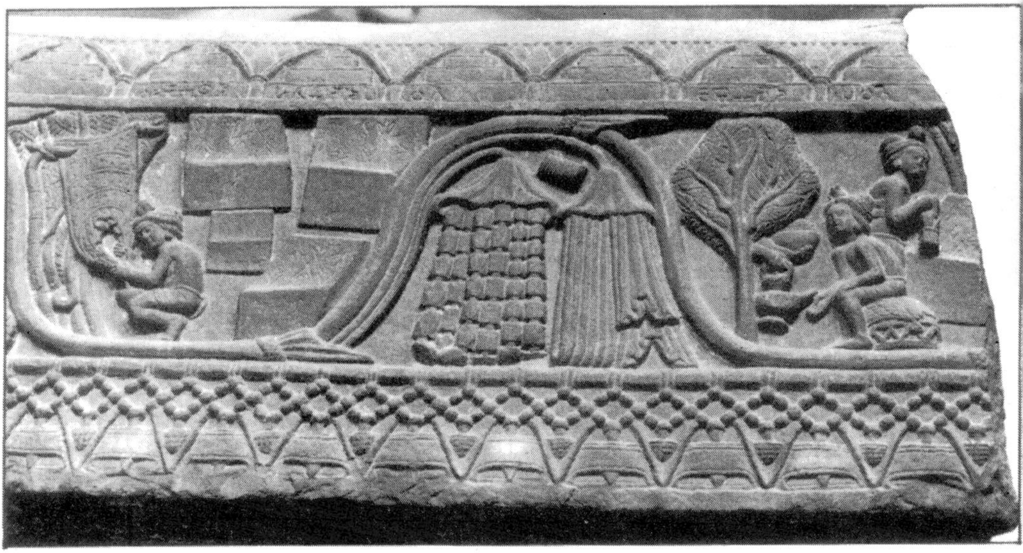

Pl. 6. Kalpalatā yielding jewellery etc. (other details are same as in Pl. 3).

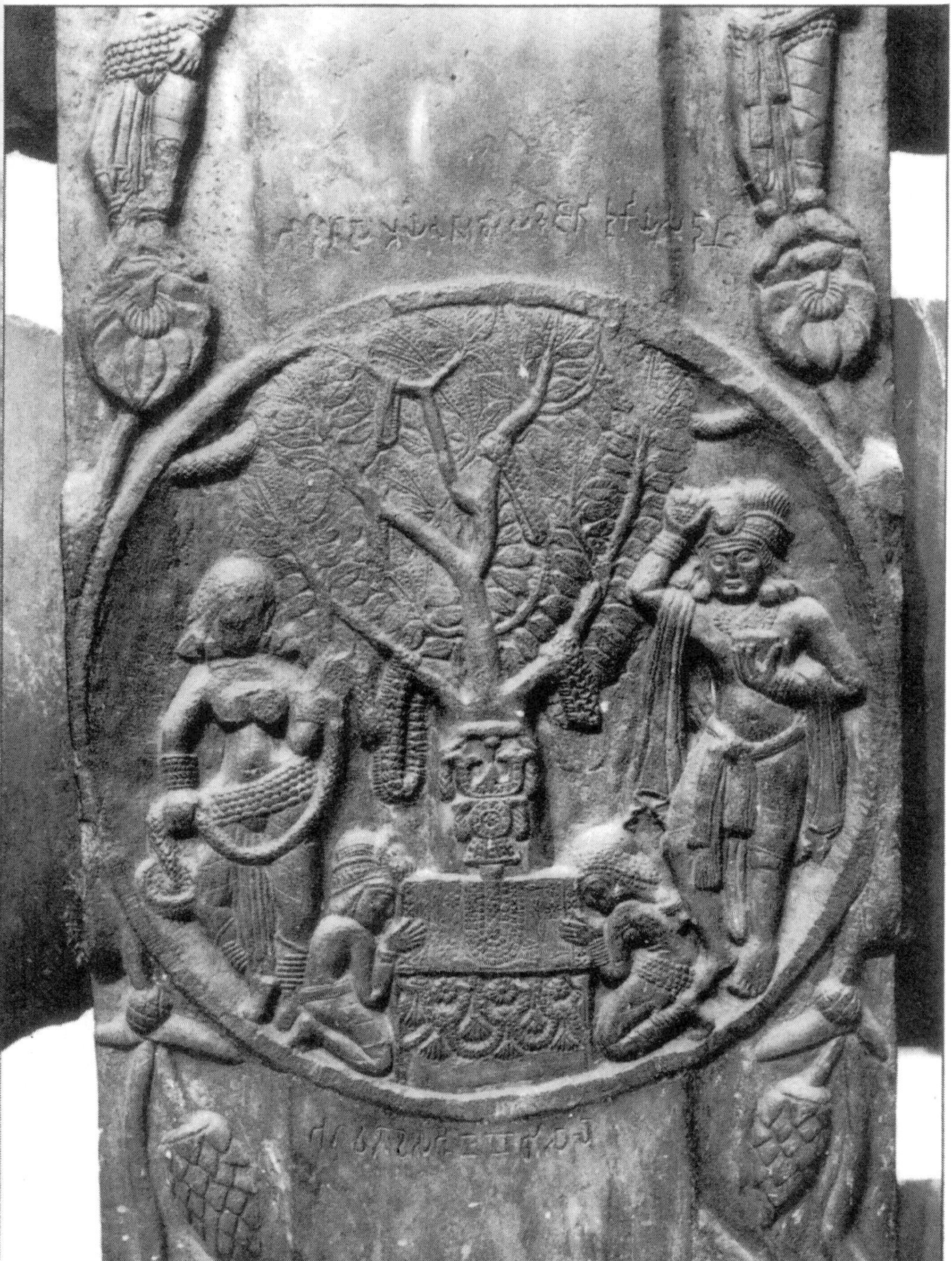

Pl. 7. Bodhi tree of Viśvabhu on a pillar (other details are same as in Pl. 3).

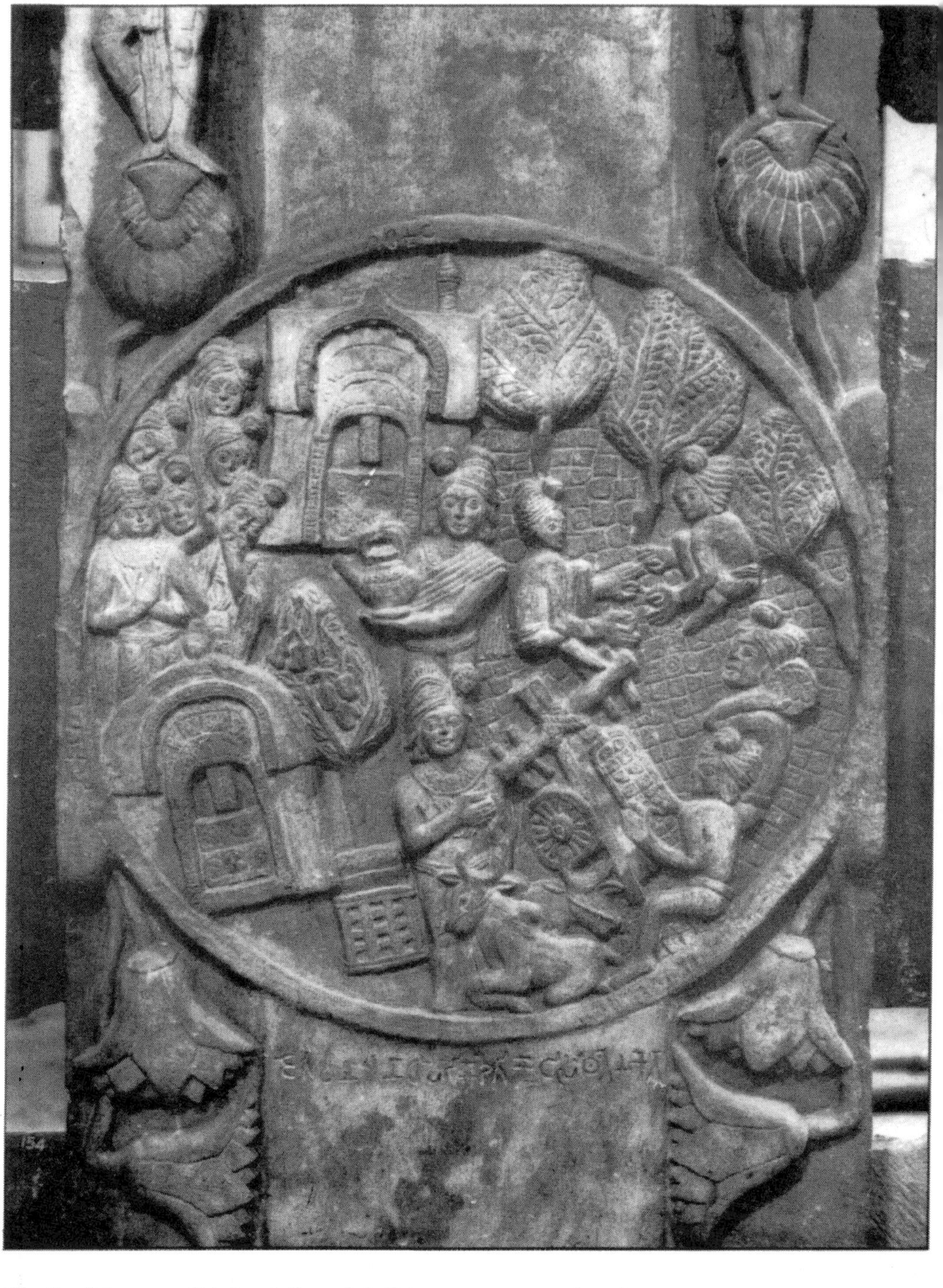

Pl. 8. Jetavana Jātaka (other details are same as above).

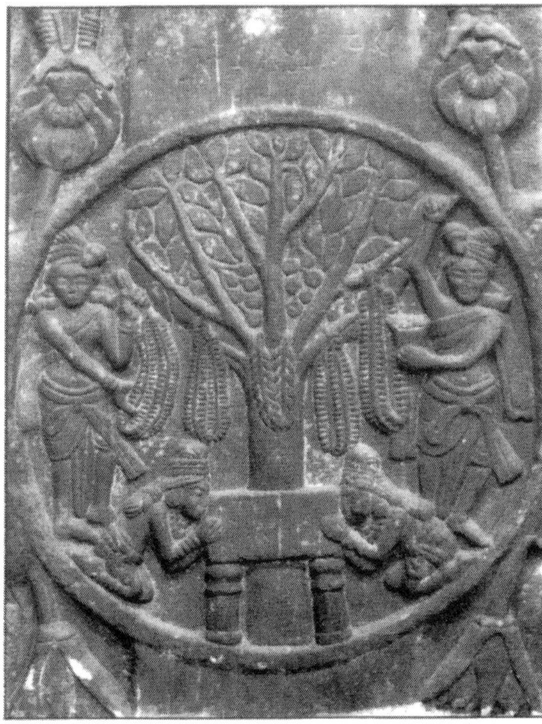

Pl. 9. Udumbara, Bodhi tree of Kanakmuni (other details are same as above).

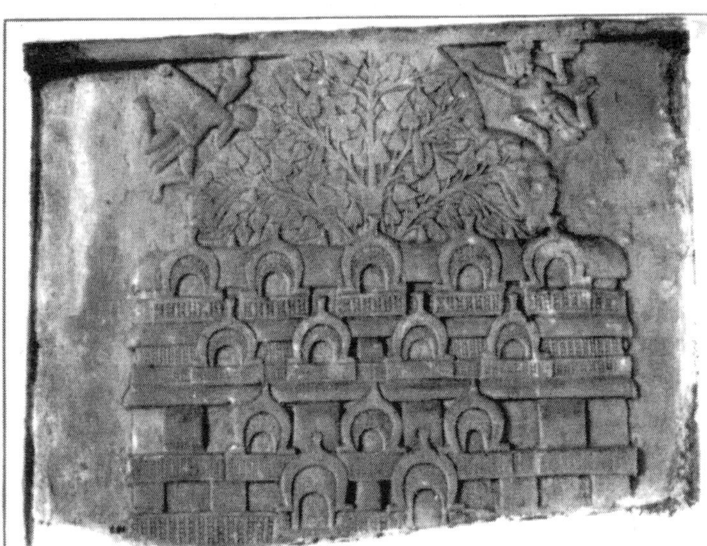

Pl. 10. Architectural fragment depicting huge aśvattha tree, Jaggayapetta (Guntur A.P.); white marble; Madras Museum; 2nd century BC.

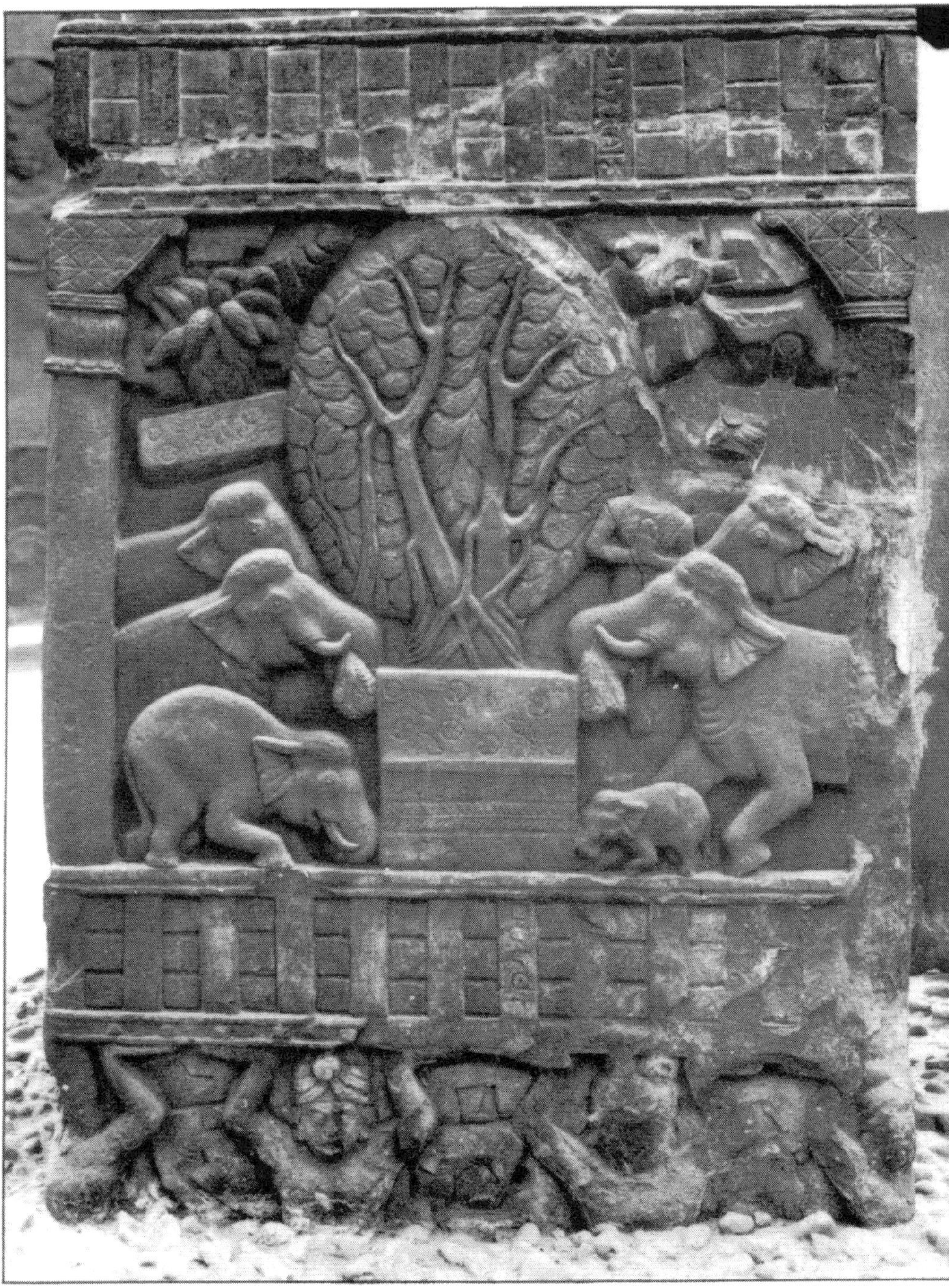

Pl. 11. Elephants paying homage to Bodhi tree; Pillar: (for details cf. Pl. 3).

Aśvattha

The *aśvattha* tree was made the basis of a profound metaphysical doctrine in Vedic times. The *Ṛgveda* (IX.5.10) mentions the cosmos as the tree of a thousand branches (*Sahasravalśa-Vanaspati*):

> O Soma, irrigate with our life-giving sap this tree which has a thousand branches, which is green and enriched with golden radiance.

From the *Atharvaveda* we learn that at the time of its composition, the *pipal* was worshipped for victory over enemies (III.6.1) and birth of the male progeny (VI. II.1).[8] *Aśvattha* is said to be abode of all gods (*Aśvatho deva-sadanaḥ)* luxuriating in the third heaven (*tritīyasyāmito divi*). In the later Vedic texts *aśvattha* is regarded as *Brahmā-taru* — the embodiment of knowledge and the Great creator. That is why *aśvattha* is called on certain occasions as 'tree of life' or the 'tree of creation'. In fact, Brahmā was born out of Viṣṇu and Viṣṇu in *Bhagavadgītā*[9] proclaims that 'He is the *aśvattha* among the trees.' A later notion reveals that *aśvattha* was fixed to be the abode of Lakṣmī. Similarly, Gobhila's *Gṛhya Sūtra* (24) is not wrong when it comments that "*aśvattha* is sacred to the Sun" because Viṣṇu is one of his *Ādityas.*[10] The *Mahābhārata* also includes *aśvattha* as one of the names of Sūrya. According to the same text[11] (Vol. X, *Anuśāsana Parva*), the man who worships *aśvattha* daily, worships the whole universe. Although the tree is mainly associated with Viṣṇu yet some consider Śiva as the patron deity of the tree. This tree is worshipped by the Brahmins daily during their evening prayer. The worshippers then walk round the tree, 7, 14, 21, 28, 35 or more times but always in multiple of seven.[12] Elwin believes[13] that sometimes the roots of *aśvattha* represent Brahmā, its bark represents Viṣṇu and its branches Mahādeva. In another mythology,[14] it is stated that Pārvati once cursed Viṣṇu, Brahmā and Śiva and they eventually transferred into *aśvattha, palāṣa* and *vaṭa* trees respectively. There is an interesting story in the *Skanda purāṇa* in which Suvarcās, the wife of Dadhīci is believed to have entered the roots of *aśvattha* tree and cut open her womb; the foetus from Dadhīci came out, it was an incarnation of Rudra; he was the renowned sage Pippalāda.[15] According to the *Śiva purāṇa,* Pippalāda was the aspect of Rudra himself born at the root of the *pipal* tree (*atha rudraḥ pippalādo's-śvatha-mūla mahāprabhu*).[16] The *Padma purāṇa* records that there is no other form of Viṣṇu on the earth like the holy fig tree, and the god in this form is most adorable.[17]

In an iconographic text[18] the goddess Bhūtamātā is supposed to have her abode under a fig tree. In the same text, abode of Kumārī is prescribed under a fig or *udumbara* tree.[19]

It is an age old concept that *apasarās* inhabit the sacred fig tree in which their cymbals and lutes resound. In the *Ṛgveda,* the *apasarās* are considered as celestial water nymphs, and are also regarded as the consort of the genius named Gaṅdharva.[20] The sphere of the *apasarās* extended to the trees is found in the later *Saṁhitās.* They are believed as inhabiting banyan and sacred fig trees.[21]

An individual tree or species of tree through association with a particular religion or historical event acquires the symbolic significance of the event as a part of its meaning. In Buddhist religion the *aśvattha* tree is regarded as very sacred, because Gautama Buddha attained Enlightenment under the friendly shade of this tree (Tree of knowledge). That is why this tree is called the *bodhi*–tree of *Śākyamuni.* It is considered by Buddhists both the source of life for all beings and the tree of Enlightenment. Besides, there was struggle between the conservatives and liberals in the Buddhist world for the idea of allowing image worship to lay devotees. The conservative circle opposed the idea of image worship. But at one stage, the followers of the said faith were allowed to show their respect to Buddha through some iconic symbols of which a tree within railing is one which is popularly known as *bodhi*-tree. That tree within railing represents Buddha can well be confirmed by an inscribed panel at Bharhut which says *Bhagavato Śākamunino Bodha.* On the basis of the text Cunningham refers that *Śākyamuni* once said to his main disciple Ānanda to bring one of the branches of that tree under which he attained salvation. His wish was accordingly met and the branch was planted inside the *vihāra* at Vaiśālī. Further, Buddha is known to have told that "He who worships it will receive the same reward as if he worshipped me in person."[22] The Buddhist texts *Nidankantha* and *Vinaya Pitaka: Mahavagga* (I, 1-4) have also referred to the account of Enlightenment of Buddha. According to the *Mahapadana Suttana,* the *bodhi*-tree of Buddha was an *aśvattha.*[23] The *Digha Nikāya* (II, 2-8) states that the six previous Buddhas were each enlightened under different species of trees.

That Emperor Aśoka loved to worship *bodhi*-tree is maintained in a certain portion of *Divyāvadāna.* But a contradictory view has been narrated by Hiuen Tsang who refers that a *bodhi*-tree was cut down by Aśoka himself. While going through the rock cut Edicts of Aśoka it can be presumed that

Hiuen Tsang's remark about the Emperor was baseless.[24] On the contrary, king Aśoka sent his son Mahendra and later his daughter Sanghamitta to Ceylon for propagating Buddhism there. A branch of the very *bodhi*-tree under which the Buddha had gained Enlightenment at Bodhgaya, was taken to Śrī Lankā and it was planted at Anurādhapura.[25]

The Jains also consider the trees sacred. The *Samavāyanga Sūtra* gives a list of past, present and future Tirthāṅkaras and records a list of *caitya-vṛkṣas* of all twenty-four Tirthāṅkaras of this age in the *Bharata Kṣetra.*[26] The *aśvattha* is regarded as the *caitya* tree of the fourteenth Tirthāṅkara Anantanātha in both sects of Jainism (i.e. Digambara and Śvetāmbara). A list of trees worshipped by ten classes of Bhavanvāsī gods is mentioned in the *Suthānānga Sūtra* (10.3, Su. 766). But a different list with some variations is supplied by the *Tiloyapannathi* (4.913 ff). According to the latter text, the *caitya* tree of Asura Kumara is *aśvattha* in both the sects of Jainism.[27]

In Christian world also, the fig tree is held with great esteem. In the Bible, the 'Tree of Life' in the Garden of Eden was the fig tree, symbolical of the male creative power.[28] The Christians believe that cross may also be referred to as a symbol of the 'Tree of Life' that stands in the Garden of Eden. The wood from true cross was believed to have the power to restore the dead to life. A variety of different trees are credited with being the wood chosen for Christ's cross: cedar, dogwood, mesquite, ash and oak.

Bilva

The word '*bilva*' is the name of wood apple tree (*Aegle marmelos*) which finds frequent mention in the Vedic texts. A mythical account is found in the *Taittirīya Saṁhitā* (II. i.8.1-2), which deals with the origin and significance of the *bilva* tree. According to this myth, the gods thought of making atonement for yonder sun who did not shine. They restored the brilliance of *Sūrya* by offering him a white cow. It is further said that the *bilva*-tree was born at the very reappearance of yonder sun. The sacrificial post of *bilva*-wood is used to acquire Brāhmaṇ-splendour and good place because of its divine origin. A similar type of mythical account of the divine birth of this tree is found in the *Maitrāyāṇī Saṁhitā* (III.9.3). As per this myth, yonder sun was here only but the gods stole him away from here to yonder world. It was from his brilliance that the *bilva*-tree was born, and he who desires Brāhmaṇ-splendour employs the sacrificial post of *bilva.* The same text also refers to the birth of *parṇa* and *khadira* trees. According to *Śatapatha Brāhmaṇa* (XII.4.4.8-9), the *bilva* was born out of the marrow of the Prajāpati which flowed from the ears. Elsewhere also,[29] the *bilva* and *udumbara* trees have been highly placed and eulogised:

> *mahā́m vaí bhadró bilvo bhadrá udumbaráh*
> *mahā́m abhiktá bādhate mahātaḥ sādhú khodánam.*
> (*AVŚ.* XX.136.15).

The same verse is also mentioned in the *Ṛgveda* (kh.v.22.10) and may be rendered as follows:

> Great, indeed, is the good *bilva*, great is the good *udumbara*, the great one presses on the knees (rendering for *abhijñu*), a good thing is the amorous sport of the great one.

The *Ṛgveda* further informs us that *bilva*-tree, the lord of trees, is born out most probably from the heat (*tapas*) of Prajāpati (*tapaśó dhi jātó Vánaspátis-táva vṛkṣo tha bilváḥ*).[30]

In some of the *Dharmasūtras* and very frequently in the *Śaiva Upaniṣads,* the *bilva* has got another name *śrīphala,* the fruit of plenty. In *Bilvopaniṣad* (7; 8; 16; 17; 18) and *Śivopaniṣad* (iv. 59) Lord Śiva is said to have a special liking for *bilva* tree (especially for its leaves) and is mainly connected with the Śaiva and Śākta cults. Generally, it is believed that no worship of Lord Śiva is possible without the leaf of this tree. To *Bilvopaniṣad* (8) the *bilva*-tree is nothing but the form of Lord Śiva. That is why even with a single leaf of *bilva* Lord Śiva becomes very much pleased.[31] In the same text (21), the worship of the *bilva*-tree is referred to at par with the worship of the Lord Śiva himself and its trefoliate leaf symbolizes the three functions—creation, preservation and destruction of the Lord as well as his three eyes.[32] Thus in Hindu mythology Śiva is

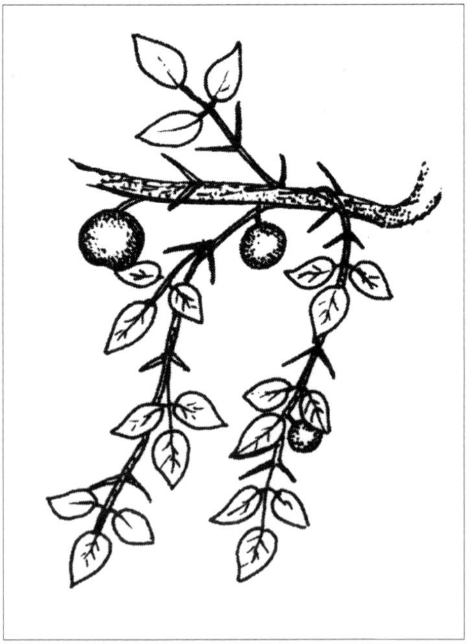

deeply connected with this tree, and is also called *Vilvadanda,* one endowed with staff of *bilva*-tree.

Bilva is also considered as one of the most sacred trees in the *Purāṇas.* According to *Garuḍa Purāṇa,* Sundara Sen, the vicious king of Arunda went out hunting and took rest in a bower of *bilva*-tree. There was a Śiva-liṅga in the bower. Some *bilva* leaves fell on the liṅga because king was plucking them. The plucking of the leaves made dust rise, and to lay down the dust king sprinkled water on the tree. During this process, some water dripped down on the Śiva-liṅga. Incidentally, an arrow fell down from the king's quiver; while bending to pick it up his chest touched the Śiva-liṅga. Having touched, bathed and worshipped the Śiva-liṅga with *bilva* leaves on the night of a fast (*vratam*) kept on *Śivarātri*, the king got his vision of Śiva.[33] A different version of the story is given in another legend.[34] As per this legend, a hunter climbed a *bilva* tree to shoot a deer. While waiting for deer he got bored, and just to kill the time he started plucking the leaves of the tree and throwing them down on a Śiva-liṅga which was installed under this tree. The hunter had a vision of Śiva telling him, "I make myself visible to you for it is not the way you worship that is important but the worship itself". The hunter had a vision of Śiva even by the accidental fall of leaves on Śiva-liṅga. It is believed that from this day onwards, the tree and its trefoliate leaves became sacred. In yet another interesting legend[35] the merit of offering a sacrifice of *bilva* fruit is given. In *Rāmāyaṇa*, it is said that before the start of battle of Rāma and Rāvaṇa, Brahmā took Rāma to a *bilva* tree growing on the seashore to invoke Devi on the *Krishṇa navamī tithi.* Rāma eulogised Devi and she assured him with a voice from heaven that he would be victorious.

In the *Baṇihi Purāṇa* and Tāntrika folklore, Lakṣmī is believed to have been born as a sacred cow and from her dung arose the *bilva* tree. Since the tree is affiliated with Lakṣmī, it is also called *Śrī-vṛkṣa,* the tree of prosperity and good fortune.[36] At another place,[37] both Lakṣmī and Saraswatī are mentioned as wives of Viṣṇu. Lakṣmī once got enraged over Viṣṇu because he loved Saraswatī more. She started worship of Śiva and was engaged in meditation for a long time but Śiva did not appear before her. And after a while Lakṣmī became the *bilva* tree and now Śiva dwells in the tree. Similarly, an interesting story is recorded in the *Brihaddharma Purāṇa*. Lakṣmī usually worshipped Śiva by offering him one thousand lotus buds. One day when she was going to worship Śiva, she found the lotus buds short by two. She decided to cut off her breasts and substitute them for the missing lotus buds, because her husband Viṣṇu always compared her breasts to lotus buds. When she cut off her breast Śiva got satisfied with her worship and sacrifice, appeared before her and said that her breasts would grow into a *bilva* tree.[38]

At the great Durgā-*Pūjā* festival in the autumn, Durgā is invoked on a twig of *bilva* tree. The festival is a rejoicing at the promising crops in the field. In this festival goddess Durgā along with nine leaves is worshipped. On the morning of the first day of *Pūjā,* nine branches with nine leaves are tied together with a plant of *Clitoriaternate alba,* and a twig bearing a pair of fruits with suitable *mantras* is stuck in the bundle. Before cutting the twig the following mantras are recited:

> *Śrīphala* tree, you are born on the mountain Mandarā, Meru Kailāśa, and at the top of Himavat, you are always a favourite of Ambikā. Born on the top of the Seri hill *śrīphala*, you are resting place of prosperity, I take you away to worship you as Durgā herself.
>
> Om Vilva tree, most prosperous, always favourite of Śaṅkara, I worship the Devi, having taken away your branch, O Lord, you must not mind the pain generated by the separation of your branch. I vow to the bilva tree born on Himalaya mountain, favourite of Parvasa and embraced by Śiva. You are auspicious in action and a favourite of Bhagavatī, for the sake of Bhavāni's words give me all success.

The bundle is then placed by the side of idols and the goddesses presiding over each plant are then separately invoked. Different injunctions have been prescribed to worship them.[39]

In Hindu iconography *bilva* plays an important role. According to *Abhilasitārthacintāmaṇi* (3.1.888) and *Viṣṇudharmottara Purāṇa* (III. 82.1-16), the goddess Lakṣmī should hold a *bilva*-fruit (*Śrīphala*) in one of her hands. In *Śilparatna* also, the two-handed variety of Lakṣmī holds a *bilva*-fruit in one of her hands. In the opinion of Coomaraswamy, Lakṣmī is connected with vegetation and the *bilva* (wood-apple) tree is especially related to her.[40] The *Śrītatvanidhi* informs that the images of *Kārttikeya* should be depicted with a fruit (or leaf) of a *bilva* tree on his head.[41] The image of Bāla-Gaṇapati is prescribed to carry a wood-apple in his trunk. Similarly, Taruṇa-Gaṇapati should hold a wood-apple in one of his hands.[42]

Banyan

The banyan tree has been held in great adoration since Vedic times. This tree is also called as *Bahupāda,* one with many feet and is a symbol of long life, and associated with divinity. *Vaṭa* has a special place in Indian literature and is often described as *Guru* and as an *akṣaya vṛkṣa*. According to *Gītā* (15.1) what was known in Vedic times as the imperishable *pipala* tree, *Avyaya Aśvattha*, became later known as *Akṣaya vaṭa*, the Eternal banyan Tree[43] (*Ūrdhamūlamadhaḥ Śākhamaśvatthaṁ prāhuravyayam).* The *Aitareya Brāhmaṇa* records that a certain king was asked to drink its milk leaving aside the juice of *soma* plant. Similarly, in the *Rāmāyaṇa* of Vālmīki and *Uttara-rāmacarita* of Bhavabhūti, this tree has been mentioned as the undying one (*Akṣaya vaṭa*) which was situated on the confluence of Gaṅgā, Yamunā and Sarasvatī at Pryāga (Allahabad). It is said that Sītā offered her *pūjā* to this tree before going south with Rāma during their exile. Huen Tsiang has mentioned the existence of this tree at Prayāga in his travels also.[44]

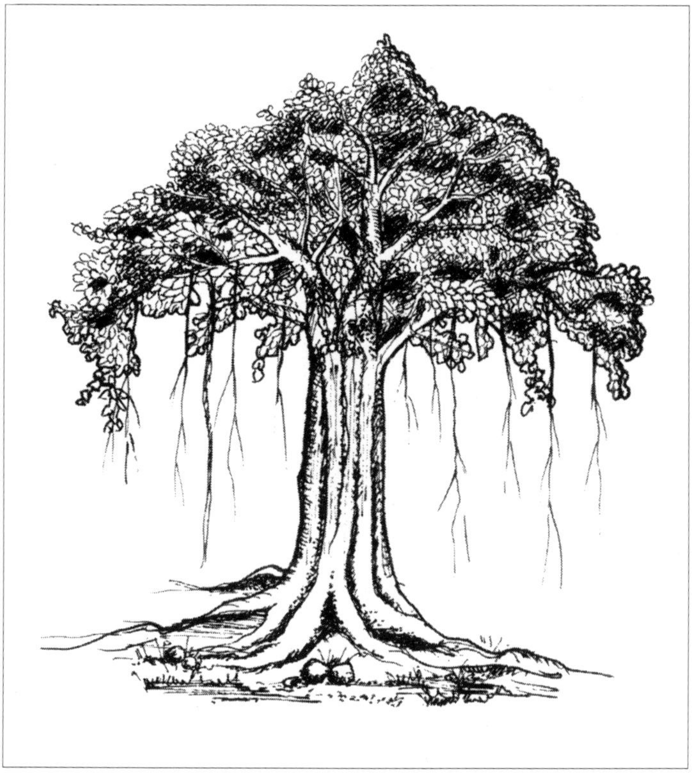

The banyan is called as the crested one and has its deities too. It symbolises Śiva and is, therefore, held sacred. Dakṣiṇāmūrti, the aspect of Śiva as a teacher, communicates the truth silently to his pupils, seated under the banyan tree of knowledge. The tree is also a symbol of Brahmā and grows in Puṣkara *dvīpa* as his special abode.[45] It was under a banyan that Satyavāna died and his wife Sāvitrī began her famed argument with the Lord of

Death, at the end of which she emerged triumphant and won for her husband his life. On every Saturday of the month of *Jyeṣṭha* women pray this tree for long life of their husbands. In the states of Bihar and Uttar Pradesh, women worship this tree and recite the story of *Bata-Sāvitrī*. Similarly, in Maharashtra and Gujarat women worship this tree to honour the memory of Sāvitrī on the 15th day of the dark-half of the month of *Jyeṣṭha* (May-June).[46]

The *purāṇas* have also glorified this tree. As per *Matsya Purāṇa*, during the universal deluge at the end of an epoch Lord Kṛṣṇa in his child form sleeps on a leaf of *nyagrodha*. In *Viṣṇu Purāṇa*, the tree is compared to Viṣṇu: "As the wide-spreading *nyagrodha* tree is compressed in a small seed, so at the time of dissolution, the whole universe is compressed in thee as its germ. As the *nyagrodha* germinates from the seed and becomes first a shoot and then rises into loftiness, so the created world proceeds from thee and expands into multitude."[47] According to *Brahmā Purāṇa* (103.5), Śiva is associated with the Indian fig tree (*vaṭa*). When demon Hiraṇyākṣa entered the sacrificial ground of one Priyavrata, all gods fled away or hid themselves; Śiva entered the *vaṭa* tree.[48] Interestingly, the *Skanda Purāṇa* (V.1.70.41; 43-44) has referred to *vaṭamātaraḥ* (Mothers of *vaṭa* tree).[49] It records that the *vaṭamātaraḥ* Brahmāṇī, Kumārī, etc. were created by Brahmā to kill the demon Andhaka, near a *vaṭa* tree, hence they became famous by that name. On the new moon day of *Śrāvaṇa* they are said to be worshipped at Avanti. The said *Purāṇa*[50] further refers to the worship of *Bhūtamātṛkā* from the first dark in *Vaiśākha* and lasts till 14th. Her abode is said to be an old tree and by her side a holy *vaṭa* tree or a branch of the tree may be planted. Caṇḍikā, a form of Pārvati or Durgā is mentioned to be at the root of the *vaṭa* tree.[51] It is a general belief that banyan planted in front of temples is tenanted by either Viṣṇu or Śiva, and the trees planted in public places have lesser divinities such as *yakṣa, kinnara,* or *gandharva*.[52] The *Purāṇas* further mention that Cāmuṇḍā should have her abode in a funeral ground under a *vaṭa* tree.[53] The goddess Maṅgalā is said to be the root of a *vaṭa* tree. Similarly, Śrī mātā was installed near a *nyagrodha* tree.[54] In some parts of the south India, Aiyanar, the guardian deity of the village sits under this tree.

In *Matsya Purāṇa*, the banyan tree is called *kalpavṛkṣa* (wish-fulfilling tree),[55] whereas, the *Jambu* and *Kadamba* trees respectively are *kalpavṛkṣas* in the *Mahābhārata* and *Bhāgavata Purāṇa*.[56] Sometimes, the *pārijāta* and the *mandāra* are considered as the wish-fulfilling trees. Incidentally, a reference may be made to the 12th century Bengali poet Govardhana Ācārya, who records that the *vaṭa* tree is the abode of Brahmā, Lakṣmī, Kuvera and Ṣhasthi.[57] Another 16th century Bengali poet also refers to the *vaṭa* tree as abode of Ṣhasthi.[58]

The banyan tree is often grown in close proximity with the *neem* tree. To the Hindus, the intertwined branches of the two trees are a holy union and are normally not cut down. Of other holy trees and plants, the banyan is sacred to *Kāla* or time. The tree enjoys a kind of immortality. When a man plants a banyan or *aśvattha,* he repeats a prayer to the following effect: "May I abide in heaven as many years as this tree continues growing on the earth."[59]

In the Buddhist world, three trees are associated with the attachment of Omniscience by Buddha. These trees are known as: the tree of Enlightenment (*aśvattha*), tree of the Goatherd (*nyagrodha*), tree of the serpent king Muchalinda. Among the separate representations of *bodhi*-trees of the seven Buddhas, *nyagrodha* is the tree of Enlightenment of Kaśyapa *muni.*[60] This tree is perhaps called as *mahāśāka vṛkṣa* in the Pali *Ambattha sutta* of the *Digha Nikāya* (c. 400 BC), where Buddha says to Ambattha, "My ancestors lived at the foot of the Himalayas where there was a great ancient and very strong tree (*mahāśāka vṛkṣa*), hence they were called Shākyas. Our dynasty was founded by Okkako of *Āditya gotra.*" (Apparently, *Āditya gotra* refers to the *Āditya sampradāya*).

In Jain mythology, spirits connected with tree worship are assigned to the *Vyāntara* gods. These *Vyāntaras* are subdivided into eight groups, *piśacās, bhūtas, yakṣas, kinnaras, kiṁpuruṣas, mahārajās* (*nāgas*) and *gandharvas.* As per Śvetāmbara traditions, each group has on its crest the tree symbol in the following order: *kadamba, śulasa, vaṭa, khaṭvāṅga, aśoka, campaka, nāga,* and *tumbaru.* But the Digambara list substitutes the *badari*-tree for the *khaṭvāṅga. Khaṭvāṅga* alone does not seem to be the name of the tree in the Śvetāmbara list. In Jain iconographical texts, *kevala-vṛkṣa* of Tirthāṅkara Ṛṣabhanātha is *nyagrodha* (*vaṭa*) tree in both the sects[61] (i.e. Śvetāmbara and Digambara).

Khadira

The *khadira* is mentioned from the *Ṛgveda* onwards as a tree with hard wood (*AV.* X.6.6), and is considered sacred both by the Hindus and the Buddhists. There is also mention of it in the *Bhāgavata Purāṇa* and other ancient Indian texts. The *Garuḍa Purāṇa* has recorded the names of the flowers offered in various months of the year to the various deities. In *Āśvina* god Suradhipa, lord of celestials is worshipped with flowers of *vakula,* twigs of *mādhavi,* champaka flowers and twigs of *khadira.*[62] According to the *Skanda Purāṇa* (II.5.7.27 ff), among other flowers, the flower of the *khadira* tree is favourite to Viṣṇu. All the nine plants which are believed to control the destiny of a man are associated with different planets. The planet *Maṅgala* (Mars), hence *Manglavāra* or Tuesday is identified with Kārttikeya and *khadira* is sacred to him.[63] A myth regarding the birth of *khadira* is mentioned in the *Vāmana Purāṇa.* As per this myth, *khadira* took his birth from the middle body of Brahmā.[64] The sacrificial post, sacrificial ladle *(Surva)* and sacrificial fire are made of *khadira* wood.

The *khadira* also finds mention in the Buddhist Jātaka stories. It is believed that when Brahmādatta was the king of Benares, Bodhisattva was born as a wood-pecker in the *khadira-vana.* Since he lived in the *khadira-vana* (acacia trees), he was called *Khadiravaniya.*[65]

Kadamba

Kadamba tree is closely associated with Lord Kṛṣṇa and it might have been a common tree in the age of *Mahābhārata.* The tree is held sacred by the followers of Kṛṣṇa. The flowers of this tree are offered at the temples dedicated to Lord Kṛṣṇa in memory of his swinging from its branches and dancing under the tree with the milk-maids (*gopīs*) of Vrindāvana. According to *Bhāgavata Purāṇa* (X.2.1 ff), Kṛṣṇa stole the clothes of the *gopīs* while they were bathing naked in the river Yamunā and took them on the *kadamba* tree. The *Skanda Purāṇa* (III.2.9.108-111) finds mention of the various deities as presiding deities of various *gotras.* Interestingly, some of these include tree-goddesses which include *Kadamba.* It is believed that some tree-goddesses changed into family goddesses.[66] For an auspicious occasion special consecration of a jar is enjoined (*Kalaśa-adhivāsa*) which is filled with twigs of *kadamba* besides other things.[67] In connection with the vows in relation to Śiva, various incenses are prescribed in various months, by the *Vāmana Purāṇa* (17.32 ff). The same *Purāṇa* prescribes the incense of *kadamba* tree in the month of *Māgha.* In *Viṣṇu Purāṇa* four sacred mountains are recorded: Mandāra, Gandhamadana, Vipula and Supārśva and on each of them grows a tree, *kadamba, jambu, aśvattha, vaṭa,* each tree spreading over 1100 yojanas and towering like banners.[68] As per *Bhāgavata Purāṇa,* a mango tree is present on mountain Mandāra; *jambu* on mountain Merumandara; *vaṭa* on Kamunda and *kadamba* on mount Supārśva. But the original *kadamba* tree grows on one of the mythical sacred mountains of Hindu mythology, i.e., Gomantha mountain.[69]

In *Brahmāṇḍa Purāṇa* (II.4.44.24-27), the goddess Lalitā is closely associated with foilage, select-creepers and trees as is clear from the names *nīpa-priya, kadambeśi* and *kadamba-vana-vāsinī*. Lohitayānī, the nurse of Skanda is worshipped under a *kadamba* tree. In yet another *Purāṇic* legend,[70] Brahmā and the *kadamba* are associated together.

In Jain iconography, according to Śvetāmbaras the *kadamba* tree is the symbol on the *dhvajās* of the Piścācas,[72] while in the Digambara sect *kadamba* is the *caitya-vṛkṣa* of *Bhavanavāsī* Stanita-Kumāra.

The two south Indian dynasties Pallava and Kadamba seems to be symbolic of tree worship,[72] as *Pallava* means the leaves of the tree and the *kadamba* is a very sacred tree in Hindu mythology.

Silk Cotton

The silk cotton tree is also an object of adoration to Hindus because Brahmā, the creator, after completing his creative acts was exhausted and rested under its shade.[73] Many ancient Indian texts have described it as the tallest of trees and its fruit is regarded as poisonous.[74] Its wood is used in funeral pyres. The tree is, therefore, also called as *Yamadruma*, Yama being the god of death. It is believed that a large *śalmalī* tree grows on the mythical *Śalmalīadvīpa*, giving its name to the island.[75] The silk cotton tree is also regarded with reverence throughout west Africa.

In both the sects of Jainism (i.e. Śvetāmbara and Digambara), the *śalmalī* tree is associated with one of the ten classes of *bhavanvāsīs*.[76] In *Digambara* sect, it is the *caitya-vṛkṣa* of Suparṇa-Kumāra.

Plakṣa

That sacrificial implements were made out of the *plakṣa* tree is frequently mentioned in the *Vedas*.[77] There are also some *purāṇic* evidences which prove the said fact.[78] In the *Padma Purāṇa (Cittarakanda)*, *plakṣa* tree is associated with Brahmā. According to the legend, Śiva and Pārvatī were engaged in an amorous dalliance when the Agni *devatā* visited them in the guise of a Brahmin by the orders of *devatās* and celestial beings. Pārvatī cursed the whole host of gods and deities to be born as trees. It is because of the curse that Brahmā was converted into a *plakṣa* tree, Viṣṇu into *aśvattha* and Rudra into the *vaṭa* tree.[79] Most of the Hindus regard it sacred because of the trifoliate formation of its leaves which represents the Holy trinity—Viṣṇu, the preserver in the middle, Brahmā the creator on the left and Śiva the destroyer on the right.[80] According to *Garuḍa Purāṇa*, on the 13th day of the moon's increase in the month of *Māgha*, god Naṭeśvara should be offered *kunda* flowers and *plakṣa* twigs.[81] The red orange flowers of the tree are offered to the gods, especially to goddess Kālī. Similarly, a dye prepared from its flowers is used to sprinkle on passers-by in the spring festival of Holi. Therefore, the tree has come to be associated with Kṛṣṇa also. The *Liṅga Purāṇa* mentions that on the occasion of eclipse of the moon and the sun, one should offer the flower of the *plakṣa* tree into the fire.[82] *Plakṣa* is also sacred to planet *Soma* (moon) after whom *Somavāra* or Monday is named. According to a myth recorded in the *Vāmana Purāṇa*, *plakṣa* arose from the right side of the Yama.[83] While *Padma Purāṇa* (28.7-8) records that Sarasvatī which is said to have flown through the *plakṣa* tree is called *plakṣa-devi* hints to a mixture of the motif of tree worship and river worship.[84] Interestingly, the staff placed in the hand of a Brahmin boy at the time of his thread ceremony is made from *plakṣa* wood. When a Brāhmaṇa boy becomes a sādhu, he is given the *plakṣa* leaf to eat or he must eat off *plakṣa* leaves. In Hindu iconography, goddess Brahmāṇī is supposed to be shown seated under *plakṣa* tree.[85]

The *plakṣa* tree is considered sacred by Buddhists and Jains as well. In Buddhist *Jātakas*, this tree often figures. According to *palaṣa Jātaka*, during the reign of Brahmādatta of Benaras, Bodhisattva was born in the form of a *kiṁśuka* tree spirit.[86] In Jain canons of Digambara sect,[87] the *caitya-vṛkṣa* of Śreyāṁsanātha (11th Tīrthāṅkara) and Agni-Kumāra (Bhavanavāsī) is *plakṣa*.

Coconut

Of all fruits the coconut is perhaps the most sacred. It is offered to deities, and is considered to fulfil desires. *Nāriel* fruit is believed to be the symbol of Śiva because of three black spots as Śiva has three eyes.[88] The priests in southern Indian temples will not accept the offering of a devotee, if it does not contain a coconut. It is also worshipped as Sarasvatī, the goddess of learning. In Gujarat, every bride offers a coconut to her bridegroom and he is supposed to preserve it throughout his life. In Mysore it is worshipped as a family god. The women who nurse the desire for a son, are given a coconut as *prasād* by the priest. Even in olden days it was a custom to present it to the king as a gift by the Brāhmaṇas. It is further offered as an oblation to the sacred fire in all the sacrifices.[89] There is a common belief in western India, that the sea in high tides may be appeased by offering the coconut.[90] At Chaupati in Bombay, a number of devotees are seen making their offering to the Lord of waters on the full-moon day.

According to *Mārkaṇḍeya Purāṇa* (6.12), the coconut tree figures in the description of the forest visited by Baladeva.[91] Besides, Gopinath Rao[92] believes that the image of Bhakti-vighneśvara should hold a coconut in one of his four hands.

Rudrākṣa

The *Bhāgavata Purāṇa* (XI.2.54), informs us that a Vaiṣṇava devotee should wear a *rudrākṣa.*[93] *Rudrākṣa* beads originated from the tears that Śiva shed when the Tripuras were destroyed as mentioned in the *Skanda Purāṇa.*[94] In yet another myth it is said that Pārvatī strung *rudrākṣa* fruits as jewellery on the direction of Śiva.[95] The *rudrākṣa* is considered to be sacred, Rudra being the name of *Śiva* and *akṣa* means tears. The *Agni Purāṇa* informs that god himself gave the methods of *rudrākṣa* beads to be worn.[96]

Snuhi

Snuhi tree is associated with Manasā. This tree is worshipped by women for seeking the blessing for their child. It is a general belief among the followers of the Manasā Devi that on the fifth day of the dark half of the moon in the month of *Śrāvaṇa,* goddess Manasā appears on the tree, with eight serpents with their hoods spread.[97]

Mādhavī Latā

In ancient Indian literature, *mādhavī latā* is frequently mentioned. In *Viṣṇu Purāṇa.* Madhavī is the wife of Viṣṇu as Mādhava, and the plant has been named accordingly.[98]

Amalaka

Amalaka (*Dhatrica*) tree is very sacred to both Śiva and Viṣṇu. The leaves of the tree are essential in the worship of the said deities. The tree is also sacred to both Lakṣmī and Pārvati as recorded in the *Bṛhaddharma Purāṇa.*[99] It is worshipped on *Śivarātri* day with flowers and fruits just as in the worship of deity. Besides, *amalaki* is considered a plant which was transformed into a beautiful woman to entice Viṣṇu away from the charms of Vrindā.[100]

Udumbara

According to *Atharvaveda*, the sacrificial ladle and amulets were made out of *udumbara* tree.[101] The seat of god Vivasvan, who is worshipped at the end of *Soma* sacrifice is made out of this wood. There is a belief that during the night of Dipāvalī all the gods gather together on the top of this tree and they pluck all its blossoms. The roots of the tree are considered as Brahmā, its bark as Viṣṇu and branches as Śiva. The tree is compared with Viṣṇu because one of the names of Viṣṇu is *Udumbara*. Women worship this tree for prosperity and offspring.[102]

The tree is sacred to Buddhists as well. In fact, *udumbara* is the *bodhi* tree of Kanakamuni.

Mango Tree

The mango tree is of great religious significance in India. Hindus consider it the symbol of Prajāpati, Lord of all creation. Interestingly, the mango tree in *Brahmāsaras* is in the shape of Brahmā.[103] According to a *purāṇic* story Śiva during his separation from Pārvatī sat under a mango tree, and was united to Pārvatī by the grace of Lalitā.[104] The small branches and pieces of mango tree are used in sacrificial rites. Its flowers are dedicated to moon on the second day of the *Māgha* as well as to Madana, the god of love.

Mango tree is also considered sacred by the Buddhists and Jains. The Buddhists consider the tree holy ever since Lord Buddha was presented with a grove of mango trees, while in both sects of Jainism, *āmra* is the *caitya-vṛkṣa* of the eighteenth Tīrthāṅkara Arānātha. Goddess Ambikā had her abode under a mango tree also.[105]

Child Live Tree

Hindu women consider the Child Live Tree (*Jivaka*) as sacred and worship it. The rosaries made out of the stones of the fruits are worn by those parents whose children do not survive. They consider them to possess divine powers and keep the children in good health.[106]

Plantain

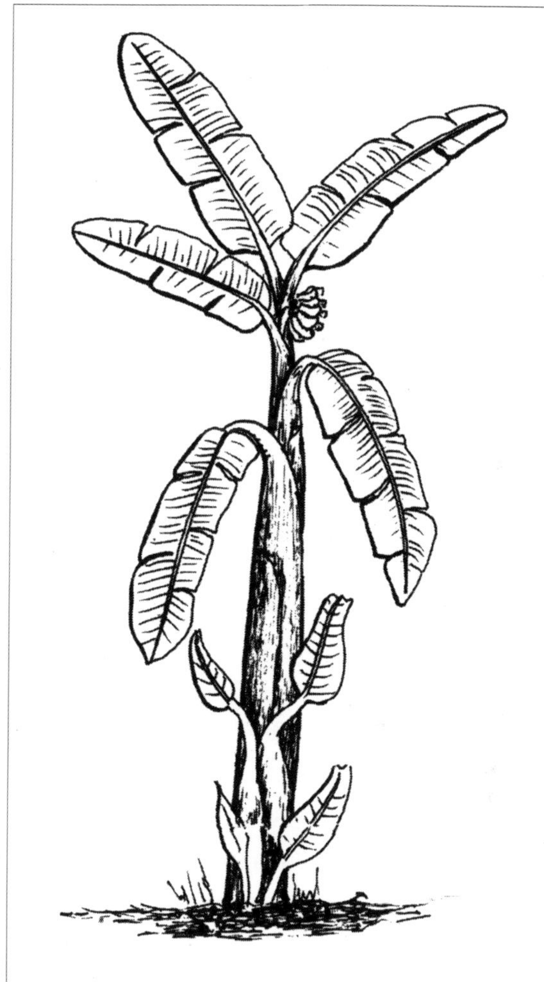

Plantain (*Kadali*) is regarded very sacred by Hindus. Women desiring male progeny worship it in the month of *Kārtika*. The plant is auspicious to both Vaiṣṇavites and Śaivites as it is considered to be an incarnation of Pārvatī, the wife of Śiva, and of Lakṣmī, the wife of Viṣṇu.[107] It is noteworthy that the plantain deity identified with Lakṣmī and Pārvati is an agricultural deity called *Nava-patrikā*. A life size statue of the goddess is carved out of the plant and dressed like a bride.[108] The image is mainly worshipped by women for the gift of a husband, a child or for a prosperous life. Besides, the image of goddess Nandā Devi is also carved out of the trunks of the plant. The leaves of the plant are especially used in the worship of Satyanārāyaṇa.[109]

Tulsi

The servants of Yama do not come to this house in the vicinity of which there is a grove of tulsi, due to the house having the nature of a holy place. O brāhmaṇa, the tulsi grove is auspicious and removes all sins.

She (i.e. the tulsi plant) was formerly planted by Viṣṇu for the good of all the worlds. The leaf and flower of tulsi are valued in all good works.

There is the proximity of Viṣṇu, where there is tulsi grove. Brahmā also (lives) there, and also Lakṣmī with all the hosts of gods.

Padma Purāṇa IV.22.22

The *tulsi* is the object of greatest adoration than any other plant at present worshipped in India. It is not merely sacred to Viṣṇu or to his consort Lakṣmī; it is pervaded by the essence of these deities, and is itself worshipped as a deity and prayed accordingly. The plant is worshipped all over the year but special importance is attached to its *pūjā* in the month of *Kārtika*. The following prayer is often addressed to it: "I adore the tulsi in whose roots are all the sacred places of pilgrimage, in whose centre are all the deities, and in whose upper branches are all the *Vedas.*"[110] It is believed to have married Viṣṇu on the eleventh day of the bright half of the month of *Kārtika,* hence it is known as *Haripriyā*. The Vaiṣṇava devotee offers his daily meals to Viṣṇu by putting a leaf of *tulsi* in his food. Indian women plant a *tulsi* sapling in their house and worship twice a day for removing all the sins, and for gaining wealth and happiness in the world.[111] *Tulsi* is also regarded as the mother and hence is called *Tulsi Mātā.*

In Jain mythology, *tulsi* plant is the *caitya vṛkṣa* of Bhutas.[112]

Ber

The *Rāmāyaṇa* and *Mahābhārata* have referred to Indian jujube (*ber*) at many places. Its fruits are offered to Śiva and at the same time are associated with Indra. *Vadari* is also sacred to Viṣṇu, and Viṣṇu is called Badrinātha, the Lord of *Badarī*, the jujube tree.[113] It is said that the holy river Gaṅgā arises from below a big *vadari* tree growing on Mount Kailāsh.[114]

Although Sikhs do not believe in the sacredness of trees yet there is one tree of jujube growing in the Golden Temple complex of Amritsar. This particular tree is held sacred by the Sikhs and is known as the tree which removes sorrow.

Śāla

The trees which are associated with the birth of Buddha include *śāla.* The other trees connected with the legend of his birth are the mango, the *aśoka* and the *palaṣa.* The great demise of Gautama Buddha also took place in a grove of *śāla* trees. Therefore, the tree is held with great esteem by Buddhists because it is connected with two great events of Buddha, i.e., nativity and *nirvāṇa.* In *Bhaddasala Jātaka*, the *śala* tree was the Bodhisattva himself.[115]

Śāla tree is mentioned in the *Rāmāyaṇa* also, and was held sacred

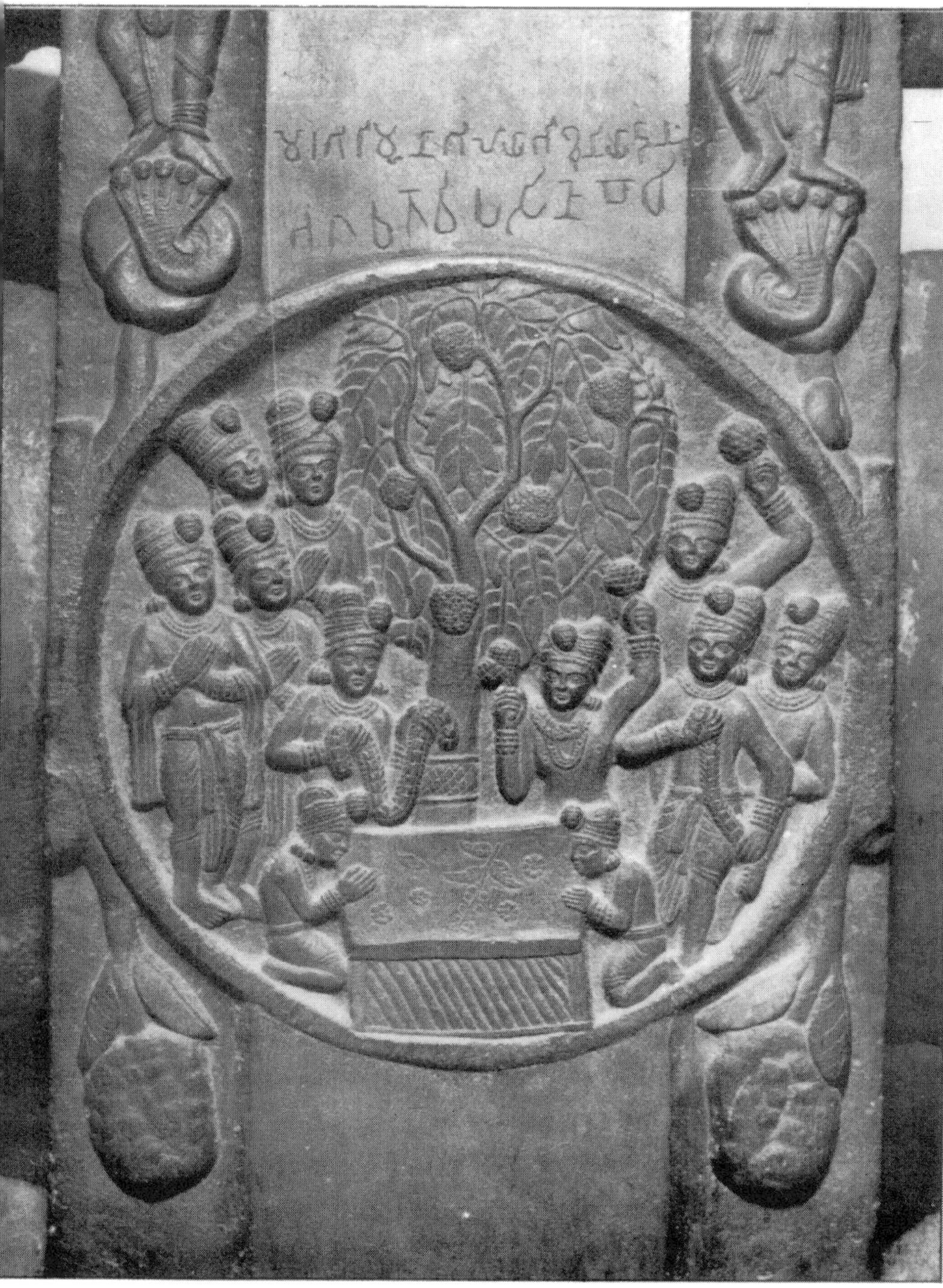

Pl. 12. Patali tree, Bodhi tree of Buddha Vipasyin; Pillar; (cf. Pl. 3 for other details).

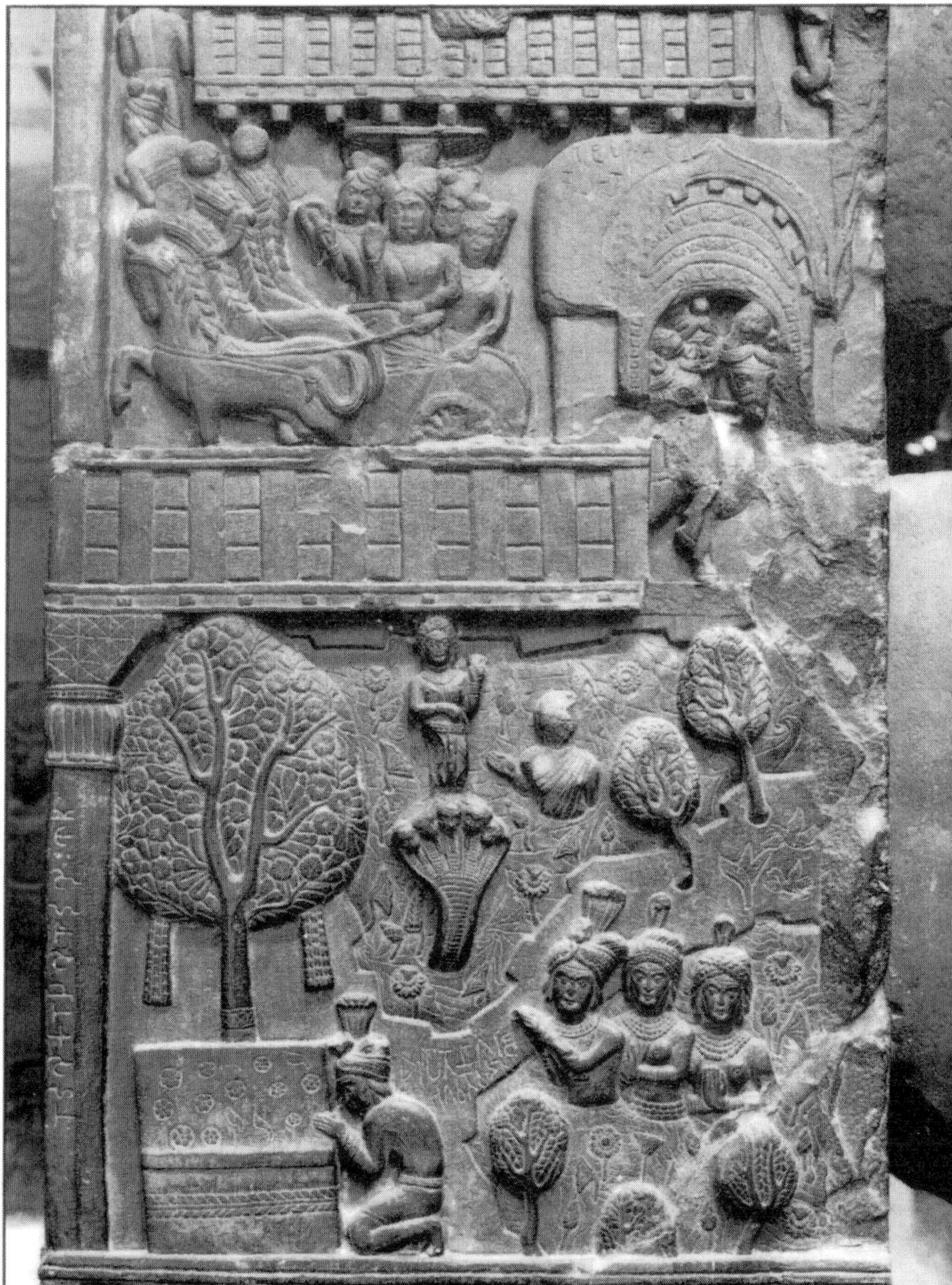

Pl. 13. Nāga King Erapata worshipping Bodhi tree; Bharhut Stupa, Great railing, South gate, Corner pillar; Sandstone, Indian Museum, Calcutta; 2nd century BC.

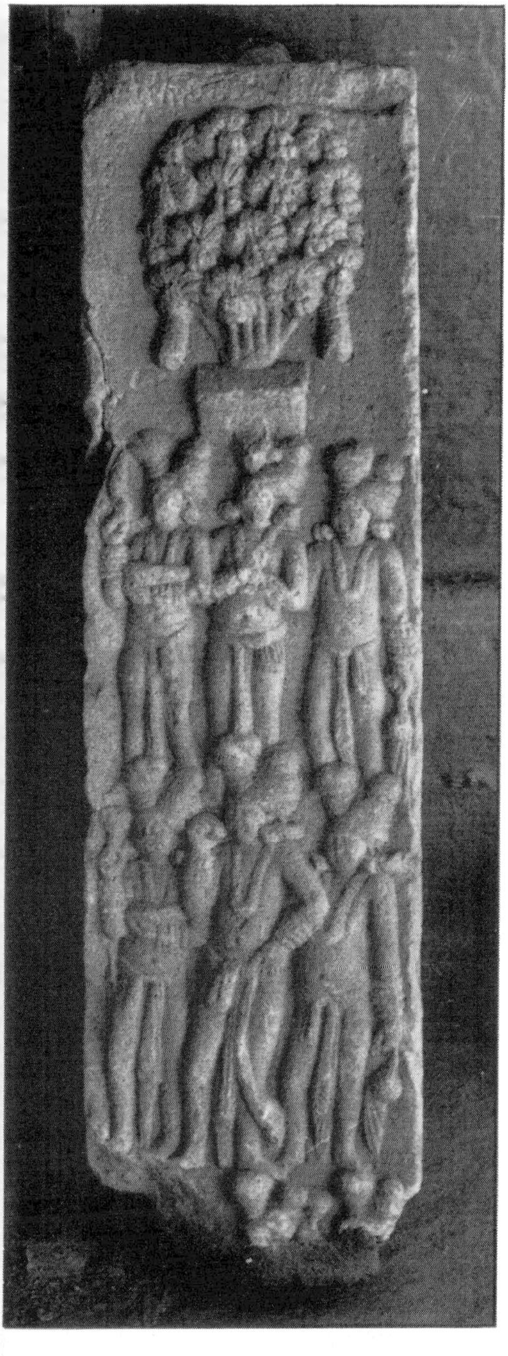

14. Tree within railing; Besnagar (M.P.), Railing Pillar; Sandstone; Central Museum, Gwalior; 2nd century BC.

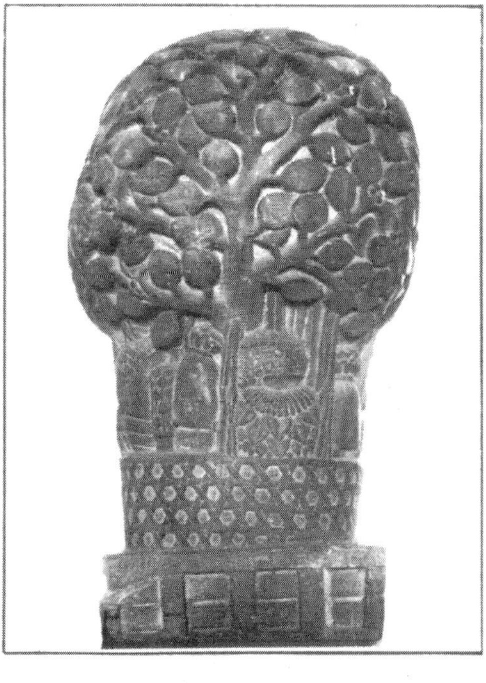

Pl. 15. Kalpavṛkṣa; Besnagar; Sandstone; Indian Museum, Calcutta, 2nd century BC.

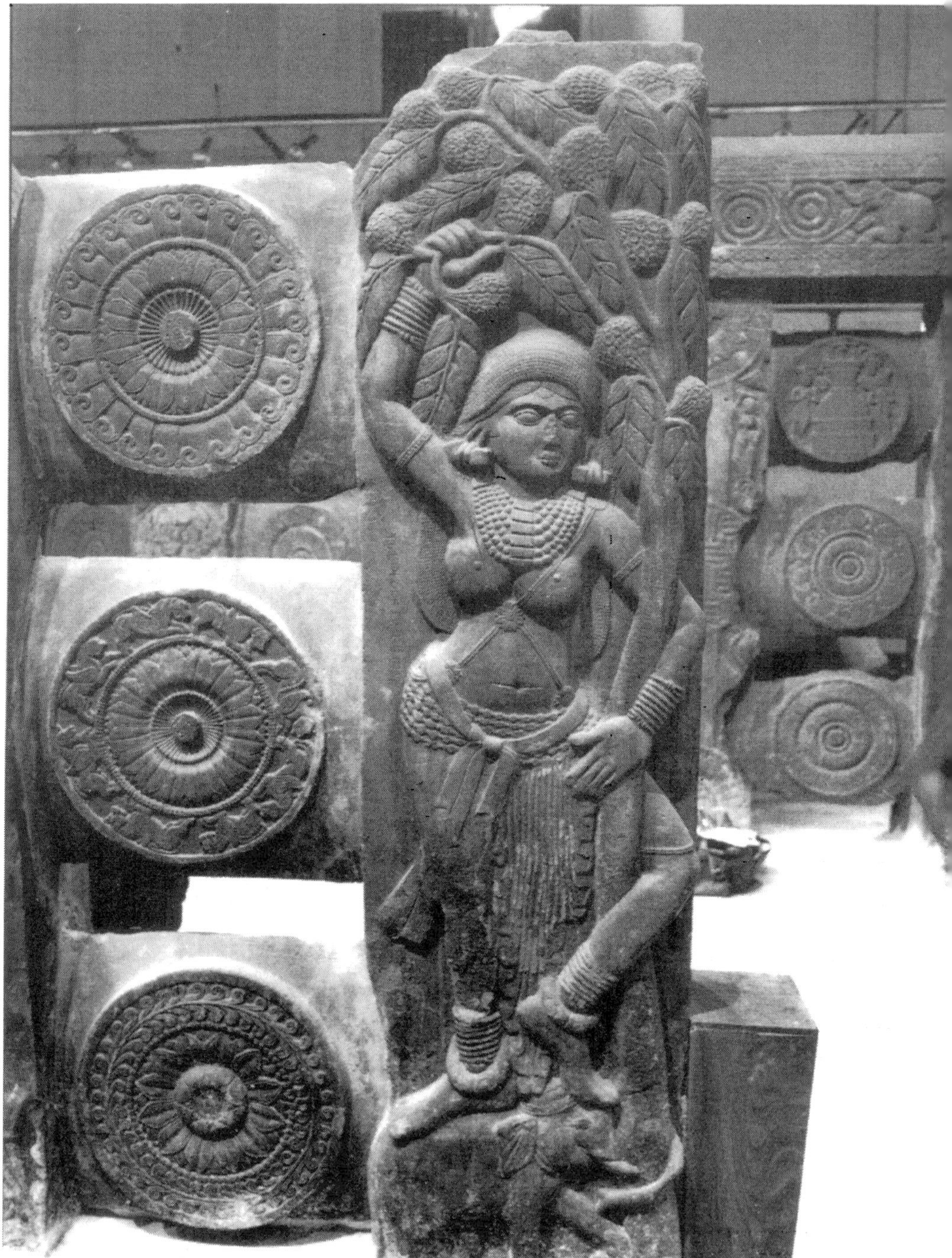

Pl. 16. Culakoka Devatā; Pillar; (cf. Pl. 13 for other details).

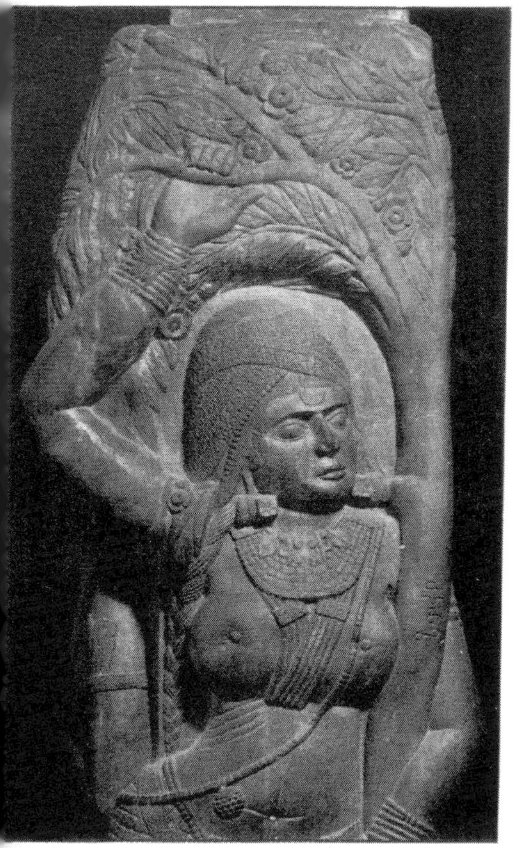

Pl. 17. Yakṣi Candra bust; north gate; (cf. Pl. 13 for other details).

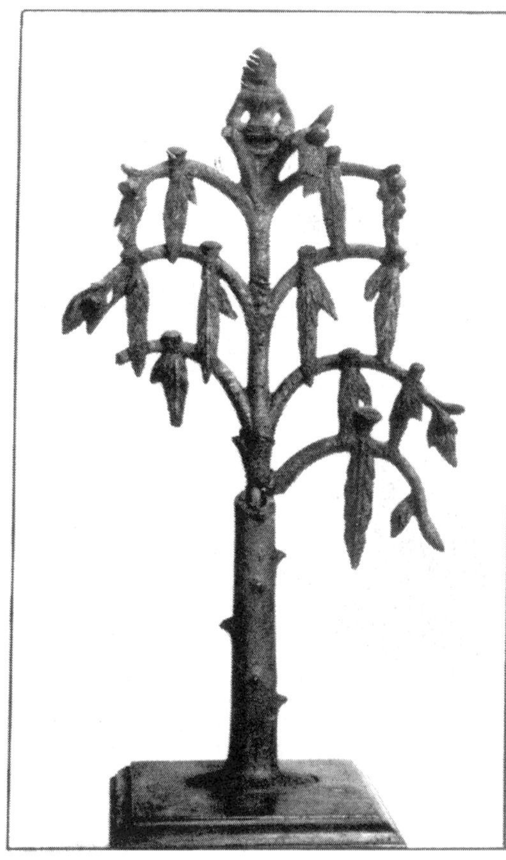

Pl. 18. Kalpavṛkṣa with female figure; Chausa (Sahabad-Bihar); Bronze; Patna Museum; 1st century BC.

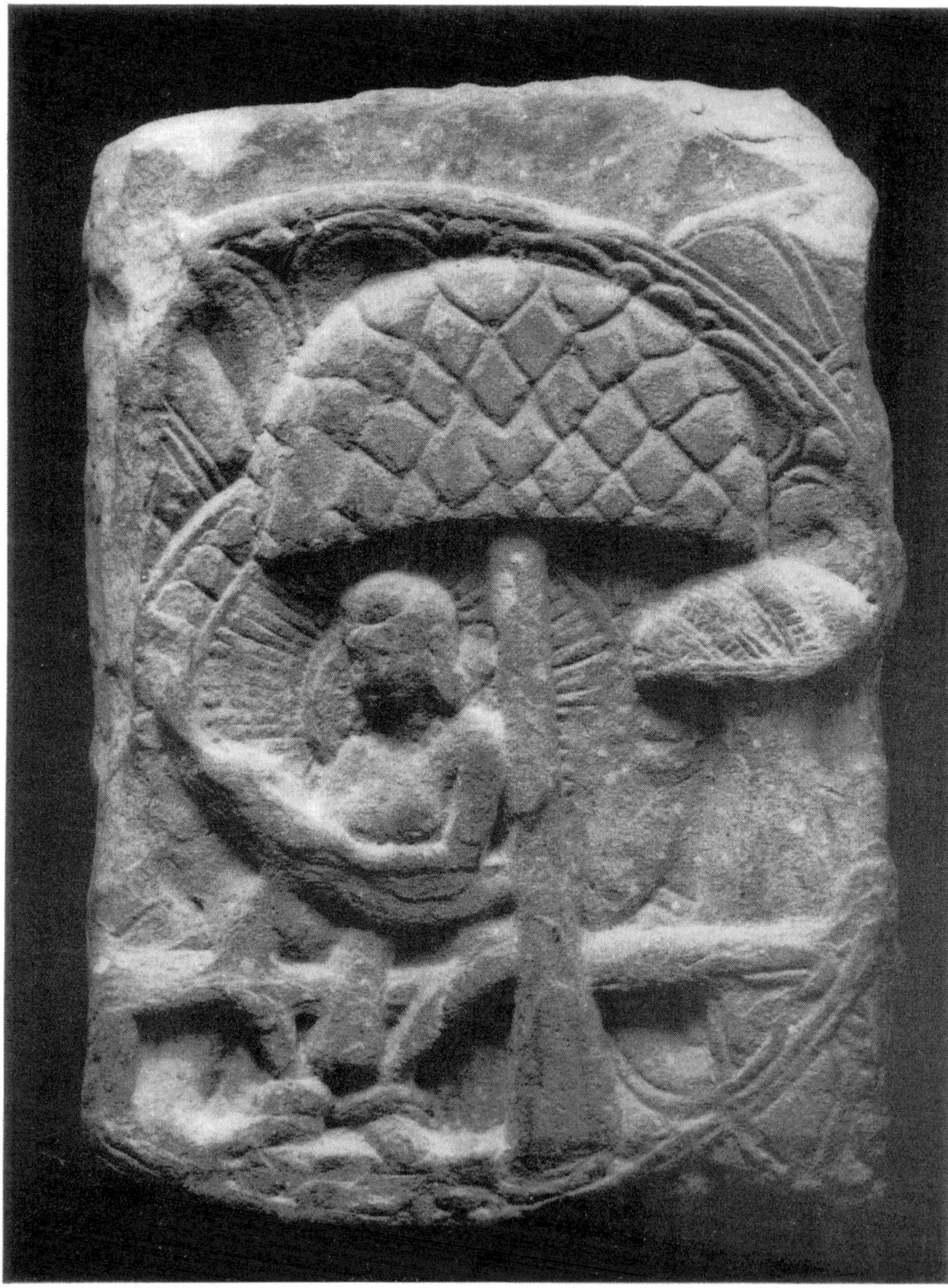

Pl. 19. Lady playing a harp under a tree; Gopalpur (Mathura); Red sandstone; Government Museum, Mathura; 1st century BC.

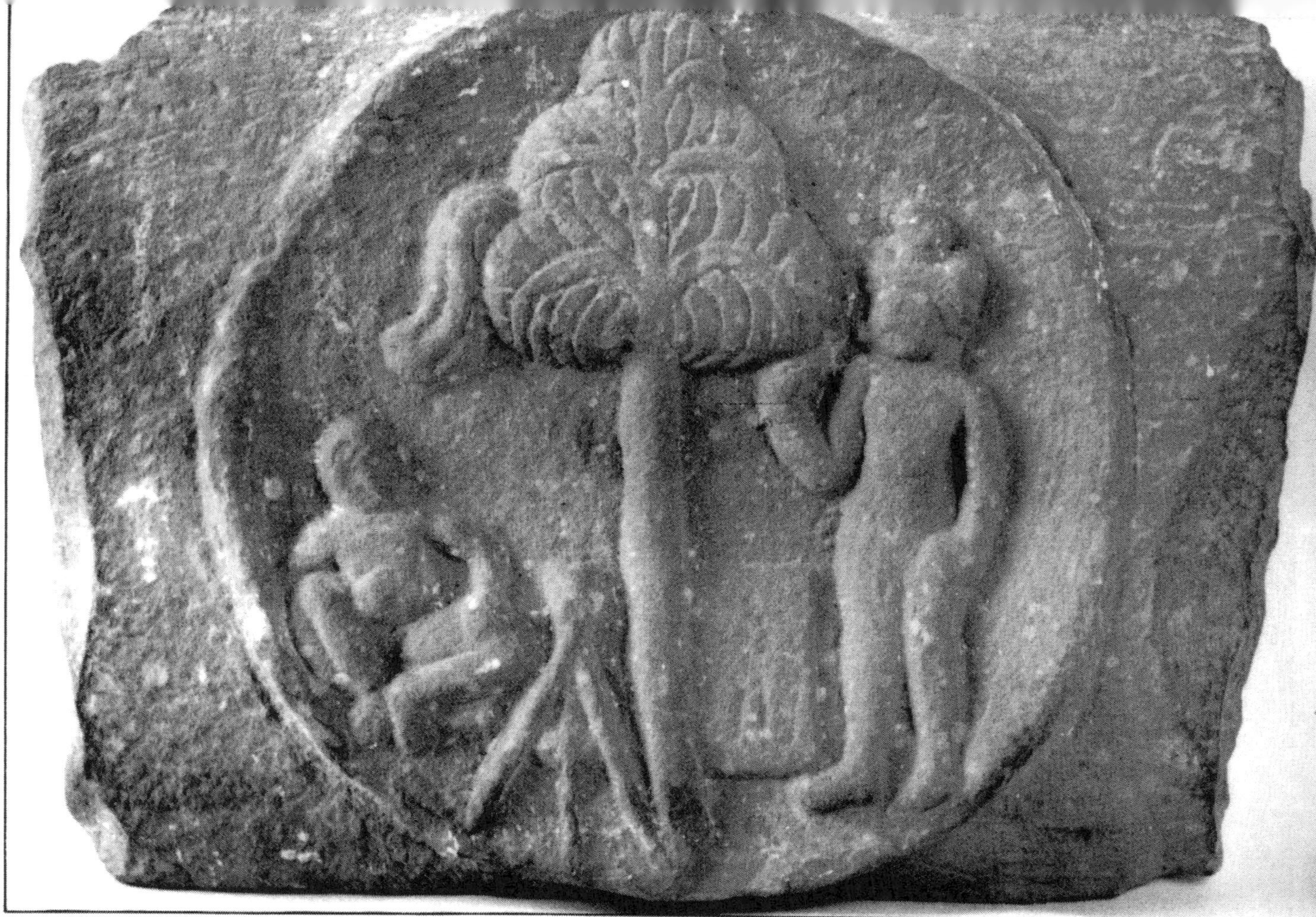

Pl. 20. Jātaka Scene (?) on crossbar; Mathura; Red sandstone; Patna Museum; 1st century BC.

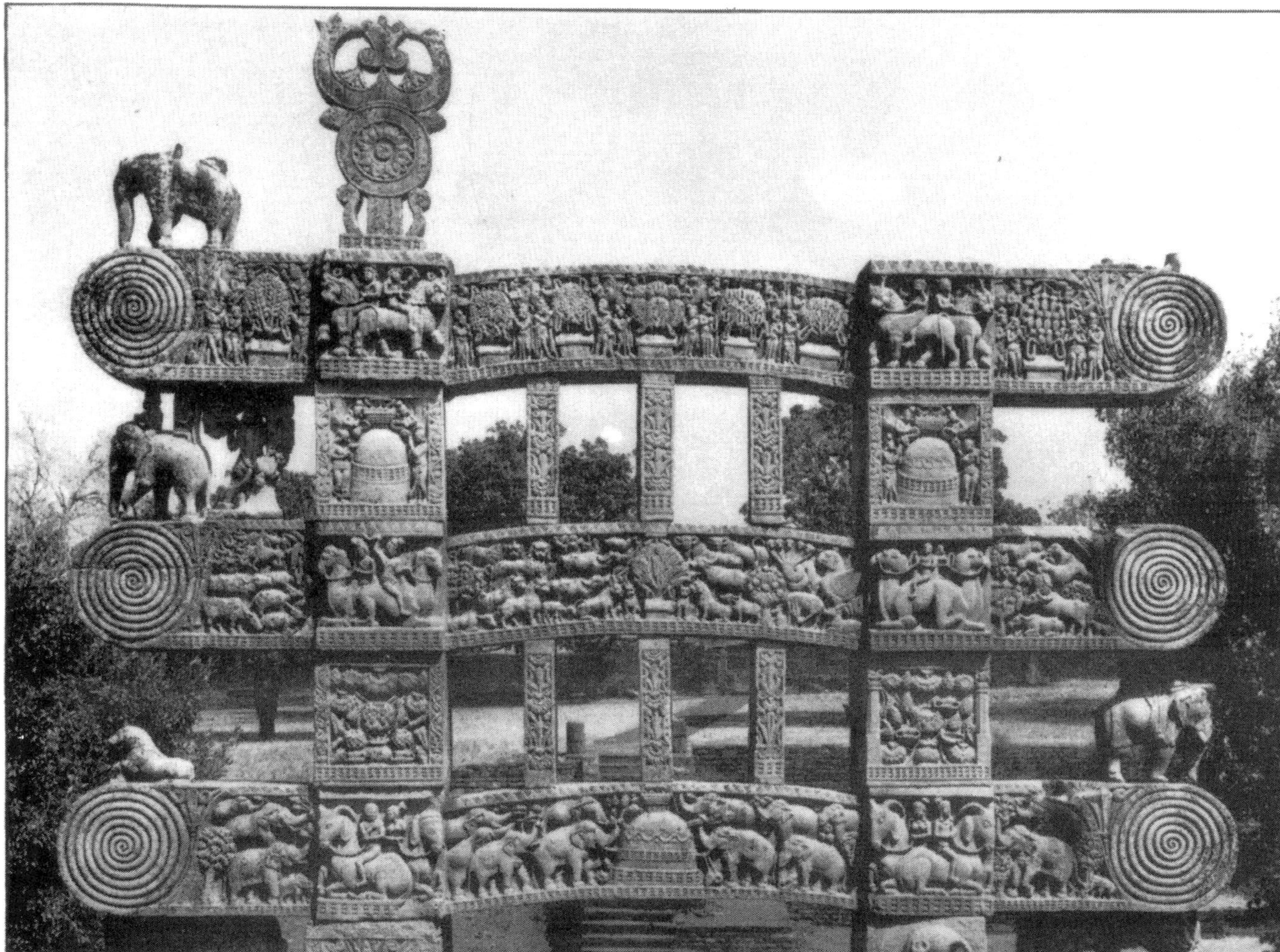

Pl. 21. Bodhi trees of seven Manusi Buddhas; Sanchi (M.P.) Stupa I, Eastern Gate...

by Hindus.[116] It is associated with Viṣṇu. Those desiring offspring should worship the tree in blossom.

In both the sects of Jainism, *śāla* is the *caitya-vṛkṣa* of Tīrthaṅkara Mahāvīra. It is *caitya-vṛkṣa* of Śvetāmbara Tīrthaṅkara Sambhavanātha[117] also.

Śamī

The mention of *śamī* tree is found in *Atharvaveda* and later texts.[118] The *Mahābhārata* has recorded a story regarding the sacredness of the *śamī* wood as *Agni* resided for a while in it.[119] Besides, *śamī* or acacia is a goddess on her own account and is supposed to contain fire. It is worshipped for removing guilt and destroying the enemies.[120] Rudra is an embodiment of fire; Śiva or *Rudra* is considered as a *yūpa* post made of *śamī*.[121]

Lotus

The symbol of lotus is frequently seen in Hindu and Buddhist art and literature. Hindus associated the lotus with Brahmā, the creator. As per a myth, a stalk of lotus arose from the navel of Viṣṇu as he lay reposing on his serpent couch, Ananta, in the celestial waters. And the lotus which bore Brahmā is believed as a manifestation of Goddess Padma herself,[122] who represents cosmic fertility and female generative organ; hence the womb of all creation, or the seat of divinity and spiritual power. The lotus is also sacred because of Viṣṇu who used to offer one thousand lotus buds daily to Śiva.

Lotus is also associated with several divinities belonging to different pantheons. It is the seat of Sarasvatī, the goddess of learning. At places it rises from the immortal navel of Viṣṇu or the Cosmic deity whose 'awakening' throws up the lotus as the seat of Brahmā, the genius of emanation.[123] Lotus is often shown in the hands of Viṣṇu, Sūrya and has intimate relation with Lakṣmī.

It also symbolises Buddha's nativity. Even Bodhisattva Padmapāṇi invariably holds lotus in his hand. Further, Jain Tīrthaṅkaras Padmaprabha and Neminātha have respectively red lotus and blue lotus as Lañchhanas. Often a five-petalled lotus symbol called the *Siddha Cakra* is sculpted on Jain temples. It is perhaps based on the concept of the *Pañca Parameṣṭhins* or the five supreme ones in Jainism, i.e. *Arhat* (Tīrthaṅkara), *Siddha*, *Ācāryas*, *Upādhyāy* and *Sādhus*.[124]

Aśoka

Aśoka is one of the sacred trees of Hindus and is especially worshipped on the 13th day of the month *Caitra*. Etymologically, *aśoka* means 'Without grief', the tree believed to be a remover of sorrow. It is said that the tree was blessed by Śiva to be immortal as his wife Pārvatī worshipped him with its flowers, hence the tree remains evergreen.[125] According to *Bhaviṣya Purāṇa*, *aśoka* tree is related to Mahādeva.[126] The tree is the symbol of love, and is dedicated to Kāmadeva (Madana), the Hindu god of love. Interestingly, *aśoka* is one of the names of Lord Viṣṇu. Sitā, the wife of Rāma is believed to have taken refuge in a grove of *aśokas* when she escaped from caress of the demon (Rāvaṇa). The śākatas before worshipping goddess Durgā, worship nine leaves of nine different trees. Like *navapatrikās*, Durgā is also represented in nine different forms *(navadurgās)*. One of her aspects is *Śokarohitā* and she may be the personification of the *aśoka* leaves of the *navapatrikās*.[127]

Aśoka is also associated with Buddhist religion. Buddhists worship *aśoka* tree because Buddha was born under it. Later on, *aśoka* was gradually associated with many other Buddhist divinities. Rakta Lokeśvara, an aspect of Avalokiteśvara rules under an *aśok*a tree.[128] Mahāśrī-Tārā has *Aśokakānta* as one of the four attendants, who holds *aśoka pallava* in one of her two hands. Similarly, Vajraṅanga (a form of Mañjuśrī) holds an *aśoka pallava* in one of his four hands. *Nispanna-Yogāvali* refers that Marichi also holds *aśoka pallava* in one of her eight hands.[129]

Aśoka tree is also associated with the attainment of omniscience of Jain muni Mahāvīra. According to the Jains, his initiation under the tree was attended by the gods.[130] The Śvetāmbara Tīrthāṅkara Mallinātha and Kinnaras are also associated with *aśoka* tree.

NOTES AND REFERENCES

1. Sengupta, S. (Ed.), *Tree Symbol Worship in India*, Calcutta, 1965, p. 3.
2. Sinha, B.C., *Tree Worship in Ancient India,* New Delhi, 1979, pp. 38-42.
3. Miller, J., *The Vision of Cosmic Order in the Vedas,* London, 1985, pp. 246-47.
4. Das, A.C., Ṛgvedic *India*, Calcutta, 1927, IInd Ed. (Revised), p. 62.
5. Macdonell, A.A., *Vedic Mythology,* Varanasi, Delhi, 1971, p. 112.
6. Miller, J., *op.cit.,* p. 248.

7. Cf. Sinha, B.C., *op.cit.*, p. 42; see also H.T. Colebrooke, *Essays on Religion and Philosophy*, 1976.
8. Goyal, S.R., *A Religious History of Ancient India*, Meerut, 1984, p. 29.
9. *Bhāgavadgītā*, X. 2b; cf. Biswas, T.K. and P.K. Debnath, "Aśvattha (*Ficus Religiosa Linn*): A Cultural and Medicinal Observation," *Vishveshvaranand Indological Journal*, Vol. XII, nos. I & II, 1974, p. 41.
10. *Ibid.*
11. Ganguli, K.M., *op.cit.*, Vol. X, p. 268.
12. Ragozin, A.A., *Vedic India*, Delhi, 1961, p. 29.
13. Elwin, V., *Tribal Myths of Orissa*, Bombay, 1954, p. 129.
14. Biswas, T.K. and P.K. Debnath, *op.cit.*, p. 41.
15. Dange, S.A., *Encyclopaedia of Purāṇic Beliefs and Practices*, Vol. IV, New Delhi, 1989, p. 1243.
16. *Ibid.*
17. Bhatt, G.P. (Ed.), *Ancient Indian Tradition and Mythology*, Vol. 39; *Padma Purāṇa*, Pt. I, Delhi, 1988, p. 764.
18. Rao, T.A. Gopinath, *Elements of Hindu Iconography*, Vol. I, Parts I & II, Madras, 1914, reprinted in New York (1968), p. 362.
19. *Ibid.*, p. 387.
20. Macdonell, A.A., *op.cit.*, p. 134.
21. *Ibid.*
22. Cunningham, A., *The Stūpa of Bharhut*, 1979, p. 106.
23. Finegan, J., *The Archaeology of World Religions*, London, 1952, p. 253.
24. Biswas, T.K. and P.K. Debnath, *op.cit.*, p. 43.
25. Finegan, J., *op.cit.*, p. 297.
26. Shah, U.P., *Jaina Rūpa Maṇḍana*, New Delhi,1987, p. 26.
27. *Ibid.*, p. 57.
28. Chakravarti, M., *The Concept of Rudra-Śiva Through the Ages*, Delhi, 1986, p. 111.
29. Cf. Patyal, H.C., "The significance of the Aegle Mardelos (Bilva) in the Veda", *Vishveshvaranand Indological Journal*, Vol. XII, Nos. I & II, 1974, p. 267.
30. *Ibid.*
31. *Ibid.*, p. 271.
32. *Ibid.*, p. 272; see also Werner, K. (Ed.), *Symbols in Art and Religion*, Delhi, 1991, p. 169.
33. Dutt, M.N., *Garuḍa Purāṇa*, Calcutta, 1908, p. 365.
34. Dubois, J.A., *Hindu Manners, Customs and Ceremonies*, Oxford, 1906, p. 707.
35. Gupta, S.M., *Plant, Myths and Traditions in India*, New Delhi, 1991, revised Second Edition, p. 16.
36. *Ibid.*, pp. 14, 15.
37. *Ibid.*, p. 15.

38. *Ibid.*, p. 14.
39. Cf. *Phallic Tree Worship Cults Arborum*, Varanasi, 1971, pp. 11-12.
40. Coomaraswamy, A.K., *The Eastern Art*, I, p. 178, quoted from Sahai, B., *Iconography of Minor Hindu and Buddhist Deities*, New Delhi, 1975, pp. 161-62.
41. Rao, T.A. Gopinath, *op.cit.*, pp. 436-37.
42. *Ibid.*, p. 52.
43. Agrawala, V.S., *op.cit.*, p. 116; *Nyagrodha* finds its mention in the *Atharvaveda* and the later literature. According to *Taittirīya Saṁhitā* (VII, 4, 12, I), the sacrificial bows (*Camasa*) were made of its wood (see Macdonell, A.A. & A.B. Keith, *Vedic Index of Names and Subjects*, Vols. I & II, Delhi, 1958, p. 462).
44. Sengupta, S. (Ed.), *op.cit.*, pp. 5-6; the descendent of this original immortal tree still stands in the fort of Allahabad.
45. Gupta, S.M., *op.cit.*, pp. 47-49.
46. Sengupta, S. (Ed.), *op.cit.*, p. 6.
47. Wilson, H.H., *Viṣṇu Purāṇa*, Calcutta, 1961, p. 166.
48. Dange, S.A., *op.cit.*, Vol. II, 1987, p. 402.
49. *Ibid.*, p. 692.
50. *Ibid.*, p. 703.
51. *Ibid.*, p. 706.
52. Gupta, S.M., *op.cit.*, p. 49.
53. *Agni Purāṇa*, Ch. 50. 21-22 and Ch. 144. 30-37; *Matsya Purāṇa*. Ch. 261. 33-37; references quoted from Sahai, B., *op.cit.*, p. 198.
54. Dange, S.A., *op.cit.*, p. 407.
55. Agarwala, V.S., *Matsya Purāṇa: A Study*, Varanasi, 1963, p. 188.
56. Ganguli, K.M., *op.cit.*, Vol. V, p. 19; see also Gupta, S.M., *op.cit.*, p. 48.
57. Maity, P.K., *op.cit.*, p. 321.
58. *Ibid.*
59. Williams, M., *Religious Thought and Life in India*, Calcutta, 1978, reprinted, p. 337.
60. Gupta, S.M., *op.cit.*, p. 49.
61. Shah, U.P., *op.cit.*, p. 51.
62. Gupta, S.M., *op.cit.*, p. 13.
63. *Ibid.*, p. 10.
64. *Ibid.*, pp. 10-11.
65. Cf. fn. 68 above.
66. Dange, S.A., *op.cit.*, pp. 733-36.
67. *Ibid.*, Vol. III, p. 931.
68. Wilson, H.H., *op.cit.*, p. 136.
69. Gupta, S.M., *op.cit.*, p. 18.

70. *Ibid.*, p. 8.
71. Shah, U.P., *op.cit.*, pp. 57-58.
72. Saletore, R.N., *op.cit.*, Vol. II, New Delhi, 1981, p. 624; according to *Varāha Purāṇa* (149, 55), at a place called kadamba a stream is said to flow out from the *kadamba* tree, and the tree is said to show blossoms only on the bright 12th *Māgha,* in the noon.
73. Gupta, S.M., *op.cit.*, pp. 22-23.
74. Macdonell, A.A., and A.B. Keith, *op.cit.*, p. 354.
75. Same as fn. 79 above.
76. Shah, U.P., *op.cit.*, pp. 57-58.
77. Macdonell, A.A. and A.B. Keith, *op.cit.*, p. 500.
78. *Bhaviṣya Purāṇa* (*Madhyana Khanda,* 10.17 ff-22), reference quoted from Dange, S.A., *op.cit.*, Vol. I, p. 77.
79. Gupta, S.M., *op.cit.*, p. 24.
80. *Ibid.*, p. 23.
81. Dutt, M.N., *op.cit.*, p. 355.
82. Dange, S.A., *op.cit.*, Vol. II, p. 472.
83. Cf. Gupta, S.M., *op.cit.*, pp. 10-11.
84. Dange, S.A., *op.cit.*, Vol. I, p. 33.
85. Rao, T.A. Gopinath, *op.cit.*, p. 383.
86. Cowell, E.B., *The Jātaka*, English Translation, Vol. I, New Delhi (reprinted), 1990, p. 15.
87. Shah, U.P., *op.cit.*, pp. 51, 57.
88. Gupta, S.M., *op.cit.*, p. 28; in ancient times coconut was also offered to the gods instead of a human head.
89. Sengupta, S. (Ed.), *op.cit.*, pp. 10-11.
90. *Ibid.*
91. Desai, N.Y., *Ancient Indian Society, Religion and Mythology as Depicted in the Mārkaṇḍeya Purāṇa,* Baroda, 1968, p. 266.
92. Rao, T.A. Gopinath, *op.cit.*, p. 52.
93. Dange, S.A., *op.cit.*, Vol. IV, p. 1170.
94. Tripuras were devotees of Śiva but had become arrogant and started committing atrocities on mortals and celestial beings and had to be destroyed. (For details see Hazara, H.C., *Studies in the Unapurāṇas,* Vol. II, pp. 325-26).
95. Gupta, S.M., *op.cit.*, pp. 36-37.
96. For details, see Dutt, M.N., *Agni Purāṇa,* Vol. II, Varanasi, 1967, p. 120.
97. Gupta, S.M., *op.cit.*, p. 42.
98. Wilson, H.H., *op.cit.*, pp. 113-14.
99. Gupta, S.M., *op.cit.*, p. 38.
100. *Ibid.*

101. Macdonell, A.A. and A.B. Keith, *op.cit.,* p. 87.
102. Sinha, B.C., *op.cit.,* p. 28.
103. Gupta, S.M., *op.cit.,* pp. 53-54.
104. Dikshitar, V.R.R. (Ed.), *Purāṇa Index,* 2 Vols., Madras, 1951, pp. 278-79.
105. Shah, U.P., *op.cit.,* pp. 51, 210.
106. Mathur, R.C., *Systematic Botany,* Allahabad, 1965, p. 190.
107. Gupta, S.M., *op.cit.,* p. 56.
108. *Ibid.*
109. Sinha, B.C., *op.cit.,* p. 27.
110. Williams, M., *op.cit.,* p. 333.
111. Sengupta, S. (Ed.), *op.cit.,* p. 12.
112. Shah, U.P., *op.cit.,* p. 58.
113. The town of Badrināth is considered to have derived its name from the *badari* tree that once grew there (cf. Gupta, S.M., *op.cit.,* p. 102).
114. Hopkins, E.W., *Epic Mythology,* Strassburg, 1915, p. 7.
115. Gupta, S.M., *op.cit.,* p. 88.
116. Cf. Ibid., fn. 87.
117. Shah, U.P., *op.cit.,* p. 51.
118. Macdonell, A.A. and A.B. Keith, *op.cit.,* p. 354.
119. Ganguli, K.M., *op.cit.,* Vol. V, p. 133.
120. Williams, M., *op.cit.,* p. 338.
121. Gupta, S.M., *op.cit.,* p. 77.
122. *Ibid.,* p. 58.
123. Agrawala, V.S., *Indian Art,* Varanasi, 1965, p. 53.
124. Gupta, S.M., *Plants in Indian Temple Art,* Delhi, 1996, p. 128.
125. Gupta, S.M., *op.cit.,* pp. 81-82.
126. Cf. Biswas, T.K. and P.K. Debnath, "Aśoka (Saraca Indica Linn): A Cultural and Scientific Evaluation," *Indian Journal of History of Science,* Vol. 7, No. 2, 1972, p. 101.
127. *Ibid.*
128. *Ibid.,* pp. 101-2.
129. *Ibid.*
130. Cf. fn. 131 above.

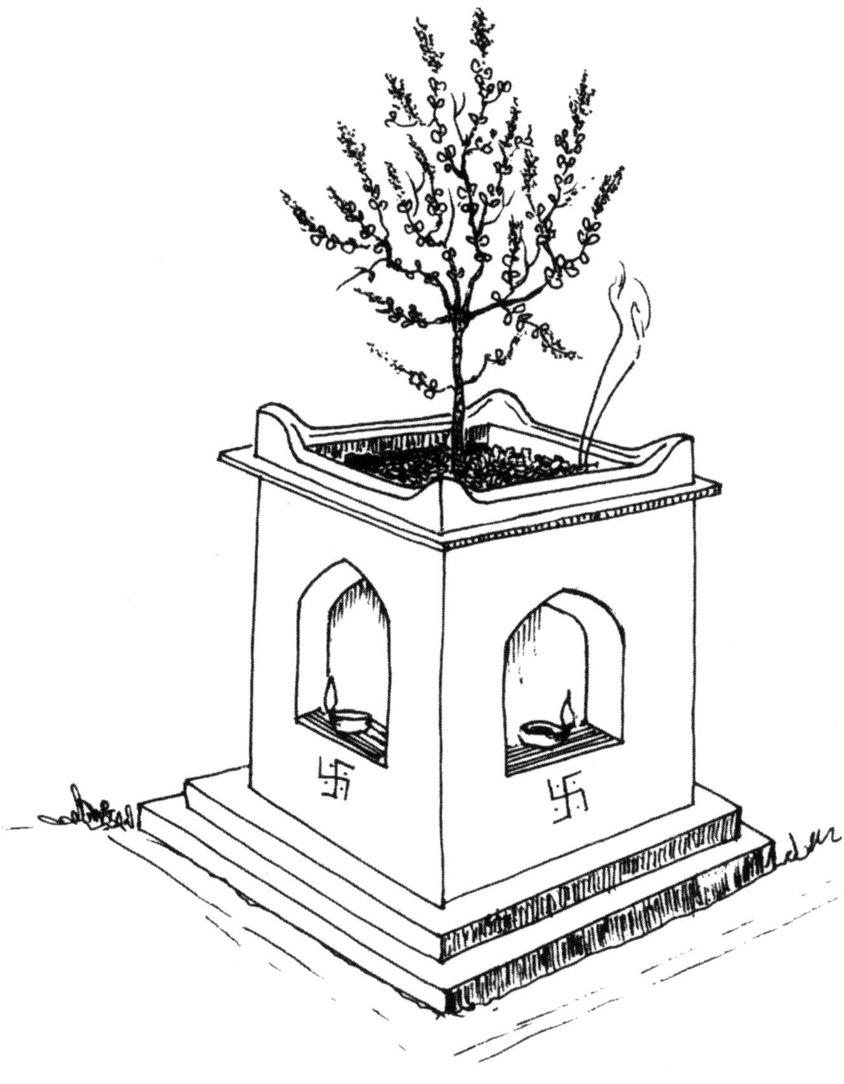

4 TREE WORSHIP IN BIO-CULTURAL CONTEXTS

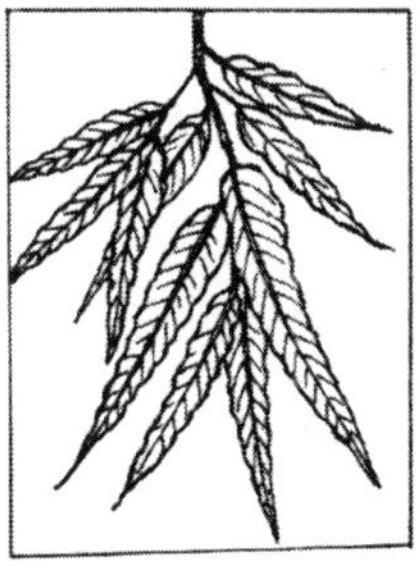

I

TREES AND ETHNO-RELIGIOUS ATTITUDES

Trees are a form of nature that represent life and the sacred continuity of the spiritual, cosmic and physical worlds. For a man trees were the only refuge in various ways before he developed agriculture and became fully civilized. They supplied him food, medicine, shelter, shadow, fuel, and even they maintained to a great extent the ecological balance. It looks that due to usefulness of certain trees, our ancestors tried to save them from the wood-cutters. Therefore, some of these trees were declared divine (*Brahmā taru*). Certain trees were also declared containing life sustaining sap and therefore, designated as tree of life (*Jivan-vṛkṣa*). Some of the trees were categorised as medicinal (*Rogī taru*). A tree often symbolizes a deity or other sacred being, or may stand for what is sacred in general. The religious beliefs that surround a tree may include as sacred any one or all of the physical parts of the tree: its trunk, branches, leaves, blossoms, sap or roots. Sacred objects constructed from the wood of special trees are also used for religious purposes.

The physical properties of trees are combined with supernatural or sacred ideas, the beliefs that surround a tree's connection with what constitutes religion in different cultures. These are not only deemed sacred in the major religions of the East and West, but also in other traditions where beliefs in the sacred are combined with beliefs in the power of ancestors, in the creation of life in birth, about death and the afterworld and about health and illness. Trees represent certain deities or ancestors, serve as mediators or links to the religious realm, and are associated with cultural beliefs in heaven or after-life. The divine concept of the trees was recognised even by the Buddhists and Jains. The notion of *caitya-vṛkṣa, bodhi-trees, kevala-vṛkṣa, jñāna-vṛkṣa* gained popularity among the Buddhists and Jains. In Brahmanical Hindu religion, *vaṭa* was identified with Śiva, *aśvattha* with Viṣṇu, lotus with Sūrya and nine leaves of nine trees (*navapatrikā*) were associated with nine different aspects of Durgā. Goddess Durgā also receives worship on Durgā Pūjā festival in a ceremonial earthen pot (*ghaṭa*), containing the waters of creation, fleshy barley sprouts and branches of the wood-apple tree (*bilva*). These together proclaim her intimate connection with the power of the fecund earth, through which she nourishes the world. The Śākambhārī aspect of the archaic Mother led to the evolution of the cult of fertility and its antiquity can be pushed back as early as the Indus civilization. *Dohada-Śālabhañjikā* in Indian art relates also to the fertility cult. The notion that a woman fertilises trees and trees fertilise a barren mother has been deeply rooted in India's ancient past. Trees fulfil all human desires. This led to the introduction of wish-fulfilling trees and creepers.

The trees may symbolize a deity either by serving as the visible embodiment of the sacred presence or by making a sacred spot that a deity frequents. Sacred trees may be the abode of deities or may be the divine beings themselves. Many religions include belief that trees have souls or are sentient sacred beings, and it was this belief which led to the cult of animism.[1] Subsequently, various deities came to be associated with trees and plants, and it was strictly prohibited to harm them in any way. Ira, the daughter of Dakṣa, is said to be the mother of trees, shrubs and creepers. She was herself the mother of three daughters, i.e., *Latā, Valli* and *Virudha*. These three daughters in turn became the mother of trees, plants and shrubs.[2] The *Mārkaṇḍeya Purāṇa* (48.3-26 468) has recorded that the trees and plants were created from the hair of Brahmā's body.[3] It is noteworthy to find a reference to the tree spirits (*Vanadevatās*) in the Kālidāsa's play *Abhijñānaśākuntalam*, where the *Vanadevatā* blesses Śakuntalā as she leaves for her husband's house.[4] The belief in *Vanadevatā* is not held by Hindus only but is a very strong Buddhist belief also as evidenced from the *Jātaka* stories.[5]

Many *vrata* rites are associated with different trees and plants. In *punya-pukura-vrata, śiva-pūja-vrata, bhāduli-vrata, kula-kulati-vrata, aśvattha-pata-vrata, yame-pukara-vrata, itu-kumara-vrata,* etc. we find indications and traces of the different stages of religious evolution.[6] The important trees, plants and leaves which are used in the *vrata*-rites include *aśvattha* tree, *tulsi* plant, *bilva* tree, *mān-kachu* plant, *susni, kalmi,* etc. Of leaves again, most commonly used are the *tulsi*-leaves, *aśvattha* leaves, *bilva* leaves, *betel* leaves, etc. and of the fruit are the betel-nut, plantain, mango, *bilva,* etc. Similarly, flowers of *mallikā, champā, mūlā, sarshe, ākanda, dhatura,* etc.[7], essential items in the magico-religious observances from very early times are most commonly used in these *vrata*-observances also. Their use enables the observer to protect against all evils; scent, colour and medicinal properties of these flowers scare away the evil spirits and give pleasure to deities and human beings.

Aśvattha is considered to be a deity itself and a special rite is observed in its honour. As per the story of the *vrata,* disrespect shown to this tree led to all sorts of calamities to the girl; however, she regained her fortune by virtue of the observance of the rite.[8] The present day villages of Bengal have also the *Devatāsthāṇa* where people observe socio-religious ceremonies and festivals which are primitive in nature. They do not worship only the trees but also the spirits dwelling therein.

The Santhals believe that human spirits live in the *bilva* tree.[9] The snake charmers in central India cure snake bites by appealing to the tree. It is regarded as 'tree of life' in the *Brāhmaṇa* literature. The married women adorn this tree for gaining favour from their husbands.

The *bilva* tree being sacred to Śiva is worshipped by the followers on the 14th phase of moon's wane between the month of *Māgha* and *Phālguna* which is *Śivarātri* day. On this day Śiva's manifestation in phallic form is celebrated. The *bilva* leaves are also offered to Śiva on Monday in the month of *Śrāvaṇa.*

The womenfolk of Bihar and Uttar Pradesh embrace this tree in order to get their desires fulfilled. The people of Kerala never eat *bilva* fruit as it signifies the head of Śiva. Besides, a fallen tree of *bilva* is never used to serve as firewood. It is said that a person who desires wealth is to offer faggots of *bilva* tree.

The trees and plants like *pipal, neem, bel, tulsi, kalam,* etc. are regarded to be the abodes of certain deities by many tribes in India. The Bhil and Bhilala communities in central India (Jhiri-Raisen) worship Baba Ind (Indra) in the form of branches of *kalam* tree. It is said that for Ind worship, the *kalam* tree is very essential. Before cutting off the branches of the tree, some rituals are performed and coconut is offered.

In rural areas of lower Assam, the chief feature of Bhatheli festival is the planting of two green bamboos in a field. The planting of bamboos perhaps recalls the Ind *parab* of the Mundas. Mundas plant *śāla* posts and the tallest one they plant as Ind-pole. The planting of tall bamboos and *śāla* suggests some kind of Indra worship. The local Assamese idea that the bamboos represent a bride and a groom may suggest the unification of heaven and earth. The *Vājasaneyī Saṁhitā* records that "When Heaven and Earth are in harmony with each other, then indeed it rains."

(cf. Goswami, 1995: 24).

In West Bengal, districts of Bankure and Midnapur, people, mostly Santhal, perform Ind *parab* in the month of August-September (*Bhadra*). They plant a tall *śāla* post. Sometimes the number may be two or three—the taller or the tallest is called the *Indradhvaja*. In Assam apparently the bamboo has conveniently replaced the *śāla* or other trees used in earlier times. The bamboo plays an important role in Magh Bihu or Maghar Domahi, Deul, Bas Pūjā and Chomangkan festivals also.

The *tulsi* is held sacred in Assam like other parts of India. In Kati Bihu festival, a light is put at the foot of the *tulsi* plant and women and children chant:

> Tulsi, O Mother Tulsi,
> you are Govinda's favourite,
> which way has Kṛṣṇa gone,
> Mother, tell us quickly.

The plant is considered symbolic of Vrinda, one of the devotees of Kṛṣṇa. The festival is held in the autumn season.

A peculiarity of Assam's Vaiṣṇavism is that the offerings made to the god include sprouted lentils, sugarcane, banana, ginger, coconut, etc., instead of sweets and cooked food.

The Boro-Kacharis of the Assam observe the Bihu or Boisagu for seven days. On the second day they offer worship to the five-ridged *siju cactus*, the symbol of Bathou or Mahadeva. The Kacharis at Daranggiri, in the Goalpara district and to the west of Guwahati, seem to possess certain local customs and traditions not found in the northern Kamrup. On the cow Bihu day Daranggiri Kacharis put leaves of the cane, the *dighlati* and the flower of the *keturi* (a shrub similar to the turmeric) under the rafters, on the fencing near the gate and in the well. They sprinkle *phaku* or *abir* on a sheaf of these three things and keep the sheaf planted upright in a corner of the yard. Next day Bathou is worshipped in this place. The sheaf is thrown away after the seventh day of Bihu.

As the Kacharis have no fixed shrine or temple, they choose an open place and prepare a longish altar for the Kherai pūjā. The pūjā is performed for the welfare of men, animals and in particular for the growth of paddy. In the main part, a *siju cactus* is planted as symbolizing Bathou Borai. A lamp and offerings like betel-nut and leaves, green bananas, and a pot of water with a gold ring and *tulsi* leaves are placed at the foot of the *siju*. This water is sprinkled on the altar. "As a symbol of creation an egg and as a symbol of truth, a piece of stone are kept in front of Bathou." In some places, the egg and the stone are buried in the ground and over the spot the *siju cactus* is planted (*ibid.*, 64).

The Mising consider *śalmalī* as a symbol of long life. The young Mising, men and woman raise a dais to the Bihu god in a nearby forest and plant a sapling of the *śālmalī* nearby. The planting of the sapling seems to suggest that like Bhatheli it also recalls one of the ancient festivals of India—the youthful festival of *Ekaśalmalī* or *Śalmalīmulankhelana*—playing round a *śalmalī* tree blindfolded and trying to seek one another. It is said that the people of the Vidharba country in central India also used to observe this festival. It is of course not known if the tree also symbolized a long life.

In Manipur, the status in society particularly of Tangkhul Nāgas was not conferred by wealth only but also by giving feasts and so winning the right to certain clothes and carving designs on the houses. To demonstrate their wealth and to get honour and great fame, they perform a ritual, a part of which is a tree-pulling ceremony accompanied by a great feast to the village community. Oak is considered the strongest and most durable for this purpose. Five oak trees with perfectly straight branches in all directions are selected for the occasion. The selected trees are felled on the same day. Usually the pits for the tree trunks are made in front of the giver's house after the teams bringing them reach the village. A ceremony is then performed during which all the five tree trunks brought are washed with rice beer. "Then the men begin to unfasten ropes and cut them into pieces. It is the priest who throws his piece of rope at the main tree. Then all the participants throwing their pieces of rope at the trunks shout, '*pilaso lo hoody*!' ('Live long!'). If they had dreamt that the main tree was a male spirit they shout, 'May you be a king!' 'And last long, long years!' If they dreamt that it was a female spirit, they shout, 'May you be a queen!' 'And last long years!' This is to symbolise that not only the trees but the folks of the village should live long lives" (Ganguli, 1993: 33). Then the trunks are lowered into the holes and in the evening villagers assemble in the giver's house for feasting. The number of ceremonial feasts given by any Tangkhul Nāga is marked on "spirit tree" mostly erected in front of his house.

The Santhals observe the *Karam parab* in *Bhadra Ekādasī* every year. The festival is observed by some non-tribal communities also. The male members after sunset cut three branches of *karam* after performing some rituals. These branches are installed in a village lane, where a community dance around the branches is performed both by young girls and boys till morning. Then branches are taken by young girls for *Visarjan*. They worship *Karamrāja* or *Vanadeva* for the good luck and wish-fulfilment of their brothers and prosperity of their families on this occasion. The tribal women observe the *vrata* on the *parab* day for the good luck and mutual understanding of the family and overall the community.

Painyyā (*Prunus cerasoides*—with light pink flowers) is considered very auspicious all over Garhwal, Kumaon and some parts of Himachal Pradesh. Its leaves, flowers and branches are used in almost every ritual and religious ceremonies.

In Garhwal Himalayas, the Pāndav *nṛtya* commences with the installation ceremony of the *painyyā* branch, which is brought amidst huge procession consisting of village folk and musicians, to the arena chosen for the performance. It remains there till the culmination of the dance, and later it is taken for *visarjan*. The Pāndav *nṛtya* is a very popular and widely practised enactment of the *Mahābhārata* lore.

The Nandā Devī festival in Almora (Kumaon) begins with selecting and cutting the banana trees, considered very auspicious for the occasion. Amidst pūjā and ritual ceremonies, the procession of local people and the priest, carries the tree to the temple complex, where they are used to make images of Nandā Devī and Sunandā, her counterpart. The images are worshipped after the *prāṇa pratiṣathā* ceremony and on the last day of the festival they are taken in a palanquin for *visarjan*. The small pieces of tree are also distributed amongst the followers as *prasāda*.[10]

In the Jammu and Kashmir state, trees are held sacred, especially those found in Hindu temples or on graves of Muslim saints (*asthan, peer baba*). The believers generally tie rags to these trees for the fulfilment of their desires. These rags are supposed to be removed after one's desire is fulfilled. The Hindus regard the *elm* as sacred to Gaṇeṣa. It was a favourite tree for shrines as well. The *deodar* (tree of gods) or Himalayan cedar is worshipped as symbol of Tripurasundrī at Devsara (Anantnag); mulberry tree is a sacred symbol of Ragnabhagvati at Tulmula (Ganderbal). The roots of *gogal dhup* (*Jurinea macrocephala*) are used by Hindus in making *dhup*, or incense. *Durva*, a kind of grass is associated with many religious rituals. Many fruits are used by Kashmiri Pandits in their religious functions. Walnuts are used on the *Śivarātri* festival. They offer walnuts soaked in earthen utensils to Śiva. These are distributed as *prasāda* after *pūja* on the 15th day of *phālguna*. In Kashmir the *Śivarātri* is celebrated from the first day of this month. The fruits like apple, apricot, grapes, peech, pomegranate (*phalamula*), etc. are essential in the *śrāda* ritual. Among vegetables the raddish is necessary for the ritual.

The *brimij* is usually found in graveyards and in the vicinity of shrines in the Jammu and Kashmir state. Some places without the discrimination of religion are sacred to both Hindu and Muslim communities. The common people avoid defecation under a tree because of the belief that good or evil spirits always reside in it. It is believed that a sapling of *kikar* (*acacia*) was brought from Mecca and was planted in the precincts of Hazratbal shrine. People adorn it while visiting the shrine on auspicious days. In the Ladakh region popular tree is held with great esteem.

Mango tree is believed to be the abode of vegetation spirits, and it can scare away evil spirits and eliminate their influences. Due to this reason, the twig of a mango tree is used in all rural ceremonies. Even marriage paṇḍāls are particularly decorated with mango leaves. In all socio-religious observances, the mango twig is put in the *jala ghaṭa*. Besides, it is customary for the people of Assam to take a little of green mango and jute leaves mixed with mustard and salt in the morning of *Garu Bihu*. Eating of tender mango on the New Year Day was an old Indian custom known as *Navamrakhadika*. The plantain plants are also used in many socio-religious rites as posts to mark four corners of the sacred spot.

Trees may represent a spiritual healing for and protection from evil. The Indian mimosa tree is believed to provide spiritual protection against wicked spells and evil eyes. The illness caused by Śītalā Mātā, the Indian goddess of smallpox, may be averted by setting up a branch of the *neem* tree just as Buddhists invoke certain sacred trees for health.

The *neem* tree (*Azadirachta indica*) is believed to have many utilitarian qualities and is held with great esteem in many parts of India. Its leaves, fruits, flowers, roots, woods all are necessary for Hindus. Vaiṣṇavites have special respect for this tree because their great ascetic Nityānanda used to sit under it. Interestingly, the banyan tree is often grown in close proximity with the *neem* tree. To the Hindus, the intertwined branches of the two trees are a holy union and are normally not cut down.

Neem is regarded as the dwelling place of deities, especially the godlings of disease. It is symbol of Śītalā, the cooler one, and the deity of pox. The patients of pox and measles etc. are provided air with *neem* twig, and many people wear armour made of branches of *neem* or *siju* to avoid cholera and pox. As per another belief, Manasā and six sisters of Śītalā also reside in *neem* tree. It is also connected with snake worship, sun worship and Nimbārka Vaiṣṇavas. The Doms of the eastern districts of the north-western provinces hold the tree sacred to Kali or Śītalā, and the Kurmis dedicate it to Kāli Bhavānī. A section of the Nath sect (*Kanpatha yogis*) use on their ear-hole like earring, a piece of *neem* branch. The wood of the tree is used for making Patgoswami of Nilpuja during Charak festival. The leaves of the tree are supposed to repel snakes.

Rabhas of Goalpara district in the south-west of Assam put certain leaves in the cattle shed as a preventive of disease of cattles. They also squirt water sanctified with *tulsi* leaves on the cattle sheds. Men take bitter food cooked with a dried fish as a precaution against diseases. Rabhas of Dudhnai prepare a food known as *pithali-sak*, a combination of strong-smelling medicinal plant, broken rice and *khar* or *alkali* prepared from banana trees. They put a little of it at the door of their cattle-shed. Among the gods and goddesses worshipped by the Rabhas include forest goddess *Kansa* also.

The betel-nut is supposed to possess the power of scaring away evil spirits. It will not be out of place to mention here that the paste of sandal-wood and turmeric also protects from evil spirits.

The coconut tree is regarded as a *kalpavṛkṣa* because of its various uses.[11] In Bengal the tree is regarded to be a Brahmin and is not allowed to be cut except by the latter.

The religious or spiritual powers may be inherent in a tree or in the elements that make up the tree. For example, the Andaman Islanders use the intrinsic qualities of hibiscus trees to aid them in their struggle to catch large turtles and fish. It is through the spiritual qualities of these trees that the Islanders are able to succeed in overcoming their prey and protect themselves from harm. The particular qualities of the tree represent essential elements of physical and spiritual life and ward off dangers associated with turtles and the sea.

In the Kati Bihu, autumn festival of Assam, the farmer plants a small bamboo in the field and lights an earthen lamp at its foot for the protection of his crop. He may also whirl a piece of bamboo and chant certain *mantras* to protect the maturing paddy from pests. Some persons light the *ākāsh bauti* or the sky-lamp hanging from a tall bamboo. The Kacharis put lamps at the foot of the *siju cactus,* symbol of their chief god Bathou, in the garden, at the granary and in the field.

The Saoras honour the banyan tree, for they believe that "it is our mother" and "source of life." As per their belief the banyan tree succoured

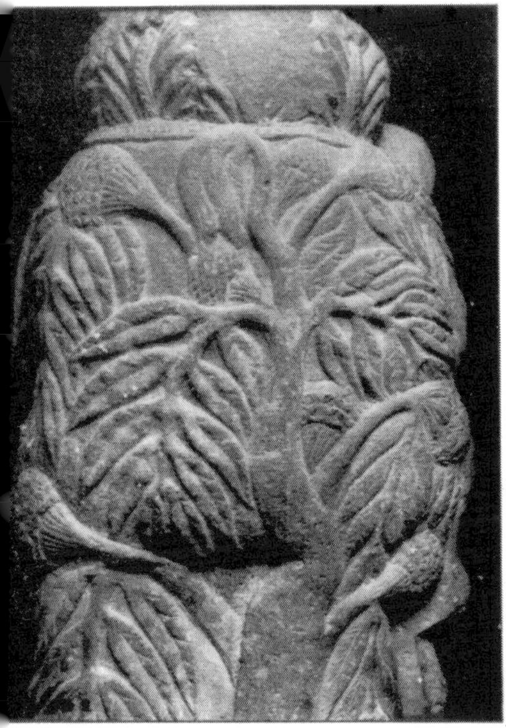

Pl. 22. Sporting ladies under aśoka tree, back view; Kota (Mathura); Red sandstone; Government Museum, Mathura; 1st century AD.

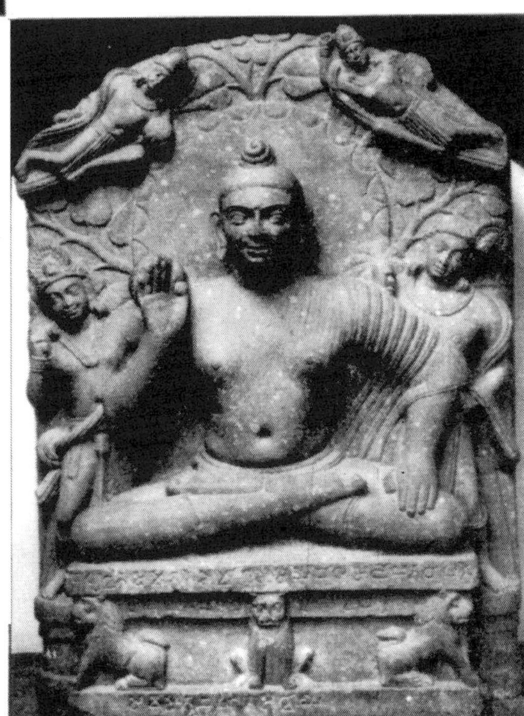

.. 23. Buddha seated under aśvattha tree; Katra Keshav Deo (Mathura); Red sandstone; Government Museum, Mathura; 1st century AD.

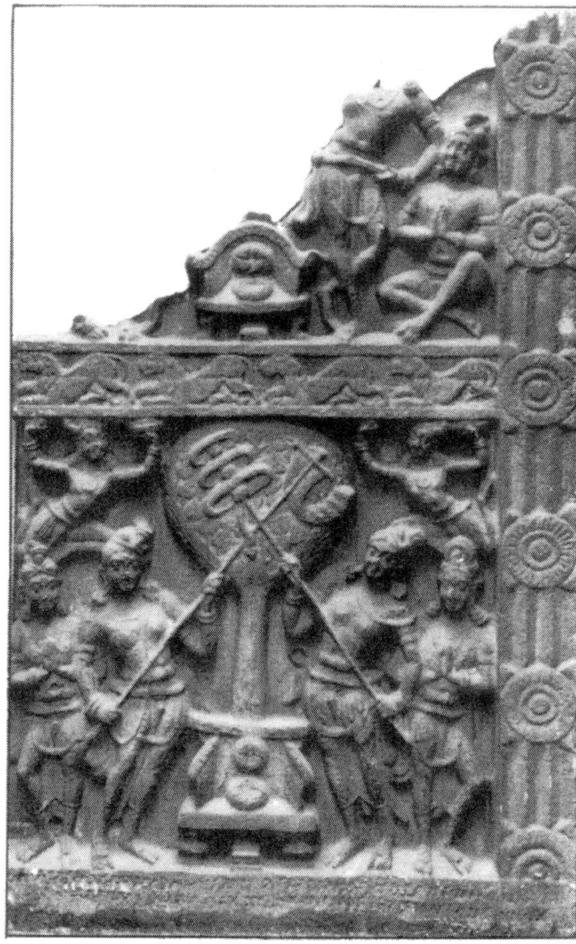

Pl. 24. Buddha's enlightenment; Amaravati (A.P.), Rail post; Limestone; Indian Museum, Calcutta, 2nd century AD.

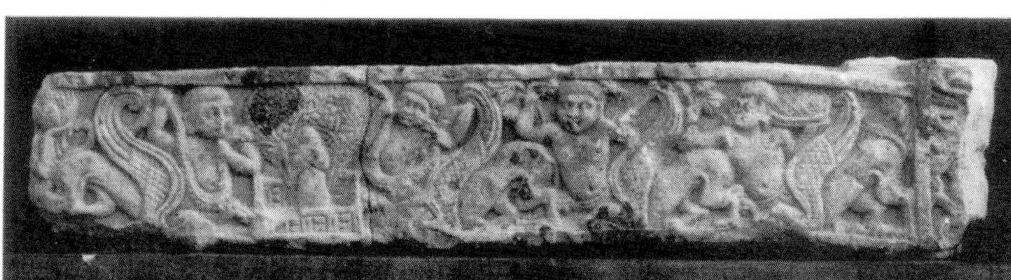

Pl. 25. Lintel showing worship of Śivaliṅga under tree; Mathura (Bhuteśara); Red sandstone; Mathura Museum; 2nd century AD.

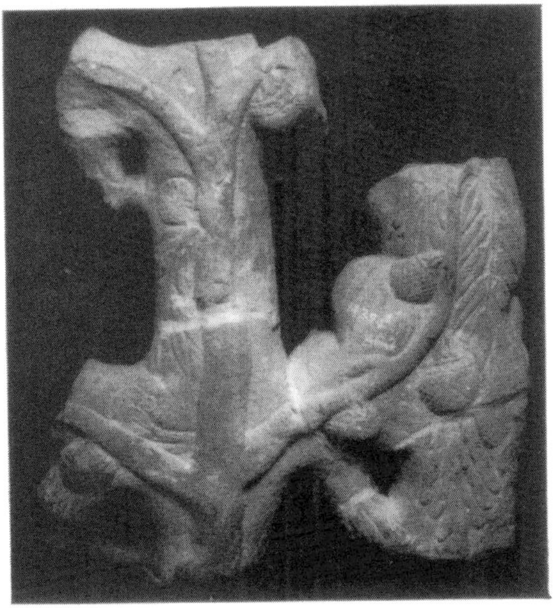

Pl. 26. Aśoka tree on the back view of Caturvyuha-Viṣṇu; Saptasamudri Kuan (Mathura); Buff sandstone; Government Museum, Mathura; 2nd century AD.

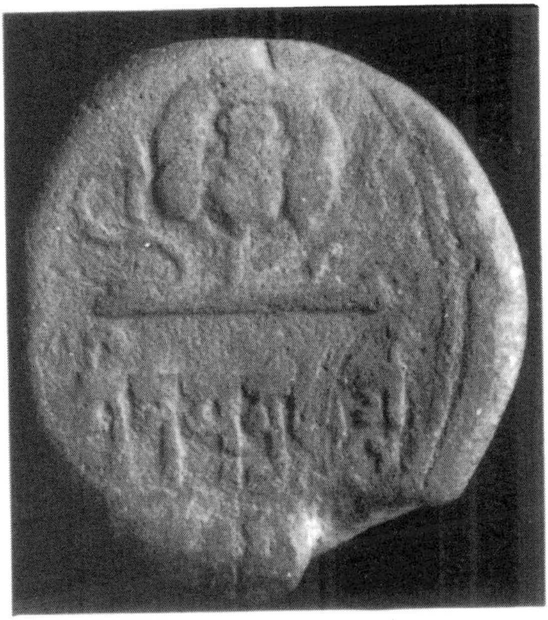

Pl. 27. Clay seal depicting a tree on its obverse above a line with designs on both sides at its upper half; India; clay; Government Museum (Mathura); 4th century AD.

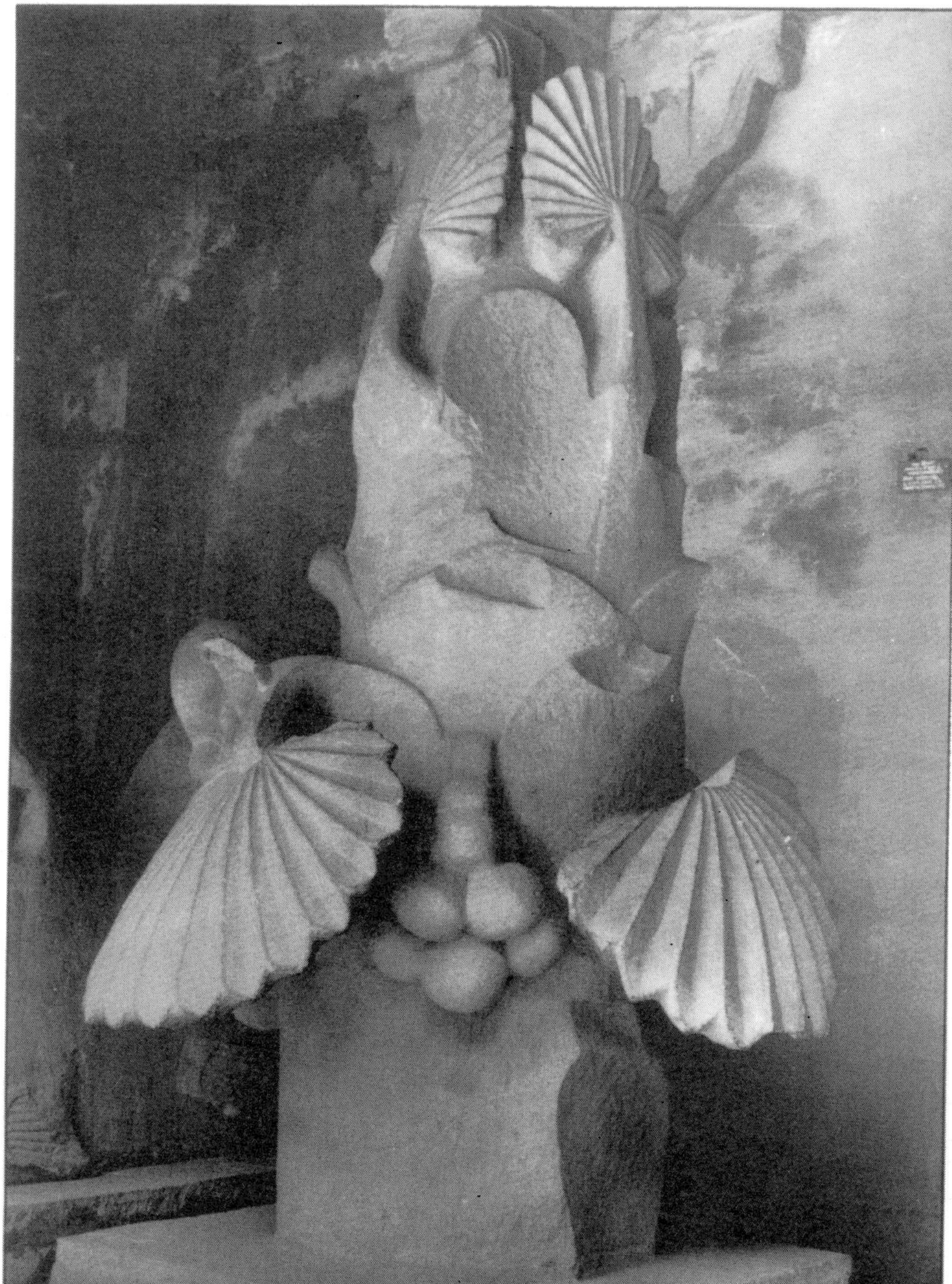

Pl. 28. Fan-palm capital; Pawaya (Gwalior, M.P.); Buff sandstone; Central Museum, Gwalior; 4th-5th century AD.

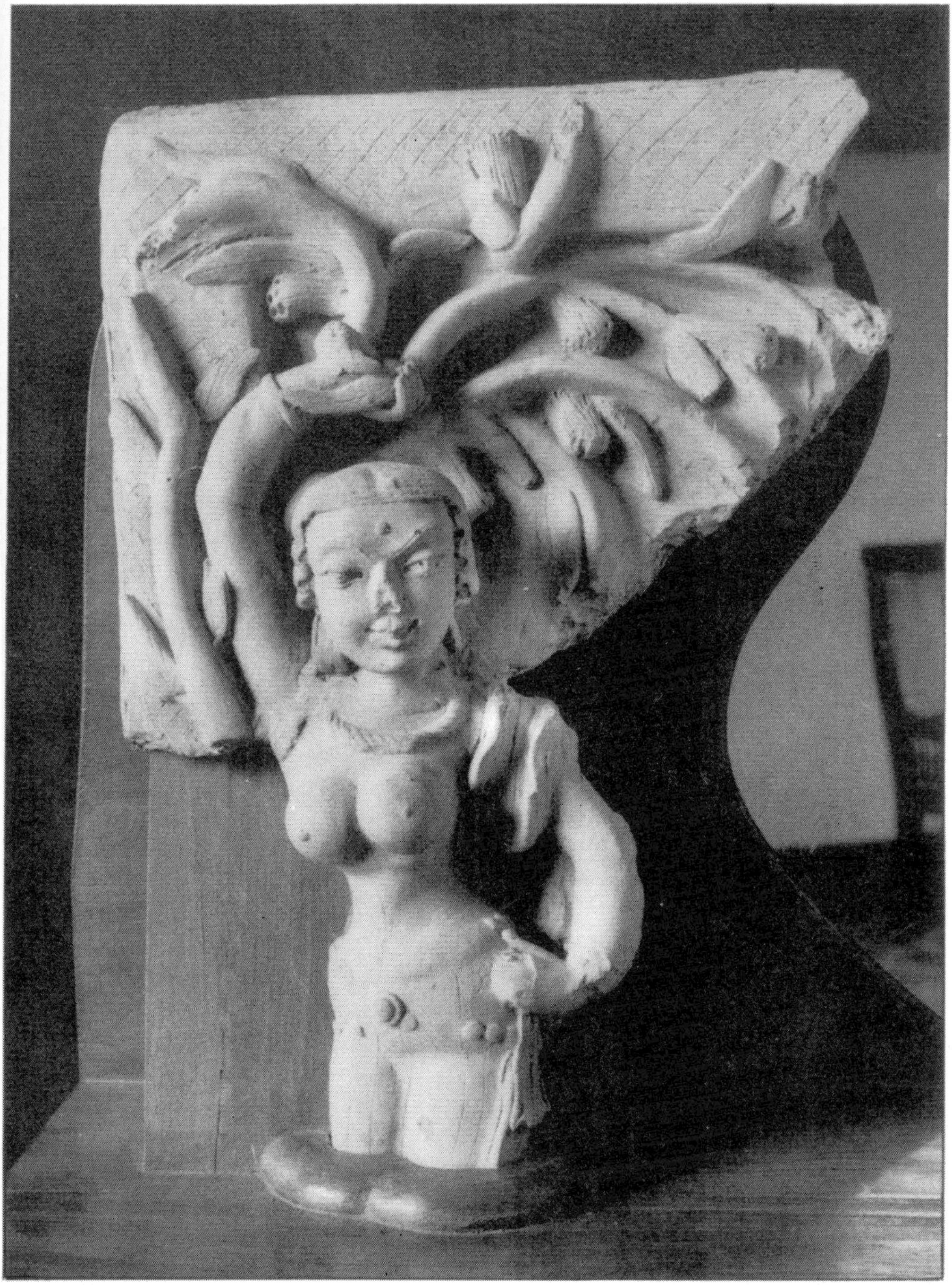

Pl. 29. Śālabhañjikā; Kopa (Basti, U.P.); Terracotta; Municipal Museum, Allahabad; 5th century AD.

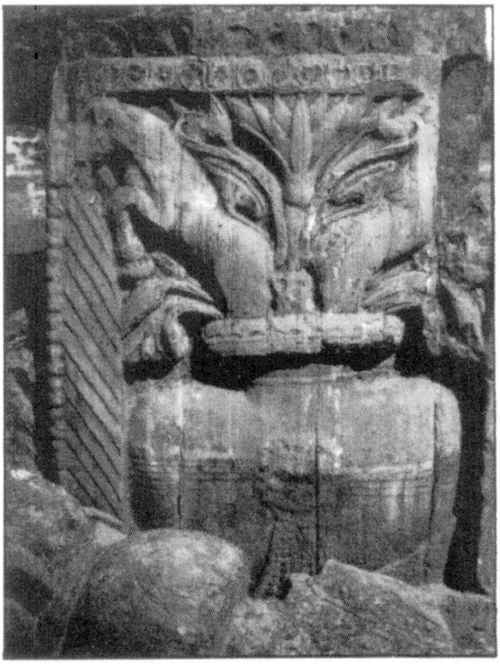

Pl. 30. Two Vyuhalas and stylised lotuse issuing out from the mouth of a pitcher (ghaṭa); Tala (Bilaspur M.P.); Jethani temple, Main entrance on south, east pillar, lower detail; stone; 6th century (late) AD

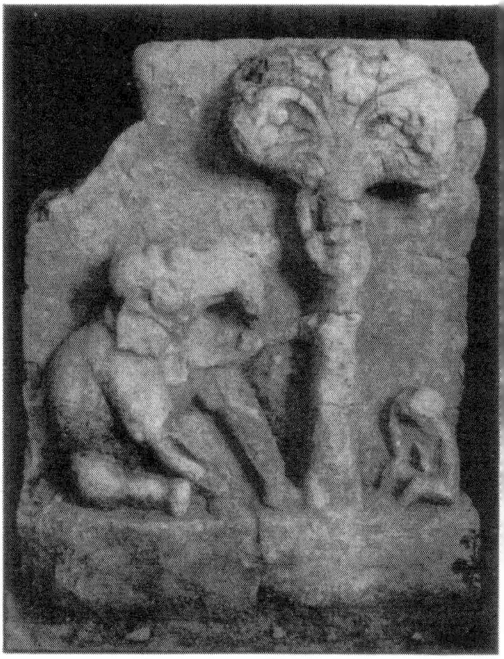

Pl. 31. A panel carved with some story; Malhar (Bilaspur, M.P.); Buff sandstone; Site Museum, Mathura; 5th-6th century AD.

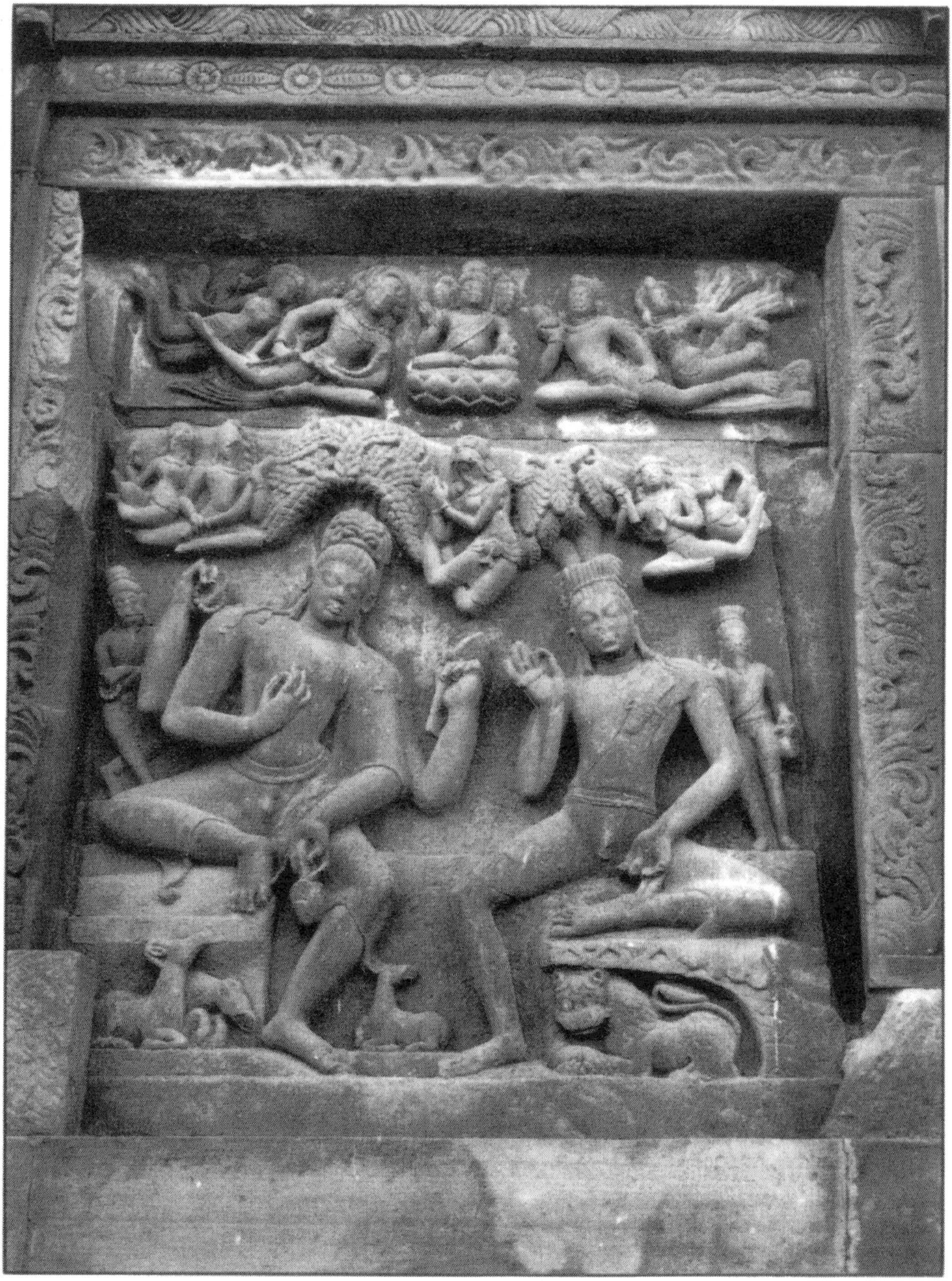

Pl. 32. Nara and Nārāyaṇa under trees; Deogarh (Lalitpur, U.P.), Dasāvatara temple, East Jaṅgha, Rathikabimba; Red sandstone; ca. AD 500-25.

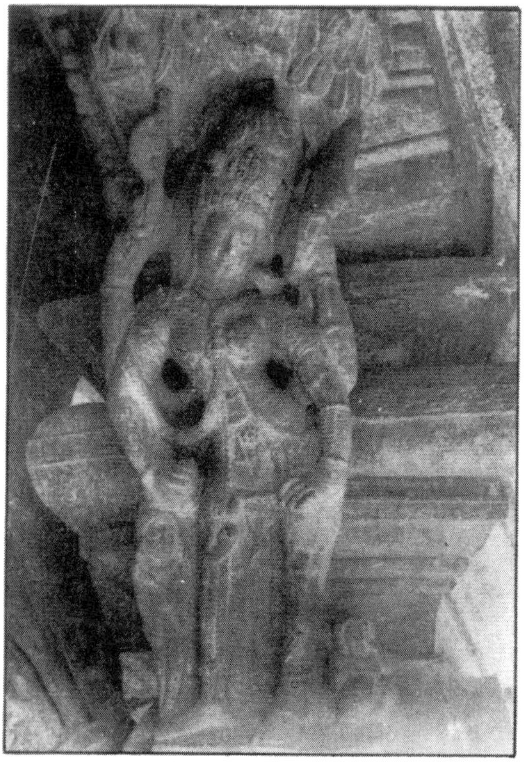

Pl. 33. Mock coronation of child Kṛṣṇ Badami (Bijapur-Karnataka), Ca 3; sandstone; ca. AD 500-78.

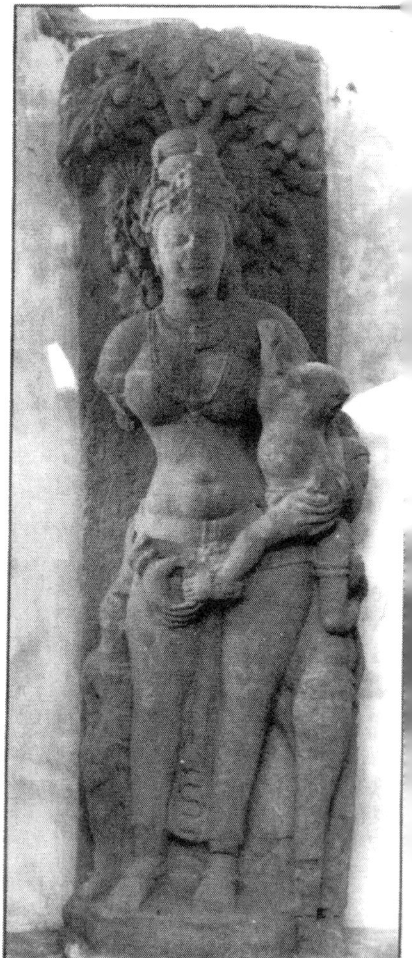

Pl. 34. Ambika standing under a mango tree; Sirpur (Raipur, M.P.); Buff sandstone; Site Museum (Sirpur); 6th century AD.

two fatherless children whose mother had abandoned them under its branches. The children would have perished but for the milk of the banyan that dripped into their mouth and fed them.

Trees offer protection from both physical and spiritual illness through their association with the divine. Certain tribes in India believe that nothing is more effective for protection against evil and spiritual problems than carved wood offerings.

In another vein, trees can be associated with a shrine dedicated to a deceased relative, who in turn becomes an ancestor. This idea of sacred tree representing the lineage or clan is an old one. For many cultures, the ancestors are the deities and are responsible for life, death and spiritual happiness. The wooden totem-pole used particularly by different tribes is not merely name or emblem of different family groups. It indicates towards special relationship between ancestors and the sacred world also (Fig. 6). It is also believed that Hindu ancestors reside on *aśvattha* tree.

A variety of trees are specifically associated with religious beliefs about the fate of the dead and the rebirth or passage of their souls to the after life. Many religions practise tree burial as the appropriate spiritual resting place for the deceased. The Khasiyas of eastern India leave the deceased in the hollow trunk of a tree. The Coorgs of south India cut down a mango tree that grows in the burial ground for the funeral pyre. The leaves of the baine palm are also associated with death and are used in funeral rituals by Coorgs. The Hindus of Bengal burn their dead with mango wood. In myth and rituals, trees serve as symbols of orientation, knowledge and life.

II

FERTILITY CULT

Ever since man evolved on this earth he studied various elements in nature. These studies led him to a firm belief that the vegetation, animals and humans all emerge from the first principle of world order, i.e., seed and womb; and both are energised by *prāṇa* (breath). However, the seed is the primary principle from which all other principles proceed. It is the "seed" of the vegetal world, the foetus of the animal world, and womb of the human world. It is the germ of life and the basic dynamic energising principle. The entire universe is its manifestation and expansion. The conception seed, *bija, garbha* and *andha* comprehended at various levels is a unifying

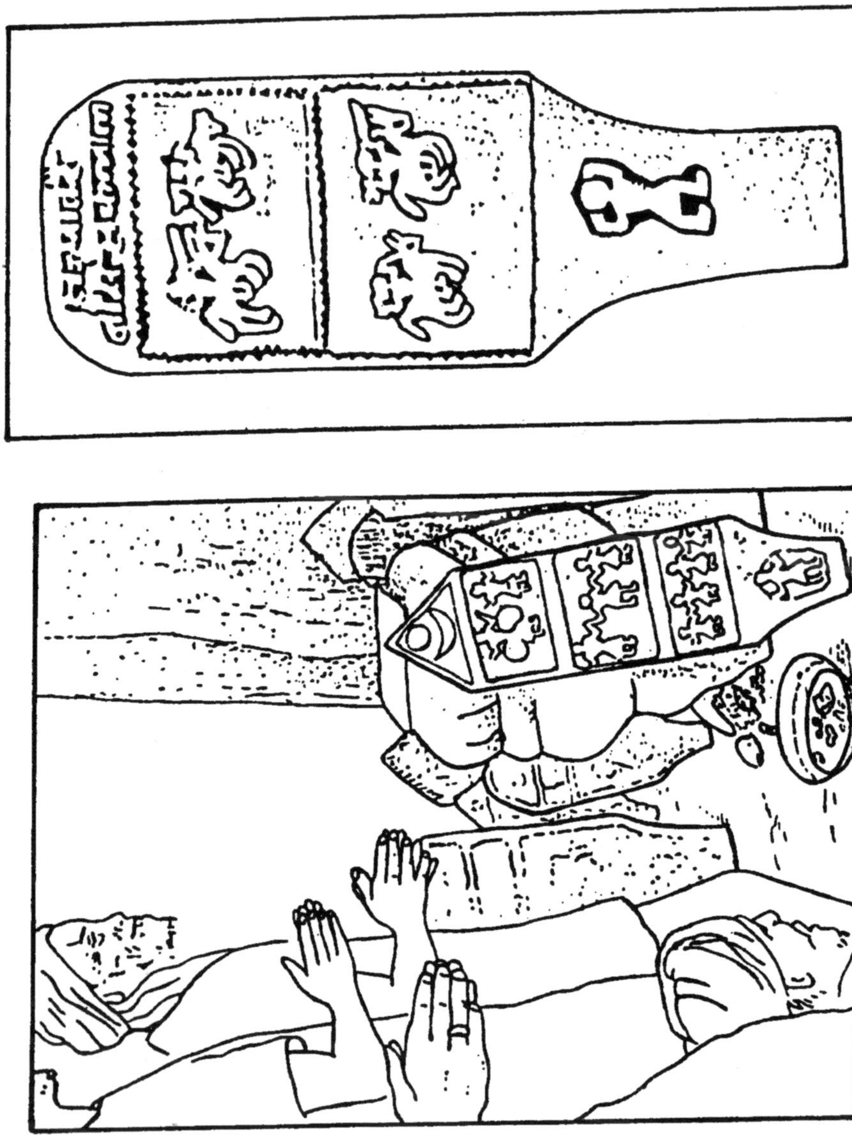

Fig. 6. *Korku men worshipping the carved wooden board under a sacred tree*; at Baba Garden in Pachmarhi town (Madhya Pradesh)

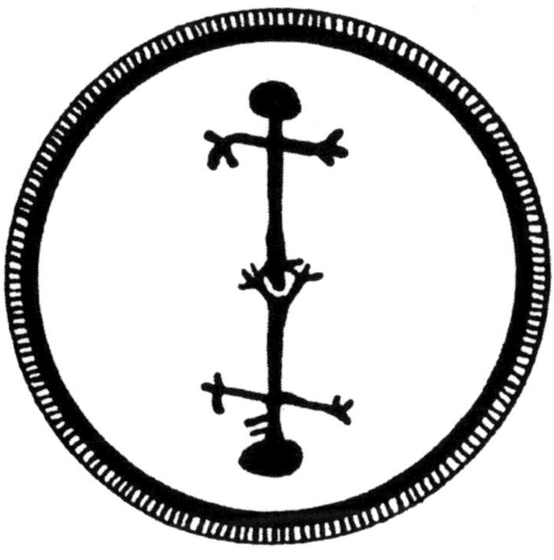

Fig. 7. *Representation of male and female;* pot; Daimabad (Maharashtra).

principle of Indian thought and art.

The Śākambhārī aspect of the archaic Mother which perhaps emerged from the above principle led to the evolution of the cult of fertility and its antiquity can be pushed back as early as the proto-historic period. The recovery of the numerous phallic stones and ring stones, the figures of the male ithyphallic horned god in association with animals who is probably the prototype of Śiva, and the figures of Mother goddess from the Indus valley and in its extensions of Gujarat, Rajasthan and Punjab indicate the prevalence of their cults in these areas.[12]

On the several seals, tree spirits of indeterminate sex are seen with a tiger or any other animal, and occasionally with worshippers (Figs. 1, 4). But not a single representation of the sexual act is reported so far from the said area. One of the earliest depictions of sexual act is reported on a pot (Fig. 7) of the chalcolithic period at Daimabad in Ahmednagar district of Maharashtra. These erotic figures are said to be symbolic representations of the union of *ātman* and *brahman* or of *puruṣa* and *prakriti* or the Male and Female principles of the universe, and the divine bliss (*ānanda*) is expressed through the state of human sexual union.[13] The coition is believed to ensure fertility of human beings which would magically enhance the fertility of earth, vegetation, animal, etc. It was considered also as a magico-protective device against calamities.[14] In historical period also, significant material on the possible connection of erotic couples with fertility cult is available.

Mother Goddess Cult

Among the numerous types of goddesses in ancient India, three types, i.e., "opulent" goddess, the personified yoni type of goddess, the pāñcacūḍa types were most popular and they directly concern us.[15] A reference may be made here of a gold plaque from Lauriya (Fig. 8) and ring-stones (Fig. 9, Pl. 1) from Murtaziganj (Patna) which depict "opulent" Mother goddesses. The

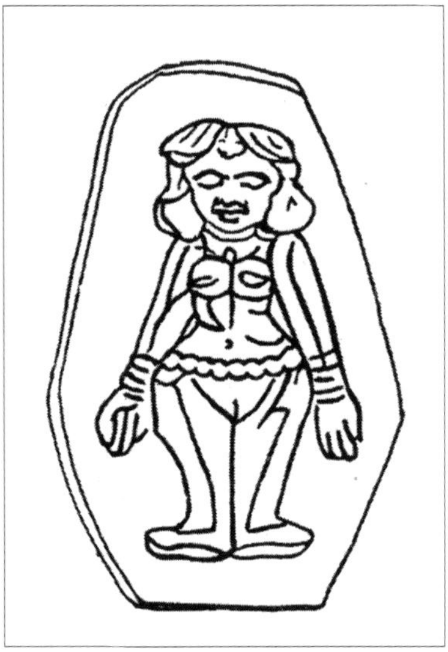

Fig. 8. "*Opulent" Mother Goddess;* Gold Plaque; Lauriya (Distt. Champaran); (courtesy: Desai 1975)

goddesses in these cases are having broad hips, exposing their sexual triangle, and depicted in frontal posture, while mother goddess in one case is depicted along with motifs of vegetation, a crescent moon, deer, lions, horses, elephants, birds, and a lotus design in the centre (Fig. 9). The association with wild beasts and the crescent moon most probably relates her to the Anāhitā-Nana-Artenis-Diana group of fertility goddesses.[16]

Another variety of goddesses, the nude goddess, generally called by M. Murray (1934) the 'Baubo' or personified *yoni* is reported in the beginning centuries of Christian era. The goddess is completely nude and displays her *yoni* (Fig. 10). A lotus emerges from her head (being headless) and she sits in frog or 'Baubo' style with legs apart (*uttānapad*). The fertility aspect of this goddess can be proved beyond doubt as even today women worship such figures and apply butter and kumkuma on the *yoni* for begetting children.[17]

The most awe-inspiring image of the nude goddess carved in dark stone is at Alampur in Andhra Pradesh (Fig. 11). About this image Stella Kramrish says, this is "Aditi" the life giving mother earth, invoked in the *Vedas* so that she may spread wide and favour us (AV XII 1.2). She is in the *uttānapad* posture, "the posture of sexual intercourse as well as giving birth". It is she who bears plants as mothers. "Plants O Ye Mothers, I hail you as goddess" (*Yajur* v. IV 2.6).[18] Another scholar suggests that the Alampur image (Fig. 11) can be the stone counterpart of the goddess *Pālaghaṭa* (Mother Earth), whose outlines suggest a similar birth giving and

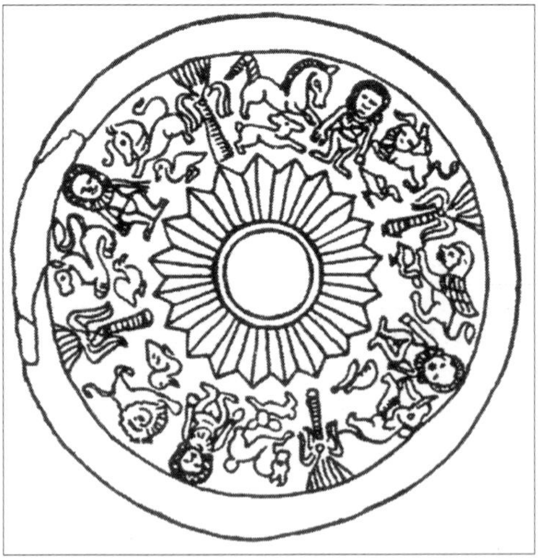

Fig. 9. *Ring stone representing "Opulent" Mother Goddess;* Murtaziganj (Patna); Patna Museum

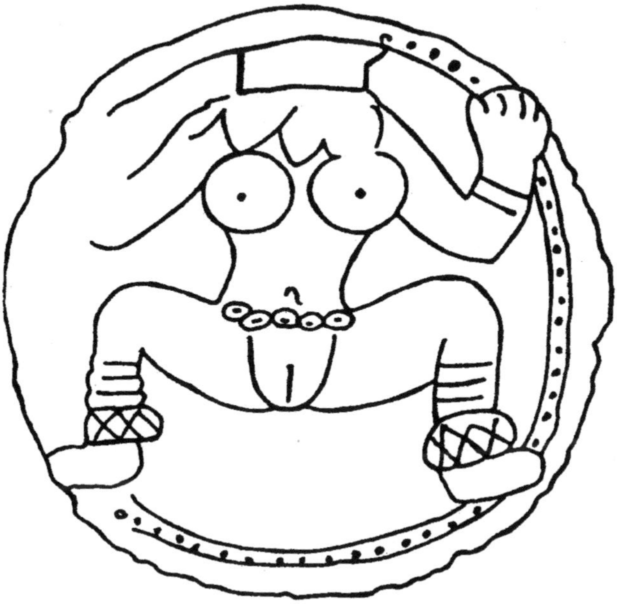

Fig. 10. *Headless nude goddess;* terracotta; Bhita, Maharashtra; (courtesy: Desai 1975)

life giving posture.[19] A Kānsarī song establishes that *Pālaghaṭa* is the position taken both for sexual act and for giving birth to a child. The primitive birth giving goddess (Fig. 12) can be deciphered in the paintings at Talaseri, Karanjvira, Dhamangaon, Gagangaon, Halapada, Ambe-sari, etc. in different shapes.[20] She is also responsible for all of vegetal life (Kānsarī) as mentioned in the song.

Interestingly, the position of *Pālaghaṭa* closely resembles the goddess giving birth to the vegetation in an Indus valley seal from Harappa (Fig. 2) in which a plant in the process of being born is shown as issuing out of her womb, and the tigers stand probable guardians to the Earth Mother's auspicious act. The present scene can be a vivid concretisation of the concept of fecundity.[21]

The divine status of yet another variety of goddesses, *Pāñcacūḍa* (Fig. 13) is established by many scholars and numerous suggestions have been made for her identification (Desai, 1975:13). She is generally adorned with five or three *āyudhas* (weapons) as ornaments in her elaborate head-dress, and her cult was prevalent in the Śuṅga period in various parts of India from Punjab to Bengal. As per V.S. Agrawala,[22] her association with an original cult of fertility may be inferred from the presence of sacred symbols on the head-dress and the necklace and also, in one instance, from the indication of nudity.

Pālaghaṭa

Etymologically, the word *Pālaghaṭa* means the pot over-flowing with plants (*Pāl*—plants, *ghaṭa*—pot) and could represent the goddess of fertility. The pot is revered as a fertility symbol among Saora tribe of Orissa and is

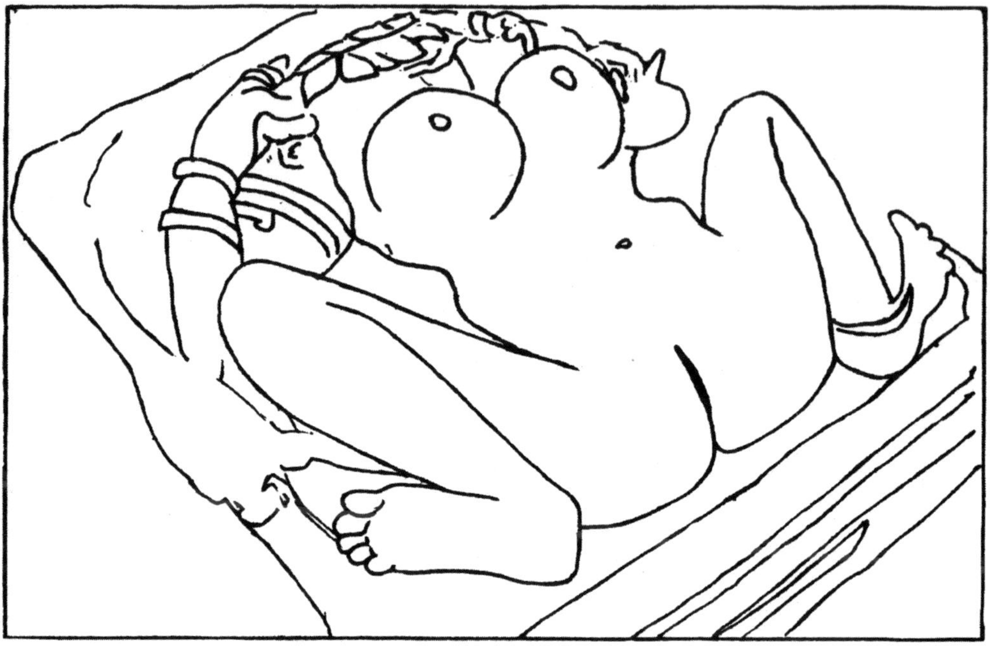

Fig. 11. *Nude goddess in Uttānapad pose;* stone; Alampur, Andhra Pradesh

associated with goddess *Pālaghaṭa*. She may also be a Bhil goddess, because Khandesh is inhabited by Bhils with whom the Warlis have an affinity.[23] *Pālaghaṭa* is generally regarded as the most ancient of goddesses, the Mother Earth, who is all sustaining principle of nature. She is central to the Warli paintings of Maharashtra and is the patron deity of marriage, without whom it cannot take place (Fig. 12). Her form varies from bare skeletal figure in the north to the triangular, decorative goddess of the south. She is shown as a strangely disembodied figure without a head or any physical feature.[24]

In Indian art, the pot of abundance or the overflowing vessel, *pūrṇaghaṭa*, is the commonest of all auspicious symbols. Its depiction is found from the early historic period rock paintings of Bhimbetka (Fig. 14). Among the earliest examples it is also found at Amaravati (Fig. 15), Bharhut and Sanchi where the pot of abundance with a mass of lotus flowers and leaves rising from it is seen or the goddess identified as Śrī Lakṣmī standing on a lotus rising from a *pūrṇaghaṭa* (Fig. 16) or as a human representation

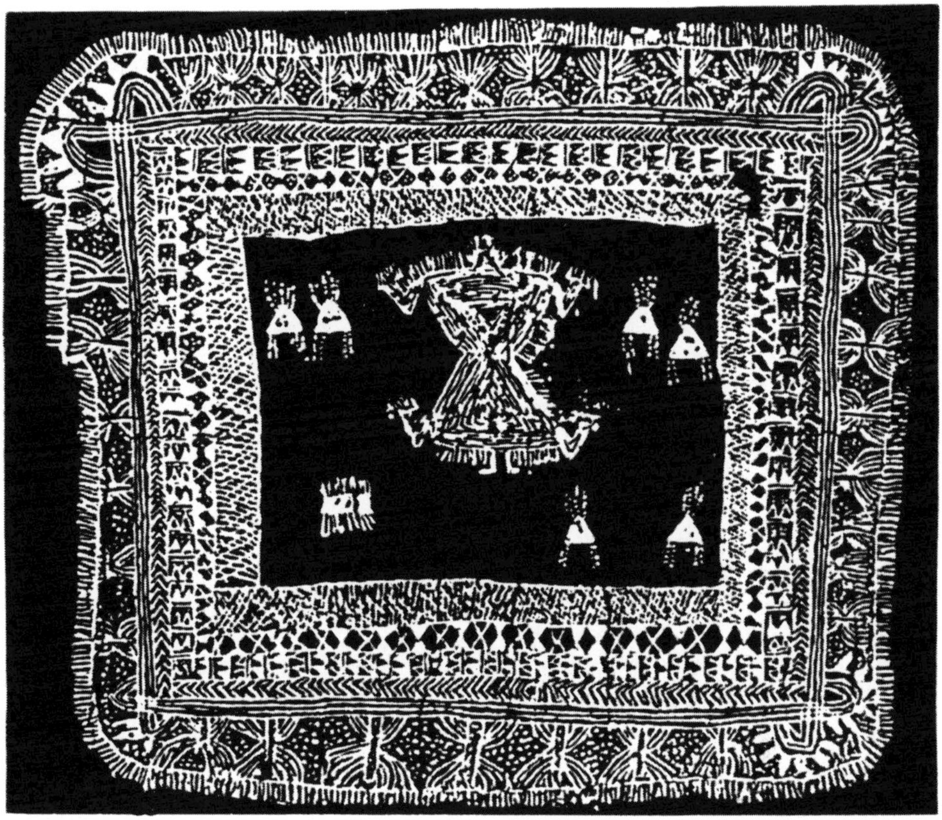

Fig. 12. *Goddess Pālaghaṭa in a Warli marriage painting from Ganjad, Maharashtra;* mural painting; (courtesy: Dalmia 1988)

of this, *Śrī Lakṣmī* standing or seated on a lotus. In *Śrī Sūkta* her fertility aspect is clearly revealed and is called *ārdrā* (moist), green as plant, olive, etc. She is regarded as a guardian deity of farmers. Coomaraswamy (1965) has drawn attention to her role as goddess of fertility and love. He opines that vase alone should be regarded as aniconic symbol of and equivalent to goddess herself. It is the womb of creation which encapsulates birth, life and death of all living things. Here, a reference may be made of the Jethani temple at Tala in Bilaspur (M.P.), which shows a huge pitcher (*ghaṭa*), from the mouth of which are seen issuing out two *Vyuhalas,* a huge stylised lotus and its leaves (Pl. 30).

On the railing pillars of Sanchi stupa II, the association of Śrī with mithuna is clearly seen. It seems that in religious art of India, Śrī has direct bearing on the depiction of mithunas.[25] Similarly, many other pillars at Sanchi depict couples with lotus in hand and stand near goddess Śrī.[26]

The lotus is an important sacred symbol and is birthplace of goddess Śrī. The cosmic lotus is personified as the Mother goddess through whom the Absolute moves into creation. It thus acts as womb of creation, the womb of the universe and support of the universe.

Iconographically speaking, the Earth goddess carries ears of corn and thereby she is related to fertility and cultivation; Śiva wears *patra-kuṇḍala* on the right and *śaṅkha-kuṇḍala* on the left ear, he is symbolised as Ardhanārīśvara and known thereby as god of creation; Kārttikeya holds a mature pomegranate partially burst open exposing thereby seeds and he is related as god of cultivation and Vasundharā. Viṣṇu is the primordial man; when he wears a garland of wild foliage and flowers (*vanamālā*), he is united with nature; this unification of man and nature leads the creation to proceed.

Śālabhañjikā/Dohada

In the magico-sexual rites women play an important role with a view to increase the fertility of the soil and vegetation, to bring rain, in general to assure agricultural fruitfulness. Interestingly, cultivation of the soil is said to be magically dependent for success on woman and is connected with her child-bearing function.[27] *Dohada-Śālabhañjikā* in Indian art also relates to the fertility cult. The notion that a woman fertilizes trees and trees fertilize a barren mother has been deeply rooted in India's ancient past.

Of the various names used for the woman and tree motif, *śālabhañjikā* and *dohada* are found to have been frequently used by Roth[28] in his article. But scholars differ with the exact meaning of these terms. To Williams,[29] the term *śālabhañjikā* means an image of *śāla* tree. According to the same author, it may also mean a game played in the east of India, a harlot, a courtesan; and also stands for a bower of branches and a large branch. In *Avadāna Śataka,* the term *śālabhañjikā* means the breaking of a branch.[30] Some scholars say that, the term *śālabhañjikā* may mean embracing a tree by a barren woman in the hope of conceiving a child. It is noteworthy that the term *śālabhañjikā* does not relate a woman exclusively with a *śāla* tree. Sometimes in the ancient Indian art, the trees are *aśoka* and mango also.[31]

According to Bloomfield[32], the term *dohada* means the craving of a pregnant woman. He further says that the term *"dohada"* also stands for

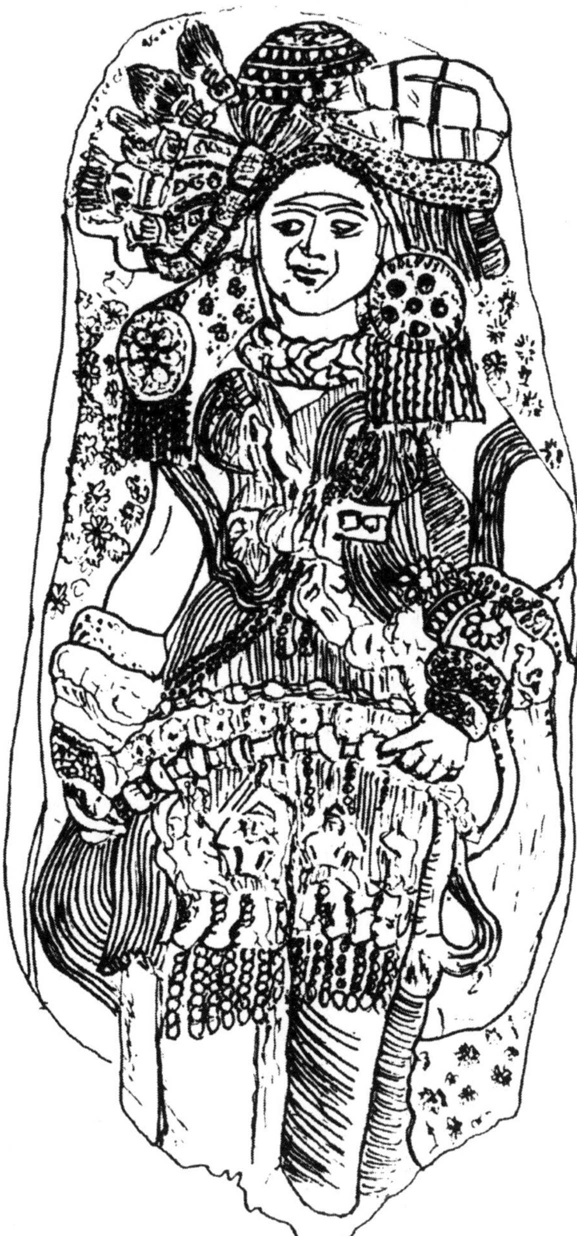

Fig. 13. *Pañcacūḍa Goddess;* Terracotta; Tamluk; Ashmolean Museum, Oxford

the presence of a second heart and second will in the body of the mother. Term "*dohada*" is perhaps derived from *dvaihṛda* and the pregnant woman may thus be called *dauhridinī*.[33] In another reference quoted in the *Raghuvaṁśa* (3.3-6), the king kisses the face of his beloved that has odour of earth and thus learns that she is in pregnancy (*dohada*). But the word "*dohada*" to Pisharoti[34] means a rite for the sake of tree, not a fertility rite but one of the fertilisation, so that trees might have flowers in abundance as was referred to earlier by Kālidāsa.

Before the birth of Bodhisattva, Māyādevī expressed her desire to play *śālakrīḍa*[35] but in the course of her play she felt labour pain. And the very pose of Māyādevī in which she delivered Bodhisattva has been described as *dohada śālabhañjikā.* In this regard Biswas[36] says, Māyādevi's case was not the case of *dohada* since she expressly declared to be freed from desires when Bodhisattva entered her

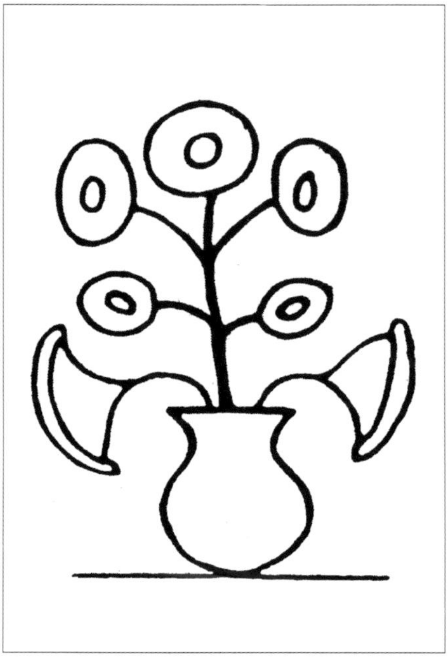

Fig. 14. *Pūrṇaghaṭa from Bhimbetka (M.P.) rock shelter*

womb and hence her pose during delivering the child should be reckoned as a pose that reminds one of a *śālabhañjikā*. The branch of the tree which Māyādevī holds during her delivery is assessed by Buddhists as a tree having amazing powers. Thus, attempts have been made to associate the terms "*śālabhañjikā*" and "*dohada*" with the notion of fertility. It seems that in the case of *śālabhañjikā,* the tree fertilises a woman and *dohada* means fertilisation given to a tree by a woman. Our epic (*Mahābhārata*, Bhīṣmaparva, 7.2-11) has recorded that barren women should approach tree spirits if they desire child. A reference here can also be made to *kalpavṛkṣa* or *kalpalatā*, as the ancient Indians believed that these trees fulfil all human desires.

As discussed above that the tree fertilises a woman and also gets fertilised by a woman, raises a question. What is then sex of a tree? Could then the term *Brahmā-taru* fit in somewhere to answer this? One finds an easy explanation if the tree is taken as *Parama Brahmā*. There are many allusions to the trees and their evident association with the cult of fertility in the pre-Buddhist literature (*Atharvaveda* [vi.8.1]; *Taittirīya Saṁhitā* [II.1.1-7]; *Aitareya Brāhmaṇa* [II.1.1]). The faith continued for centuries thereafter. The *Kālikā Purāṇa* (82.67-68) has mentioned a reference of sage Bhṛgu who advised mothers of Jāmadagnya and Viśvāmitra to embrace *aśvattha* and *udumbara* trees so that they could bear a child. According to Biswas and Debnath,[37] such instructions to barren mothers to embrace trees were not altogether fantastic and there must have been certain scientific basis for it. These scholars believe that when a woman is instructed to embrace a tree it was actually meant to obtain the sap of it through the extraction of its roots, barks, leaves, flowers and fruits.

The figures of *śālabhañjikā* which start appearing from the 2nd cent.

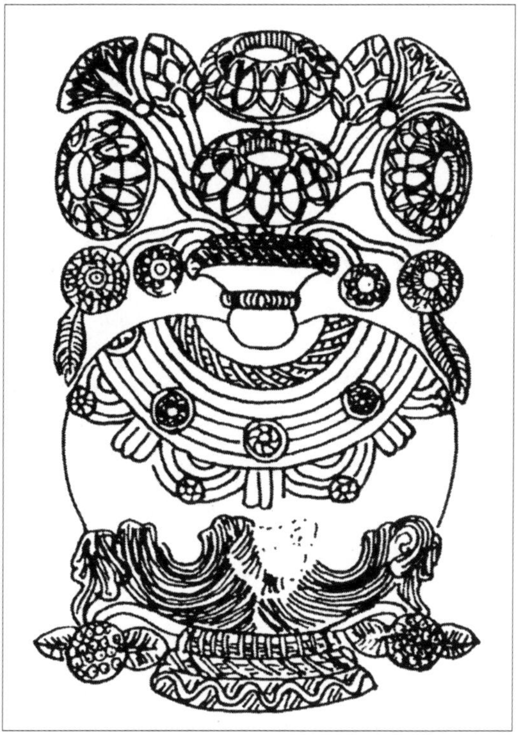

Fig. 15. *Pūrṇaghaṭa;* Amaravati

BC remained a very popular motif for centuries among the sculptors and modellers. The motif of the woman plucking flowers from a distended bough is met with on the toraṇa of Bharhut and Sanchi in the Śuṅga period and it continued on the railing pillars of the Kuṣāṇa period. It is also found in a limited number of examples in Gandhāra art of the Kusāṇa period. In Kusāṇa period, interesting motifs of *aśoka-dohada* are shown reported, in which a graceful young woman stands under an *aśoka* tree and bending low its branches with her left hand touches its stems with the left foot (Pls. 16, 17, 29). Mahāmāyā, the mother of Siddhartha Gautama standing cross-legged and bending the branch of a widespreading tree, in her longing for offspring, is commonly depicted on Buddhist shrines but apart from the Gandhara sculptures, the tree under which Siddhartha was born is usually sculpted as the *aśoka* tree even though the common belief is that he was born under *śāla* tree.

Popular Beliefs and Practices

In the olden days perhaps it was a custom for women to walk naked around the *pipal* tree in order to gain fertility (Marshall, 1931: 66). From the *Atharvaveda* (VI.II.I) we learn that at the time of its composition, the tree was worshipped for the birth of the male progeny. In the later Vedic texts, *aśvattha* is regarded as *Brahmā-taru*, the embodiment of knowledge and the great creator. That is why it is called on certain occasions as "tree of life" or the "tree of creation". The sanctity of the *pipal* tree has continued to the present day. There are many rituals connected with *aśvattha* tree. The women of northern India perform the worship of *aśvattha* for getting

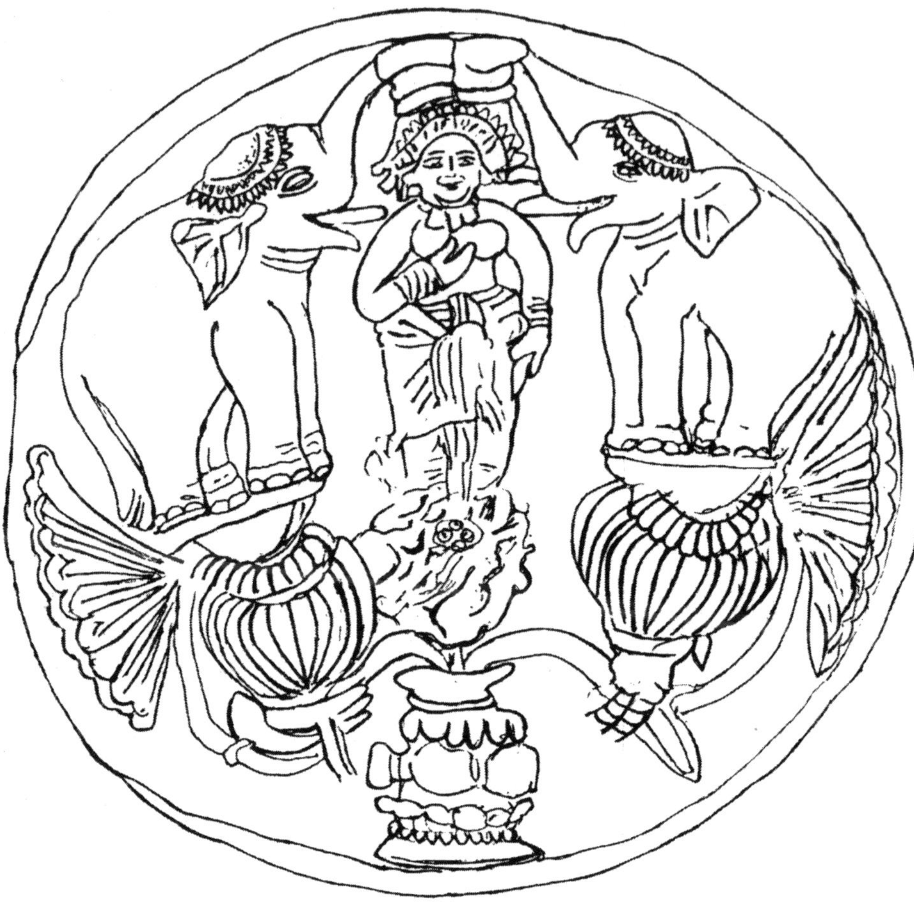

Fig. 16. *Goddess Śrī touching her own breasts;* Bharhut; Indian Museum, Calcutta

conjugal love and happiness on the fifteenth day of the black half of any month which falls on Monday (*Somavati Amāvasyā*). In Rajasthan the local women adorn this tree with their offerings in order to ward off widowhood. Similarly, womenfolk of Bengal occasionally observe the *Aśvattha pata-vrata* throughout a month commencing from last day of *Chaitra* (March-April) till the last day of *Vaiśākha* (April-May). This *vrata* is observed for gaining all-round prosperity of the family or for the fulfilment of specific desires. They make vows and tie rags to its branches in order to acquire the boon of having male offspring. In order to avert ill-luck of a girl, her marriage with the tree is performed.[38]

In all socio-religious observances, the mango twig is put in the *jala ghaṭa*. The leaves of a mango and *sīriṣa* trees are hung over the door of the birth chamber of a male child. Even marriage *pandāls* are particularly decorated with mango leaves.

The plantain plant and its fruits are always associated with the fertility cult. In *Durgā-pūjā*,[39] the plant is dressed as a woman and described as *Vana-Durgā*. Similarly, in the *Lakṣmī-pūjā* a plantain dressed as a woman is worshipped. She is considered as Lakṣmī herself. In rural Bengal the marriage *paṇḍāl* is constructed with plantains even today. They are also required in certain marriage rites. The women worship this plant on the 4th day of *Kārtika* for long life of their husbands.

The betel-nut along with betel-leaf (*pān*) is particularly associated with procreation and fertility. According to a common belief in Orissa, if a woman picks up a betel-nut from within a well while drawing water, her desire for children will be fulfilled.[40]

Like betel-nuts, coconuts are also believed to possess magical properties, and it is said that their use will ensure the birth of a large number of children. In some rites of rural Bengal, women use coconut on the occasion of what is called second marriage.[41]

Bilva is regarded as "tree of life" in the *Brāhmaṇa* literature. Married women adorn this tree for gaining favour from their husbands.

Since trees and plants were treated as animated beings, it resulted in treating them as male and female, who can be married to each other in a real, and not merely in figurative or poetical sense of the word. In this regard, Kālidāsa's *Abhijñānaśākuntam* has mentioned the marriage of a "*navamallika*" flower with a mango tree.[42] In our country, the marriage of trees is considered to be symbolic only. The marriage of trees may be performed when a woman has been married for many years and has not yet borne children. One tree representing her husband and one tree symbolising her fertility are planted side by side so that their combined growth may symbolically and spiritually increase her fertility and growth of life within her womb. Such marriages are very common in Bihar.

Certain tribes of India even perform marriage of their boys and girls with trees.[43] If it is predicted that the first marriage of the boy will break, then by marrying him to a tree, the tragedy is averted, and later he is married to a girl and she is considered his second wife. On several occasions, a girl is married to a tree with a belief that she will imbibe fertility of the tree, before she is married to a man.[44]

In the Konkan district of Western India it is believed that barrenness can be cured by planting a tree for the uneasy spirits that wander about and inhabit women, preventing conception. Under favourable circumstances the evil spirit will leave a woman suffering from barrenness to take up residence in the newly planted tree, allowing the woman to conceive.

The "marriage tree" is common in south India as a representation of male or female ancestor. This tree is necessary for all weddings and is adorned as a part of the ceremony. The practice of marrying brides to a tree is traced to matriarchal conditions, when true marriage is not recognised. The idea behind these marriages is perhaps to bring the bride and bridegroom into close association with the fertility of nature. Both woman and nature are the vehicles that carry the procreative energies. Interestingly, the fertility cycles are expressed in the growth of crops, the mating habits of animals and the menstrual flow of women and the annual return of fertility is revered as a primal act of creation.

As per existing belief at many places in India, the fertility of soil depends upon the periodic marriage of the Mother Earth with her male consort. In this connection, a reference may be made to Oran tribe of Bengal; they celebrate annually marriage of Earth with the sun god, when the *śāla* tree is in blossom. It is suggested that the union of the Earth with the sun was symbolised in the Vedic *Mahāvrata* rite.[45] The divine marriage is probably celebrated to ensure the fertility of the ground. Even today, the periodic marriage of deities in Hindu temples is celebrated with much pomp. For example, Jagannātha of the Puri shrine is married to Rukmaṇī on *Rukmaṇī haraṇa Ekādaśī* every year; the god of famous Liṅgarāja temple of Bhubanesvar is married to the deity in the Gaurī temple on *Śītalāṣaṣthī* day every year, etc. In ancient India, the Earth (*Pṛithvi*) and Heaven (*Dyauh*) were regarded as a couple and their cosmic intercourse finds mention in the *Ṛgveda*.[46]

Fertility Festivals

Many festivals of ancient and medieval India were related to the fertility cult. The important among them include Vasantotsava, Madanamahotsava, Holī and Kaumudīmahotsava. In festivals like Dolayātrā, Aśokāṣṭamī, Yakṣarātri, Damanakacaturdaśī, Ambubāchī, Nāga-pañcamī, Mitra-saptamī, Rathasaptamī, Udakasevāmahotsava, Śābrotsava etc. the fertility rites are also performed. Interestingly, use of obscene (*aślīla*) words and gestures is one of the essential features of most of these festivals. The ritual function of abuse and contumelious speech is previously found in Vedic culture. Obscene words and abusive language are believed to bring rain. Such words and jokes are usually spoken on seasonal festivals like Holī, Vasantotsava and Madanamahotsava and festivals in honour of deities.

In the festivals of Madanamahotsava, Vasantotsava and Kaumudīmahotsava, men and women meet freely and have sexual liberty.[47] There was a considerable relaxation of social restraint in respect of mixing of men and women in these festivals. It is believed that celebration of these festivals will bring luck and avert evil in general and stimulate agricultural fertility in particular.

The Bas *pūjā* or *Madanakām pūjā* festival of Assam reminds us of the ancient spring festival known as Madanamahotsava, but how Madana or Kāmadeva, the Indian god of love, came to be symbolised by bamboos is difficult to explain. Certain groups of people in the erstwhile Goalpura district are seen performing the *Bas* (*Bans*) *pūjā* ceremony of the *Madanachaturdasi* (March-April) continuously from three to five days. Two stout bamboos are ceremonially cut and washed and wrapped in cloth. The longer one is considered to be the male and is wrapped in white cloth. The shorter one is believed to be the female and is wrapped in red cloth. The significant feature of this festival is the narration of aetiological ballads describing the birth of Madana-Kām, different species of bamboo, selection of the right species, etc. Some parts of the songs have erotic tone. Sometimes even songs associating Rādhā and Kṛṣṇa are sung. The bamboos as symbolising the male and the female suggest procreation also. Only male members take part in the ceremonial activity, but women and children attend the function.

The folk festivals have considerable variations according to the areas and communities. The Hajong tribals near Garo hills put up three bamboos instead of two discussed above. The third bamboo has a peculiar function. A *jakai* (a contrivance for catching fish), a creel and a broken plough are hung up on this bamboo. Menfolk dance and sing songs carrying feeling of desire as well as pain as not getting someone. The musical instruments played on the occasion are the drum, the pipe, cymbals and the flute.

The worship of Kāmadeva at the foot of a bamboo planted for the occasion is seen in Cooch Bihar in northern Bengal on the full moon day of *Chaitra*. In Bajali area of Barpeta district, the bamboo kept leaning on a banyan tree is known as Madanmohan Gosain, a name for Kṛṣṇa, and worshipped as such.

III

ECOLOGICAL AWARENESS

The destruction of forests is most dangerous for the nation and human beings. Vanaspati has direct relation with the well being of society. Due to the pollution of the natural environment and the destruction of the forest, many diseases crop up to ruin the nation.

Caraka Saṁhitā, Vimansthan, 3.2

Forests play a vital role in maintaining the ecological balance, modifying the climate, filtering the air, controlling the run-off of water, also protecting soils, increasing the precipitation and providing habitat to animals. Trees absorb carbon and release oxygen. As per 1991 Forest Survey of India Report, the forest cover is 6,39,182 sq. km, i.e., 19.44% of the country's total geographical area. But under ecological norms, the forest cover should not be less than 33%. The tropical forest cover is supporting the richest bio-diversity and the present trend of deforestation is causing threat to bio-diversity. Once the forest cover is lost the entire ecological balance would be lost. Our forests are suffering depletion due to the lower economic level or crippling poverty, trade in timber, commercial logging, shifting cultivation in eastern Himalayas, misuse of land, transformation of forest lands to agriculture lands, residential complexes, industrial complexes, over exploitation of natural resources for fodder, fuel, conventional method of horticulture, floriculture and agriculture.

The impact of shrinking forests is devastative for human organism as deforestation is responsible for the release of carbon dioxide. The concentration of toxic gases—carbon dioxide, carbon monoxide, etc.—is responsible for the increase of global temperature and global warming. The deforestation is further responsible for the destruction of habitats of wild animals. In India recurrence of floods and droughts is due to deforestation, and economy also suffers a setback because the supply of raw materials to agro-based industries is stopped. The supply of fodder and fuel has been reduced too.

The trend of deforestation in Indian subcontinent is, therefore, causing concern to the environmentalists. The conservation of these forests is not necessary for development only but for our survival too. While realising the importance of forests, the Government of India passed a Forest

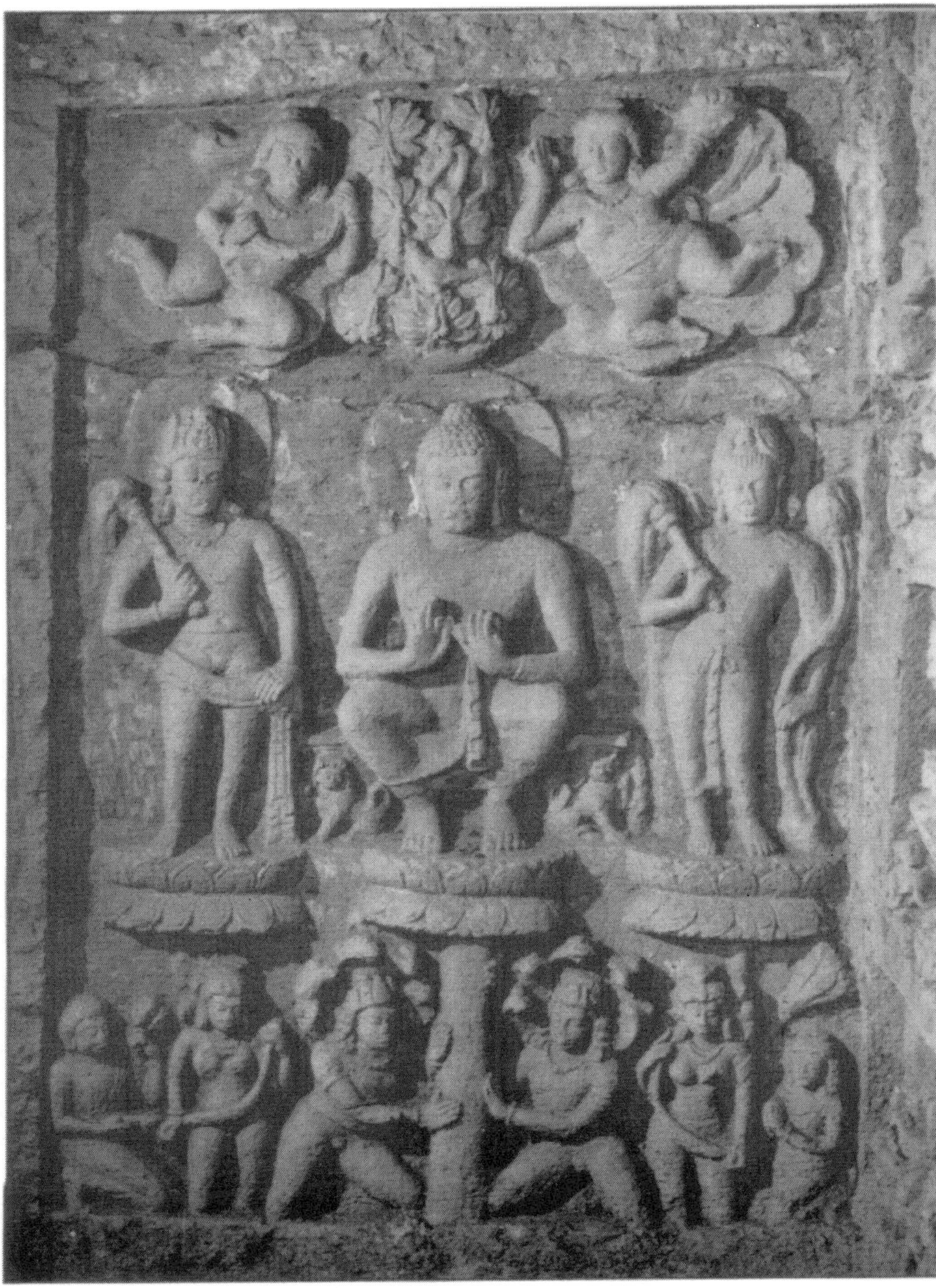

Pl. 35. Buddha seated under a tree in bhadrāsana; Kanheri (Bombay-Maharashtra), cave 90; 6th century AD.

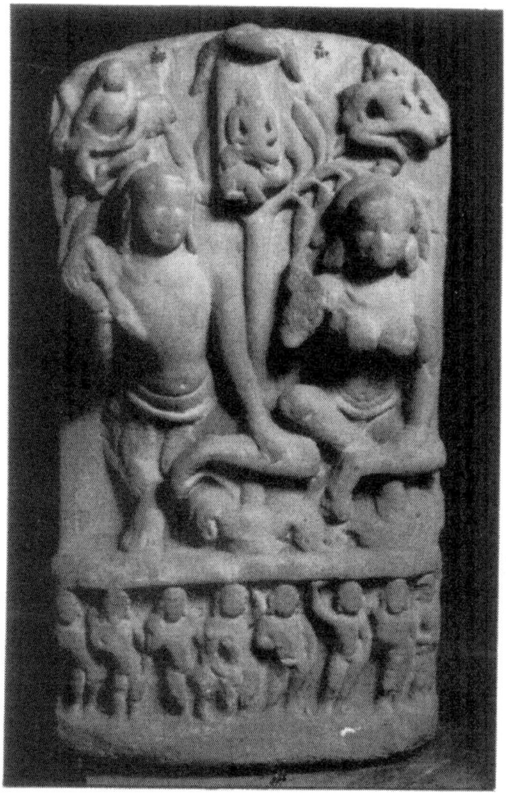

Pl. 36. Jaina couple seated under a
Sahet Mahet (Gonda, U.P.); S
Museum, Lucknow; 5th century

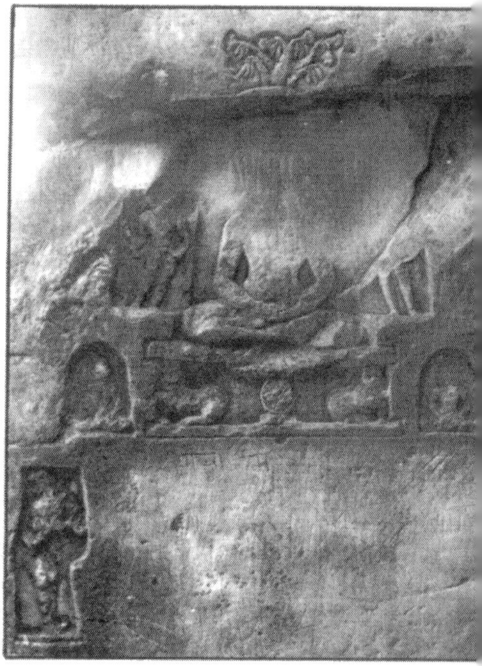

Pl. 37. Mahāvira seated under a tree; Rajgir (Nalanda); Sonabhandar cave; Sandstone; 4th-7th century AD.

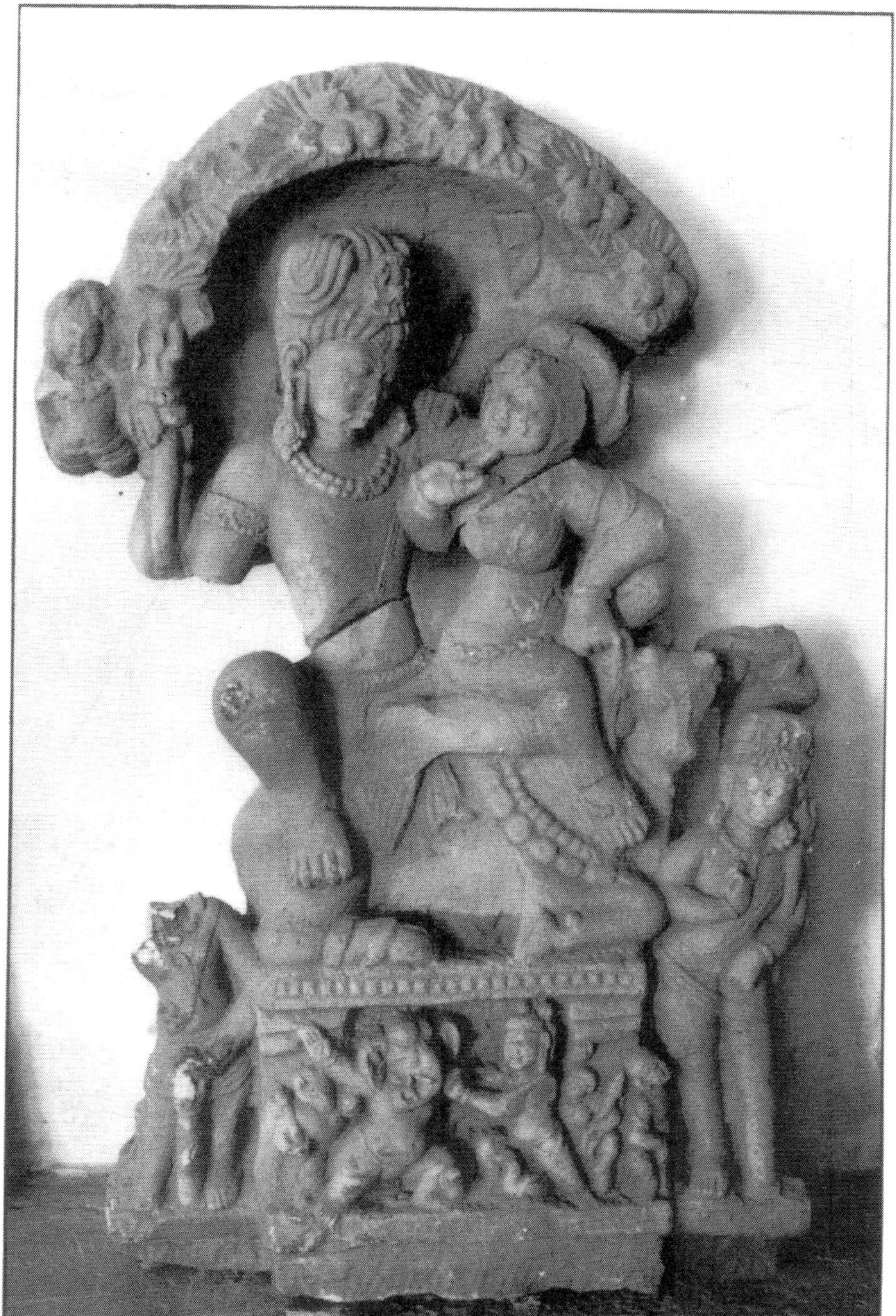

Pl. 38. Uma-Maheśvara under tree; Bhanpura (Mandasore, M.P.); State Museum (Bhanpura); 8th century AD.

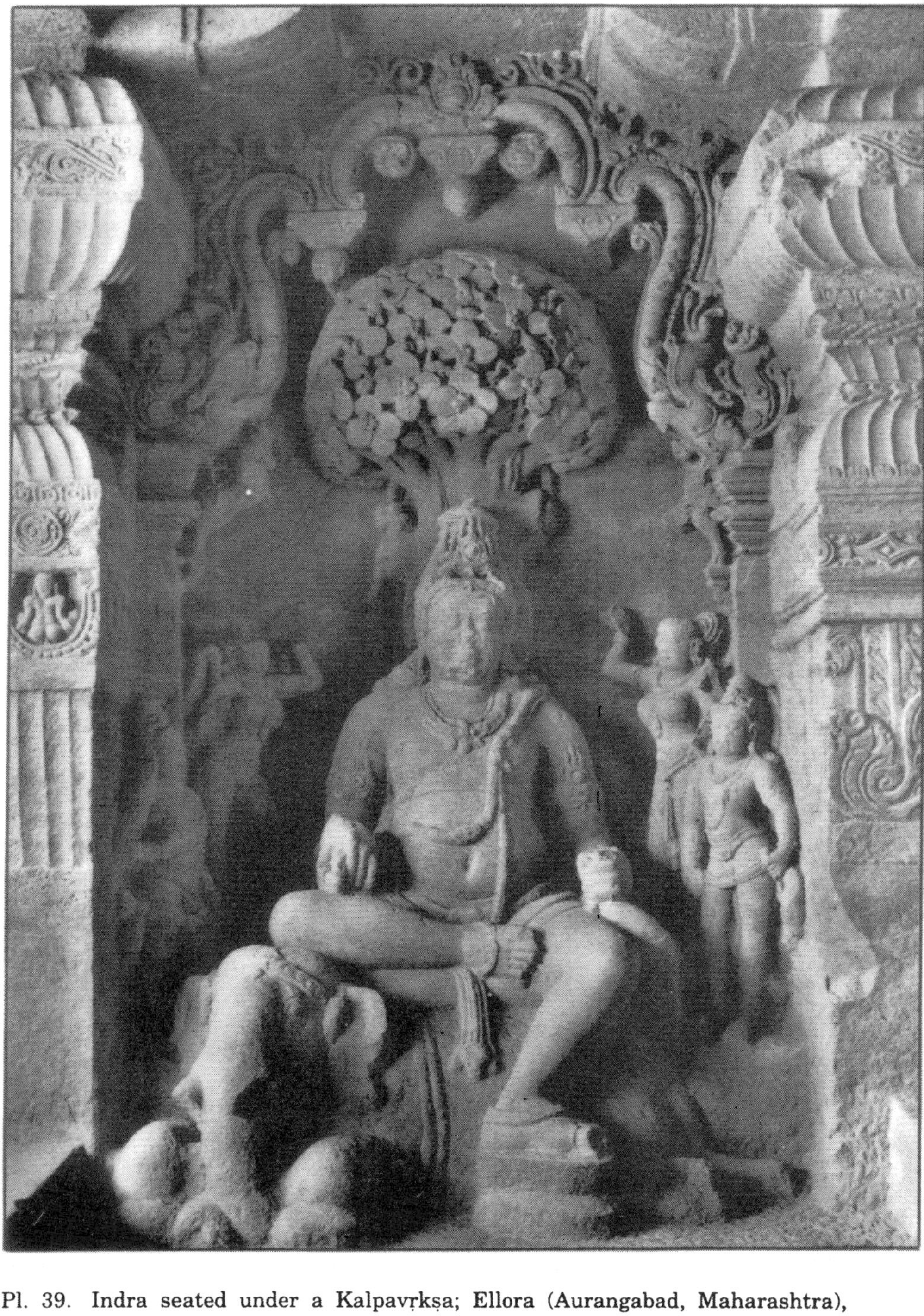

Pl. 39. Indra seated under a Kalpavṛkṣa; Ellora (Aurangabad, Maharashtra), cave 32; ca. AD 810-80.

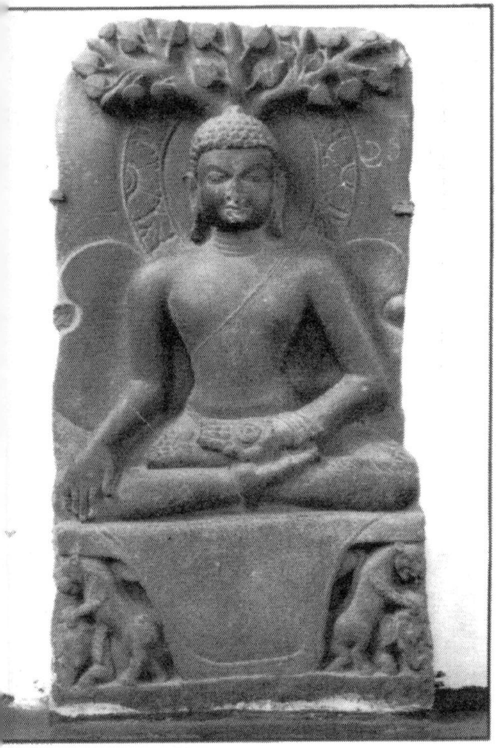

Pl. 40. Buddha seated in bhumisparśa mudrā under an aśvattha tree; Tetrawan (Patna); Black basalt; Indian Museum, Calcutta; 9th century AD.

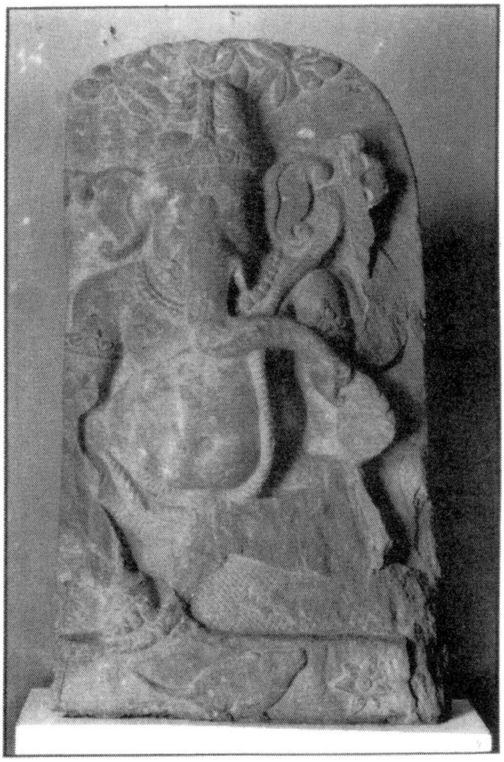

Pl. 41. Ganeśa seated in lilāsaṇa under a mango tree; Nalanda (site 3); Basalt; Nalanda Museum; 9th-10th century AD.

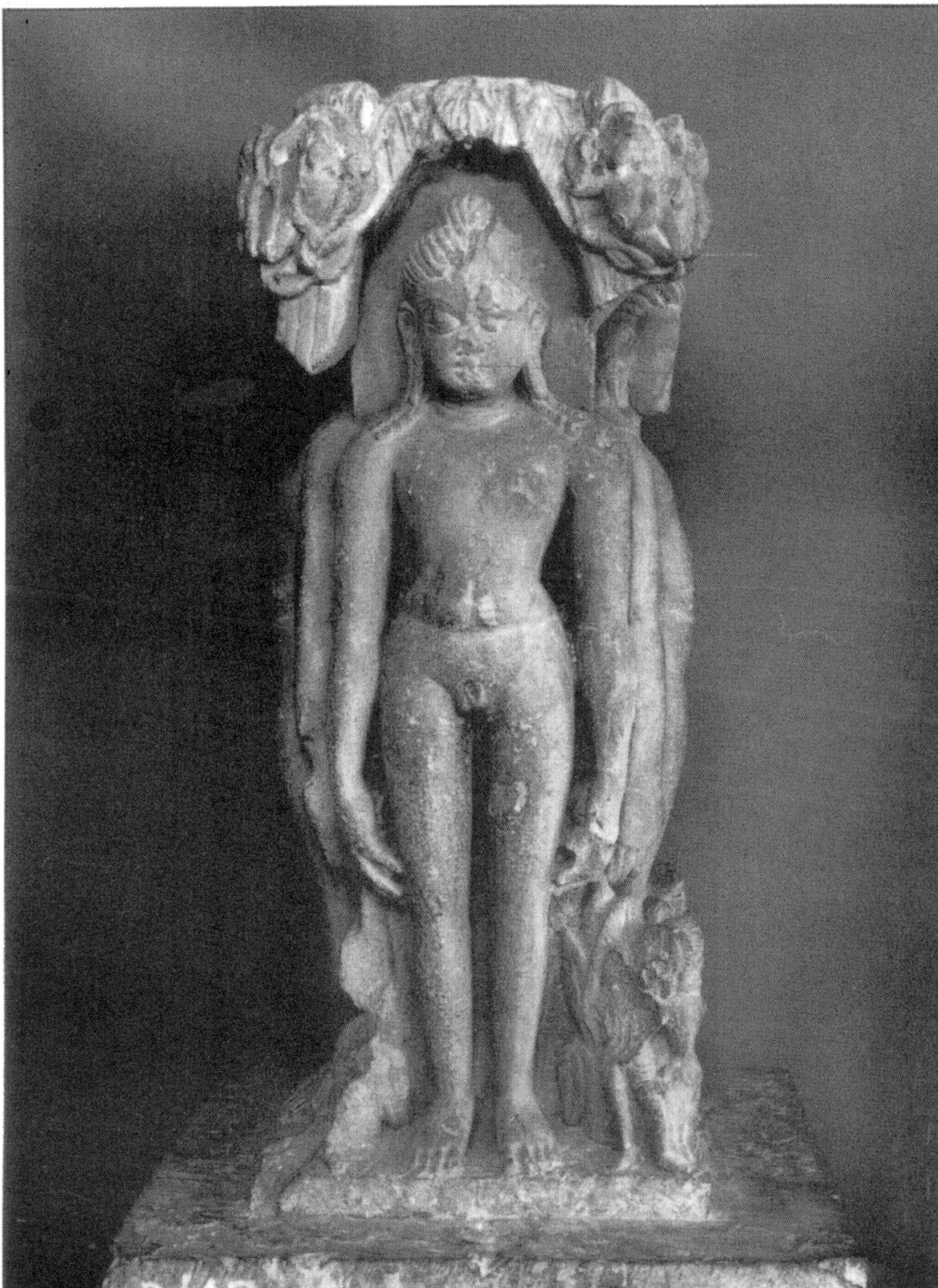

Pl. 42. Ādinātha under a nyagrodha tree; Jaghina (Bharatpur, Rajasthan); Buff sandstone; State Museum, Bharatpur; ca. AD 900.

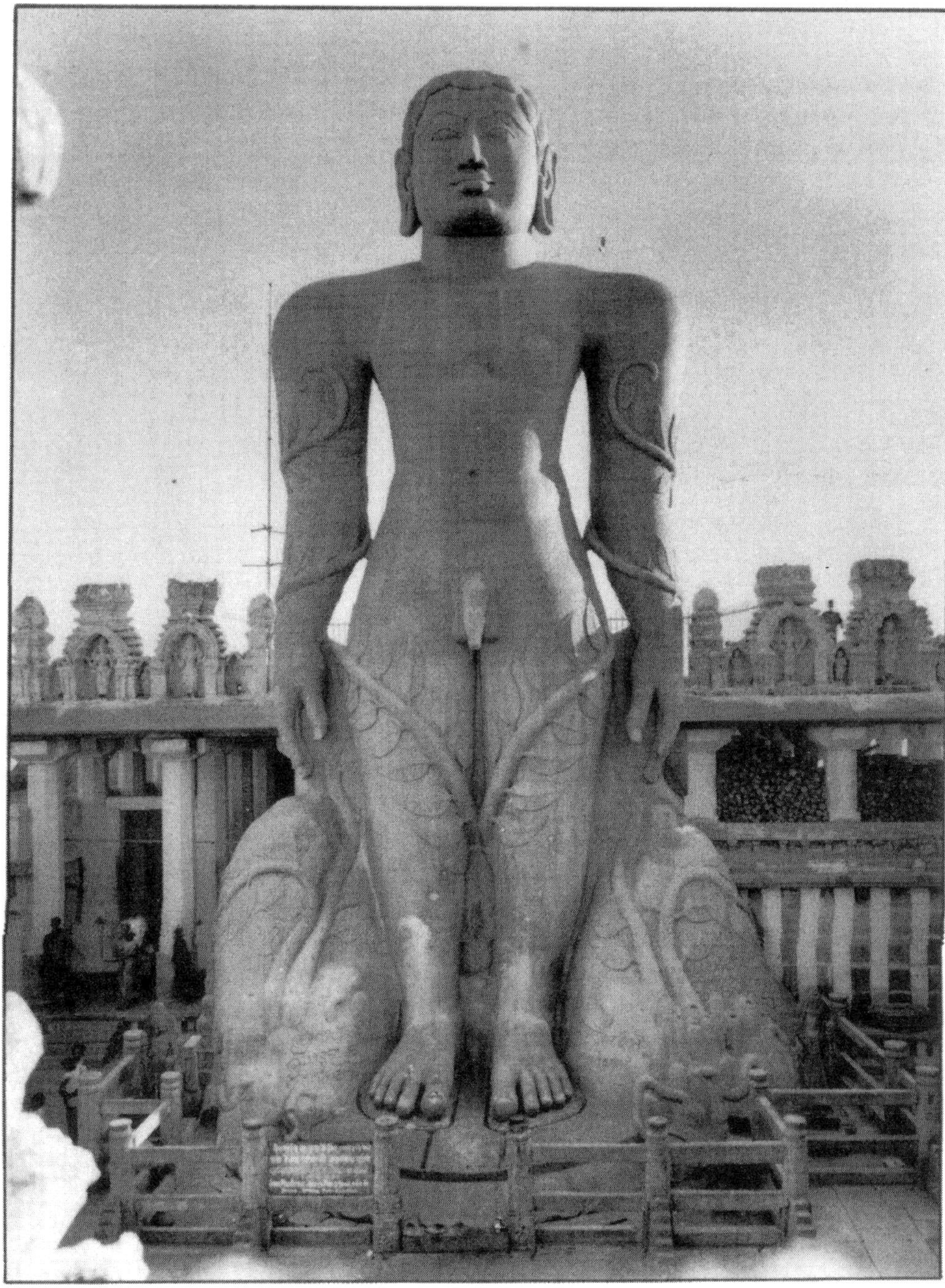

Pl. 43. Gomateśvara entwined with aśoka creepers; Sravanabelgola (Chikamagalur, Karnataka); Granite; ca. AD 983.

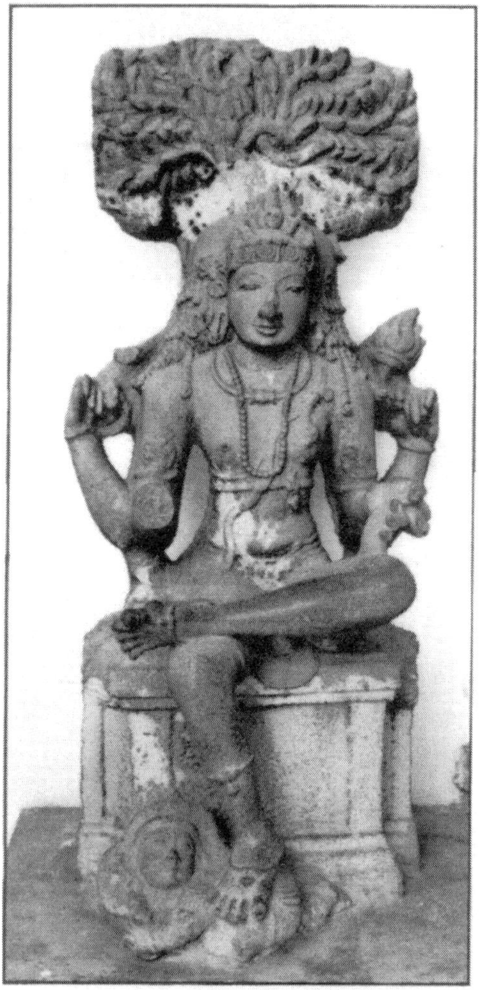

Pl. 44. Daksinamurti Śiva seated under a tree; Madras; Granite, Tanjore Art Gallery; 10th century AD.

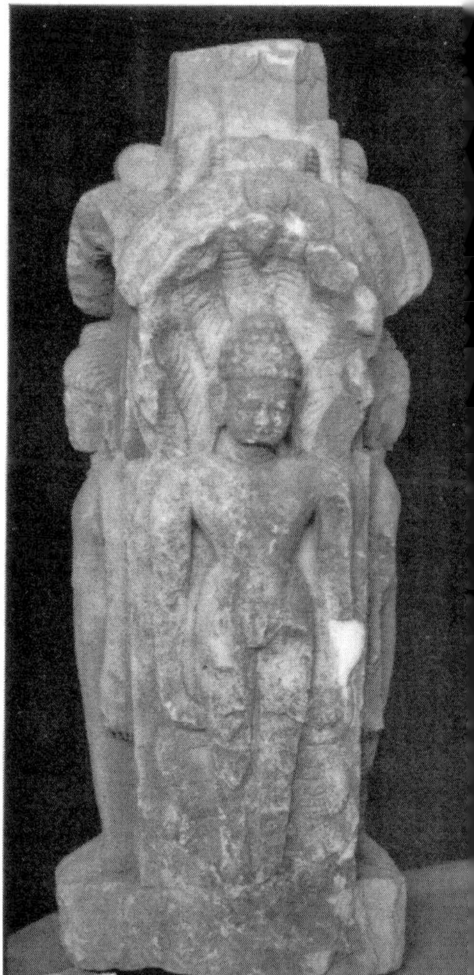

Pl. 45. Pārsvanātha under a tree, India; Buff sandstone; Bharat Kala Bhavan, Varanasi; 11th century AD.

(Conservation) Act, 1980, which prohibits diversion of forest lands for non-forest use, except with the prior permission of Central Government. In 1985, the National Waste Lands Development *Board* was set up to achieve a quantum leap in afforestation activities. Similarly, the National Forest Policy of 1952, has also been revised recently to give emphasis to the conservation and other ecological aspects of forests. A countrywide national environmental awareness campaign has been launched on a continuing basis, which seeks to create environmental awareness at the national as well as local levels by involving hundreds of grass-root level voluntary organisations working in remote parts of the country. A well known social worker Baba Amte took the initiative to conserve the natural resources. In U.P. Shri Chandi Prasad Bhatt and Shri Sunderlal Bahuguna started a campaign to save the forests and this so-called "Chipko" movement took bold steps to conserve the trees in the Himalayan region. Many social forestry schemes have been introduced by the State and Central Governments and in all schemes the main objective is to protect the green gold of the country. The Government agencies are also engaged to conserve the soils, watersheds, rare plants and trees. Women volunteers are creating awareness and film shows, television serials, lectures and debates are being organised from time to time in different parts of the country to educate the people about the benefits of forests. To reduce pressure on forests, for fuel, wood, townships in the vicinity of forests have been identified for supplying of cooking gas and kerosene, and special species are being introduced to provide best and cheaper fodder for the livestock.

The ecological awareness which is being noticed these days among the Indians even at the grass-root level is a matter of great relief. If such kind of awareness could receive support from all concerned then many difficult situations could be averted. Now the question is whether such an awareness among the Indians is only of recent origin or our ancestors in the past were also equally concerned regarding the various issues of ecology and its consequences? In the *Atharvaveda, soma* is considered to be master of the vegetation, who plays an important part in the growth of Indian flora (*soma oshadhīnāmadhipatiḥ*).[48] The *Jaīminīya Brāhmaṇa* (1.355) has mentioned the part played by *soma* in the vegetation growth as under:

> *Somam vai rājānam yat suparṇa āharat samabhinat tasya vā viprusho apatiṁstā evemā oṣadhayo abhavan sarvā u ha vai saumyā oṣadhayāḥ.*

According to *Śatapatha Brāhmaṇa*, seeds had been born, *soma* and *pṛiṭhivi* had united. The roots of vegetation predominate with *soma* contents whereas the upper portion had more of energy and dries up soon.[49] The same idea is recorded in the *Maitrāyaṇī Saṁhitā* (3.1.5) as:

> *Prācīnam vai Somīroṣadhayah. Pratīcīnam randrīḥ. Na hi prācīnam śuṣyanti, śuṣyanti praticīnam.*

In the *Śatapatha Brāhmaṇa* (2.2.4.5), the meaning of *oṣadhi* itself is to possess the energy (*Oṣam dhaya iti*). The vegetation continues to possess the energised particles from the earth which means that most of these articles get consumed. The same idea is supported by some ancient Indian texts as follows:

I. *Agnidārugato yadvad blinne dārau na driśyate,, tathaivātmā śarīrastha ṛte yogānna driśyate.*
(*Mahābhārata, Śānti-parva,* 112.56).

II. *Garbho tasyoṣadhīnām garbho vanaspatīnām, garbho viśvasya bhūtasyāgne garbho apāmasi.*
(*Maitrāyaṇī Saṁhitā,* 2.7.10).

III. *Tasmādagirdadhyata oṣadhīh praviṣhtaḥ.*
(*Kapiṣṭhala Kaṭha Saṁhitā,* 41.7).

Now here arises another question. Was this earth full of energised particles from the beginning of its formation? If it would have been so then the various stages as described above would have been turned into dry or ashen forms. It looks that the process of its getting energised and the growth of vegetation has been helpful to each other. Interestingly, some of the trees possess a large proportion of these particles which include the *śamī* tree (*Mimiosa suma*). This tree has very hard wood and is supposed to contain fire. The said fact is recorded in the *Taittirīya Brāhmaṇa* (1.1.3.11) as:

> *Prajāpatiḥ agnimasṛijata, Sā abibheta pra mā dhakṣyatīti, Tam Śamyā aśamayat*

(i.e. Prajāpati had caused the birth of Agni. He was afraid to be burnt by it. The *śamī* tree cooled it).

In the same text (1.1.3.9), similar quality of the *aśvattha* tree (*Ficus religiosa*) is narrated as under:

Agnirdevebhyo nilāyata, Aśvo rūpam kritvā So aśvatth saṁvatsaramatiṣthat. Tadaśvattha-syāśvatthatvam.

According to *Śatapatha Brāhmaṇa* (6.3.1.31; 6.3.1.26), the bamboo (*venu*) and muñja (*Sacchārum sara*) have similar qualities, and are also considered the best for the sacrificial fire.[50]

The science of plant life, *Vṛkṣayurveda*, was distinctly a comprehensive science, which existed in ancient India. Interestingly, a scientific truth was long ago expressed by Manu when he said, "All trees and plants are full of consciousness within themselves and are endowed with the feeling of pleasure and pain."[51] References to the plantation of trees and construction of pleasure gardens can be traced in *Ṛgveda* (5, 3, 8-2) and in the *Śānkhyāyana-Gṛhyasūtra* (5, 3-2). The ritual of consecration of trees was performed as ordained in the Vedas. As early as the *Rāmāyaṇa*, the planting of group of trees was held meritorious. The celebrated *Pañcavaṭī* garden where Sītā was imprisoned has been reproduced by many a religious Hindu, and should any of them not have sufficient space to cultivate the five trees, the custom is to plant them in a small pot where they are dwarfed into small shrubs. The *Pañcavaṭī* consists of *aśvattha* planted on the east side, the *bilva* on the north, the banyan on the west, the *Emblica officinalis* on the south and the *aśoka* on the south-east. But in the *Skanda Purāṇa*, constituents of a great *Pañcavaṭī* are a *bilva* in the centre, and four others on four sides; four banyans in four corners, twenty-five *aśokas* in a circle with a myrobalan on one side.[52] The science of arbori-horticulture, which was an old practice in India, came into vogue towards the middle of 19th century in the West.[53] The government provided public parks and pleasure gardens for health, recreation and enjoyment of the public. Similarly, palaces of kings and all decent houses had pleasure gardens attached to them.[54] Even in ancient dramas, epics and amatory poems, flower gardens played important part. In the words of Lord Buddha, "the forest is a peculiar organism of unlimited kindness and benevolence that makes no demand for its sustenance and extends generously the products of its life activity; it affords production to all beings, offering shade even to the axe-man who destroys it."[55] That Emperor Aśoka encouraged plantation of trees is proved by his Rock Edicts—"Thus said his sacred and gracious majesty the king: On the roads I have had banyan trees planted to give shadows to men and beasts. I have had groves of Mango trees planted."[56]

The merit of planting trees is also given in many other ancient texts. The *purāṇas* glorify trees with beautiful adjectives and encourage their plantation. It is a deep-rooted belief among Hindus that consecration of trees and gardens (parks) was means of remission of sins and attainment of heaven. Regarding this *Matsya Purāṇa* (59; 17-20) says, "If anybody plants at least one tree, then he will be able to stay in the heaven of Indra for thirty thousand years." It further elaborates, "The planter of trees according to prescribed rites liberates same number of his past and future manes, attains to highest perfection and is never reborn on earth." The same *Purāṇa* also mentions a legend, in which Pārvatī planted a sapling of *aśoka* and the gods asked her the merit of planting trees. To this Pārvatī replied: "A *vapi* is equal in fruits to 10 wells, a pond to 10 *vapis*, a son to 10 ponds and a tree is equal to 10 sons."[57] The *Matsya Purāṇa* has also suggested that a house with the following trees in the vicinity is very auspicious, viz. *aśoka, punnage, vakula, śamī, tilaka,* etc. The text further finds mention of a festival for the growth of trees (*vṛkṣotsava*), in which a cow with full udders and fully decorated with ornaments is ordained to release through the tree.[58] The merit for the performance of rite of consecration of trees and orchards is also recorded in *Agni Purāṇa* (70; 1-9) as: "The plantation of trees and construction of pleasure gardens (for the public) are conducive to purgation of sin and enjoyment of prosperity." In the same line of thought *Varāha Purāṇa* records, "He never goes to hell who plants an *aśvattha*, a *picumanda*, or a Banyan or ten jasmine or two pomegranates or five mangoes."[59] According to the *Gokarṇamāhātmya* chapter of the same *Purāṇa*, "A man by planting trees attains to the bliss as he does by the gift of cow and land. Just as a pious son saves the family, just as good but difficult rules followed with care save the performer from the hell, so also do the trees full of flowers and fruits save the planter." The *Brahmāvaivarta Purāṇa* (*Sri Kṛṣṇajanma khand*) refers that among other trees *aśoka, śiriṣa* and *kadamba* always bring peace and do good. Similarly, Varāhamihira in his *Vṛhat Saṁhitā* records that *ariṣta, aśoka, punnaga* should be planted in the garden or in the house as these are conducive to the welfare of house.[60] The *Padma Purāṇa* in its chapter on *Vṛkṣarpanam* (Chap. 26) has recorded that a man who plants trees by the roadside will enjoy bliss in heaven for as many years as there are fruits, flowers and leaves in the plant he plants. The *Purāṇa* further tells us, "Plants are like sons to a sonless man. Therefore, plant *aśvattha* tree with care, for it does work of a thousand good sons. Further the planting of *aśvattha,* leads to prosperity; as *aśoka,* to destruction of all sorrows; of *udumbara,* increases (the effect of) sacrifices; of *nimba,* to longevity; of *jambaki*, residence in heaven; of *dadima* leads to the bliss of a good wife; *dumura*, to the cure of all diseases; of *palaṣa*, to the protection of Brahmā; of *arka*, to the eternal pleasure of the solar deity; of *bilva*, to that of Śiva, and of *pātali* to that of Pārvatī; of *simsapa*, to that of apsarās (female seraphim); of *kunda*, to that of Gandharvas; of *bibhītaka*, to the increase of the number of servants, and of *vakula*, gives maid servants. The *tāla* leads to the loss of one's all children, and the *nārikela* gives many wives; *drākṣā* to all round prosperity; *keli* to physical pleasure, *ketaki* to ruin and *plakṣa* leads to permanent fame." *Aśvattha* is the most sacred tree in India. It is the only tree that gives oxygen, the *prāṇvāyu*, for more than twenty hours a day.

Trees are an important element in the cityscape. The functions of planted trees include the aesthetic improvement of an area or architectural feature, the reduction of glare produced by reflections from buildings and pavements, the lowering of temperature by shading, and the screening of undesirable sights. The selection of a species for planting in the city depends on the characteristics of the planting site and the function the tree is to perform.

The position of trees to be planted around the house was also clearly indicated in various early Indian texts. According to Varāhmihira, *plakṣa* in the north, *vaṭa* in the east, *udumbara* in the south and *aśvattha* in the west means good to house.[61] Bhattotpoda in his commentary on *Bṛhatsaṁhitā* says, *vaṭa* in front of a house is best, so are the *udumbara, aśvattha* and *plakṣa* in the south, west and north of the house respectively.[62] The *Matsya Purāṇa* has given a more elaborate description regarding position of trees and suggests "A banyan tree on the east of house is auspicious, and all desires are fulfilled; a fig tree to the south, a *pipal* tree on the west and a *plakṣa* to the north of it bring fortune to the owner".[63] But the *Agni Purāṇa* has advised that a *plakṣa* should be planted to the north of a dwelling house, the *vaṭa* on the east, mango on the south and *aśvattha* on the west. Thorny shrubs should be so planted as to edge the southern boundary of a house. Besides, the flower gardens should be laid out adjoining a dwelling house, and blooming plants or sesame should be cultivated therein.[64] In the same context *Brahmavaivarta Purāṇa* has given more elaborate description and informs that, "The coconut tree near the dwelling house confers wealth on the family, and if on the east, or north-east of an encampment, the tree is the donor of sons; the mango tree, the best of the trees is auspicious at every place, and if situated on the east gives wealth to man. The *bilva*, the *panasa*, the *jambira* and the *vadari* trees are, in all situations, conducive to prosperity, but if in the east, they give sons and on the south, confer wealth on the owner. The *jambuka, dāḍima, kadali* and *āmrātaksa* grown in all situations enrich the householder, but if grown in the east they bring friends (*bandhu*), and if in the south, intimate associates (*mitra*). They are always conducive to good, wealth and plenty of children. Betel-nut, if planted in the south or in the west leads to pleasure, and if in the north-east, comfort; wherever planted they bring prosperity. *Campakas* too, wherever planted, bring in their train purity and welfare. *Alābu, kuṣmaṇḍa, māyāmba, sukasaka, kharjjura, karkati* if planted in an encampment, the result is great good. *Vāstuka, karabilva, vārtāku, valliphala*, all these whenever planted yield beneficent results."[65] The *Sukranīti* of Śukracārya is more practical on this subject. The text has given some general instructions which include that one should lay out a fair garden to the left of the dwelling house, and should plant those trees which bear good fruits very near the village besides planting, thorny trees (*Kanṭakinah*) in forests, and expansive trees, shrubs and creepers in village if domestic, and in forests if wild.[66] It seems that in the treatment of plants, their utility aspect is distinctly kept in mind. Elsewhere, it is maintained that wild trees should not be planted either in encampments or in cities. *Vaṭa* should not be placed in an encampment because it leads to danger from thieves, but it is good for cities because its very look confers virtue (on the lookers).[67] It is a self-generating plant and does not die. In fact it acquires the form of a grove in due course of time. It is therefore associated with fertility and longevity. The presence of thorny trees like *khadira* near a house signals danger from enemies. The position of trees to be planted around a house and prohibition of several trees therein are also found in the *Gṛhya Sūtras* as in later *Śilpaśāstras.* Even elaborate attention is paid to the topic of classification of soils with characteristic flora in *Caraka* and *Suśruta*.[68]

An ancient text *Bṛhatsaṁhitā* has given discourses on the various methods of medical treatment of trees when they suffer from wounds. It is a general belief among Indian people that trees planted by them with worship after purification with bath and unction, grow with thick foliage and bear fruits and flowers in abundance.[69] Interestingly, some observations on the influence of the conjunction of certain heavenly bodies on the productivity of trees were published by experts in the science of medical treatment of trees. They were also aware of certain chemical processes used in the preparation of seeds which produced immediate germination and later prolific growth of fruits and flowers. In the same line *Agni Purāṇa* (Ch. 281) says that if the tree does not bear fruits, the stem should be examined by cutting with a knife and on the cut, apply powdered vermifuge seeds with ghee, and then water it. If fruits are destroyed before they ripen, mix the powders of horse-gram, black-gram, green-gram, barley and sesame with ghee and smear the tree and water it. Similarly, watering the tree with ghee and water makes the tree flower and yield fruits quickly. The mixture of vermifuge seed, fish and rice is a good remedy for all diseases of trees. There are some more prescriptions recorded in the above text by which trees yield more fruits and flowers.[70]

That injunctions against cuttings of trees were strict as early as the *Rāmāyaṇa,* is proved by a statement of Rāvaṇa, "I have not cut down any fig tree in the month of *Vaiśākh*, why then does the calamity befall me?"[71] The Kauṭilya's *Arthaśāstra* declared cutting of trees as a state offence and various punishments were prescribed for such acts: "For cutting off the tender sprouts of fruit trees, flower trees or shady trees in the parks near a city, a fine of 6 *paṇas* shall be imposed; for cutting off the minor branches of the same tree, 12 *paṇas*; and for cutting off of the big branches, 24 *paṇas* shall be levied. Cutting off the trunks of the same shall be punished with the first amercement; and felling the same shall be punished with the middlemost amercement. . . ."[72] The text[73] also recommends the appointment of a superintendent of forest produce, who should not only start productive works in forests, but also fix adequate fines and compensations to be levied from those who cause any damage to the forests. Some *Purāṇas* have also given threats against the destruction of useful trees. As per *Agni Purāṇa* (Ch. on *Vāruṇa-rāma pratiṣṭhā*), "Therefore never cut down trees that bear flowers and fruits if you desire the increase of your family, of your wealth and of your future happiness". It further adds that famine, epidemic and drought are caused if a man cuts down trees near temples, *caityas* and graves. The *Varāha Purāṇa* also strictly prohibits the cutting of trees while saying *'Karmaṇyāś caiva ye vṛkṣa na chheatvyā kadācana'*.[74] The *Matsya Purāṇa* (227; 11-95) categorically analyses the degree of punishment for the destruction of trees as follows: "One who fells his masters' or others' trees should be fined gold pieces; and double the fine should be imposed on those who cut a tree near a tank, a thoroughfare, or a boundary line (91-92). Those who break fruit trees, arbours, creepers and floral plants should be fined one *māsha* of gold (93). Even a man chopping grass unnecessarily should be made liable to pay fine of a *Kārṣāpaṇa* (94). Out of the fine levied for cutting trees the king should use his own discretion; he must pay the owner of the trees the price for them and rest should go to the Royal Exchequer (95)". In the time of Manu, destruction of plants became a state offence and in his code, provision was made for its punishment.[75] Thus, on the one hand, the above references allow us to conclude that the ancient *Purāṇakaras* tried to save useful trees from the impending dangers at the hands of wood-cutters, threatened them with evil consequences and prescribed their place in hell. On the other hand, the plantation of useful trees and construction of pleasure garden was encouraged, and such persons are told to inherit a place in the heaven. To prevent ruthless felling of trees, superstitions were encouraged. In ancient Indian tradition, folk deities and *yakṣas* are believed to inhabit trees, hence forbidden to cut. When it became imperative to cut a tree or a branch of tree; as for instance for making images for worship or for building a house, an alternate residence was first offered to the tree spirit before the tree was felled. Very elaborate rituals were laid down for cutting a tree or a branch of the tree. Many tribes in India are still familiar with these rituals.

The main idea of our ancestors was to maintain the ecological balance in the environment. They appear to have been seriously concerned about this natural problem and its consequences. They, therefore, tried their best to save trees, particularly those which were held useful for the survival of humanity. In order to save such trees from various damaging agencies, they identified trees with gods and goddesses; they noted different kinds of merits which could be gained for safeguarding trees and for the cause of afforestation. Thus by showing different kinds of gains, merits, etc., our ancestors encouraged people to protect the trees, to organise pleasure gardens and to save the forests. On the other hand, by prescribing various kinds of punishments, which include a life in hell, attempts were made to save the trees and forests.

However, Indian culture does not totally prohibit the use of nature. It rather encourages its use but only to the extent that its vitality is not adversely affected. A farmer has a right to cut a tree but only if he fulfils his duty to plant five trees. It always treated nature as a source of not only sustenance, survival and happiness but also as a system of which humans are an inseparable part. Our forefathers knew the close relationship between trees, rainfall, etc. They were fully aware that what exists in nature is essential for life. Trees have received a very special consideration for they are the source of fruits/food, medicines and oxygen. The concept of *kalpavṛkṣa* or the tree which gives everything and of *kāmadhenu*, the cow which fulfils all desires, represents our values towards nature and life in general.

One is surprised to learn that numerous plants are believed by the botanists to have been imported from other parts of the world, that is, they are not indigenous to our country. According to Randhawa,[76] custard apple, (*Sharifa*) and chillies were introduced into India by the Portuguese in the 16th century. But the custard tree must have been growing in India from very early times considering that it is mentioned in the *Rāmāyāṇa* and sculpted at Bharhut. Also, the chillies were grown in India much earlier is evidenced by their mention in *Śiva* and *Vāmana Purāṇa*, dated circa 6th-8th century AD.

IV

MEDICINAL TREES (*ROGĪ TARU*)

The medicinal use of plants receives due recognition since the Vedic period. One full hymn in the *Ṛgveda* (X.97) is found to be devoted to the praise of medicinal plants. In the *Atharvaveda Saṁhitā* (VI.96; VIII.7), certain plants are thought to be offspring and essence of the waters, and are declared as the embodiment of curative properties. That is why these trees are expected to bestow remedies. The same text (VI.136.1) further refers to a plant as, "A goddess born on the goddess earth. . . ." The earliest documents of Indian medicine are found mostly in the metrical parts of *Atharvaveda*. In the medicinal charms of the said text, diseases are addressed as 'demoniacal beings'. In the Vedas, "the songs are supplemented by amulets, medicines, philters and other devices of witchcraft, and show a prevalence of the magic element. This suggestive element persists throughout Hindu medicine. It forms part of its 'psychosomatic' approach to the task of healing".[77] The *Amarakoṣa* contains in one chapter the names of about three hundred medicinal vegetables. A far greater number of such medicinal plants is recorded in the *Dravyābhidhāna*, the properties of which are distinctly reflected in medical tracts of approved authority.[78] Regarding the usefulness of trees and plants, J.F. Dastur observes: "This vast subcontinent of ours with its wealth and variety of medicinal plants has accumulated through the ages a great mass of popular remedies, many of which are even today in common use throughout this country, though of course much of folk-medicine is steadily being eroded by the advancing tide of synthetic drugs. Vegetable drugs have been known all over the world for centuries, some at least for thirty centuries. About two thousand plants are mentioned in Ayurvedic, Unani and Tibbi systems of medicine."[79]

The *Mahābhārata* (Vol. X, *Anuśāsana parva*) has recommended that a man of intelligence should smear his limbs with unguents made of *priyangu, vilva, tagara* and *keśara*, because most of these plants are highly medicinal. Therefore, it seems that in ancient India, pharmacology was well developed. In the opinion of *Kūrma Purāṇa* (II.18.18 ff), the brushing twig should be from a tree that oozes out milk such as *mālatī* tree (a kind of jasmine), *apāmārga* (*Achyaranthes aspera* Linn), *bilva* and *karuvira*.[80] In the case of women, *Agni Purāṇa* (265.3-4) mentions that a woman whose foetus falls off, should be made to bathe in the pond (tank) full of lotuses; and a young woman who desires menstruation (in the event of its normal course being delayed or at the first time) should be made to bathe in a tank (or place) full of flowers.[81] The same *Purāṇa* (302.18-20) has further recorded that a woman who desires a male child should drink milk in which the roots of *aśvagandhā* and *dūrvā* are boiled; also she may drink milk boiled with the roots of the *bilva* tree (*Śrīmūlam*) and shoots of the fig tree (*Savatāṅkuram).* It is suggested that in such a situation, the juice of the shoots of the fig tree along with that of the *devi* tree should be drunk through the nose, together with that of the lotus roots, the roots of the *aśvattha* tree and the roots of *uttara*.[82] There is also a detailed description of the treatment of different diseases in the *Garuḍa Purāṇa*. A decoction of the roots of the *bilva* tree and *judūci* along with honey is recommended for the cure of vomiting in the said text (190.31 f). An unguent of *sajaksira* (milk of the *saja* tree) the powder of the *guñjā* seeds, the juice of *bhṛṅgarāja*, powder of the inner seeds of the mango mixed together to form a *lepa*, is prescribed for the growth of hair (176).[83] The text also mentions that inner portion of mango seed, *truphala, nīlī, bhṛṅgarāja* and *kāñjīkā* are mixed together to be applied as hair dye (176.9 ff).[84] The *Garuḍa Purāṇa* mentions a number of trees which have medicinal values for the treatment of the following diseases at length: fever, *atisāra* (diarrhoea), pain in ear, an old wound, eye diseases, wound from a weapon, *kuṣṭha* (skin diseases or leprosy etc.), for general bodily health, and also as remedies to gain sexual potency.[85]

The *Agniveśa Caraka Saṁhitā* contains information regarding medicinal implications of *aśoka* for centuries before and after Christ. Many legends, cultural and scientific, are connected with *aśoka.* The *Agni Purāṇa* (265.3-4) records that a woman whose foetus falls off should be made to bathe in the vicinity of the *aśoka* trees; the same holds good if her child dies as soon as he or she is delivered. In the *Garuḍa Purāṇa,* Brahmā is believed to have said that, "He who eats eight buds of *aśoka* flowers on the eighth day of the moon's increase in the month of *Chaitra,* marked by the asterism *punarvasu* suffers no bereavement in life."[86] Ayurvedic physicians prescribe the bark of the *aśoka* tree in uterine affections, especially in menorrhagia. Decoction is mainly used with milk. *Aśokaghṛta* is prepared with a decoction of the bark and clarified butter together with a number of aromatic herbs in the form of paste. The bark is used in Orissa as an astringent in cases of internal haemorrhoids, and the flowers, pounded and mixed with water, are used in haemorrhagic dysentery.[87]

Every part of *aśvattha* has medicinal value. From the days of the compilation of the *Caraka Saṁhitā,* the usefulness of *aśvattha* tree was recognised in the Ayurvedic system of medicine. Its roots and barks are used as medicine against many diseases. The decoction as well as powder of the stem bark of *aśvattha* are considered very useful in preparing medicine for several diseases including *mūtra sangrahaṇa.* The *Suśurta Saṁhitā* (500 BC) recorded the usefulness of the fruit of *aśvattha* as an useful aphrodisiac.[88] Therefore, in the eleventh century AD, *Gadanigraha* and *Cakradatta* discussed the usefulness of *aśvattha. Cakradatta* has prescribed varieties of medicines that could be made from *aśvattha* tree viz. for vomitting tendencies, for burns, for ear trouble and for sores. In the 13th century, *Śāraṅgadhara Saṁhitā* recorded the utility of this particular preparation for the treatment of uterine disorders, wounds, and as blood purifier. Further, detailed analysis as regards the name, use, attributes of *aśvattha* have been recorded in the *Dhanvantary Nighaṇṭu, Bhaiṣajya, Raja Nighaṇṭu, Bhāva Prākāśa Nighaṇṭu, Śāligrāma Nighaṇṭu* and *Bhaiṣajya Ratnāvali.* Among the late Ayurvedic texts the *Yoga Ratnākara* and *Yoga Taraṅgini* of 18th century have also mentioned about the usefulness of *aśvattha.*[89] There are so many other trees and plants whose medicinal significance is concisely recorded below.

Almost all parts of the *bilva* tree, viz., the fruit (both unripe and ripe), root-bark, leaves, rind of the fruit and flowers, are used for medicinal purposes. Its fruit is highly medicinal and cures diseases of skin by purifying the blood. The fruit is also very valuable in habitual constipation, chronic dysentery and dyspepsia.[90] It is one of the ingredients mentioned in *daśamūla* or the ten roots used in the Ayurveda. The leaves of this tree are specially effective in curing night-blindness (*Ratnaḍhi*).

The *plakṣa* tree is highly medicinal. Its barks and seeds are given for snakebites. The roots of young trees are baked and eaten by Mundari children.[91] Besides, the *gaduchi* plant yields a bitter medicine which is given to children for various ailments. The *dhātri* plant is also of a great medicinal value. The juice of *dhātri* plant is used in the treatment of eye diseases.[92] The latex of *manasā* tree is acrid, rubefacient, purgative and an expectorant. Diseases like warts and cutaneous eruptions, ear ache, asthma and ophthalmia are cured by it.[93]

Udumbara is yet another highly medicinal plant: its leaves are used in bilious affections: its bark is given to cattle in rinderpest diseases, its roots are used in diarrhoea and diabetes and the fruits of it considered stomachic and carminative and finally the latex of it is used in piles and diarrhoea.[94] The latex of banyan tree is applied in rheumatism and lumbago; and an infusion of its barks is considered a tonic and astringent, used in diarrhoea, dysentery and diabetes.[95] Besides, *Madhavī latā* is particularly useful for dermatitis. An application made of it is highly beneficial in scabies. Its bark is aromatic and is used to cure rheumatism and asthma.[96] In the composition of many drugs, the rootstock of the lotus is used. The seeds and stalks of the plant are edible. Rhizomes yield a nutritious arrowroot, given to children in diarrhoea and dysentery. Carpels are demulcent and nutritive.[97]

The *tulsi* plant is an aromatic herb and scientifically proved to be highly medicinal. Its leaves possess insecticidal and anti-bacterial properties and are used as mosquito repellent. The leaves are also used to cure fever, cough, stress and other diseases. According to *Skanda Purāṇa* (II.4-5.28), the leaves of *tulsi* plant should be eaten after meals for cleaning the mouth.[98] The juice of the leaves is stimulating and is used in catarrh and bronchitis. It is a good remedy for ear ache too. The decoction of the roots of the plant is given as a diaphoretic in malarial fevers. The seeds are given in the disorder of the genito-urinary system, and are believed to have the property of killing passion. This led to a curious custom of giving grounded seeds to young widows so that their chastity was preserved. The *tulsi* plant is also used as an antidote for snake bite.[99] While as the leaves of *pārijāta* tree are anti-bilious and expectorant, used in rheumatism and fevers, decoction of it is given in sciatica; it is laxative, diaphoretic, diuretic and anti-thelmintic. The powdered seeds are used for scurfy affections of the scalp.[100]

The leaves of the screw pine (*ketakī*) are used in leprosy, scabies and diseases of heart and brain. Anthers are used for diseases of blood. Yet another highly medicinal plant is betel. Its leaves are stimulant and chewed as a carminative after smearing it with a paste of *kathā* (catechu) along with *supāri,* cardamoms, aniseeds and grafted coconut. The leaves are used in snake bite, and the juice of its leaves is prescribed in the case of night-blindness and other eye affections. They have an essential oil used in respiratory disorders, catarrhs and is antiseptic. The bark of an *arjuna* tree is used for tanning, styptic, tonic, febrifuge and anti-dysenteric; pulverized bark of it gives relief in symptomatic hypertension, is diuretic in cirrhosis of liver. Similarly, the leaves of *neem* tree are believed to possess a curative effect, and the oil extracted from the *neem* fruit possess much medicinal value. The oil is applied to the head and the lower parts of the feet of the patient to bring down the temperature. The flowers of the tree have the properties of blood purification when used as syrup. The soap made out of it cures skin diseases and its tooth-paste is used for cleaning the teeth. On the contrary, the *śāla* tree is used medicinally as an astringent in diarrhoea and dysentery. The ripe fruits of *billiric myrobalam* (*bahira*) are astringent, used as purgative; its oil is applied to rheumatic swelling and its bark is diuretic, demulcent and purgative.

The leaves and skin of the *babul* tree possess medicinal properties which cure many ills; its gum is used as a tonic, and its small and thin branches make a fine tooth-brush which are daily used by the village folk. It will not be out of place to mention here that black gram (*masha*) has a very high protein content, and is used in various kinds of food. Its root is narcotic and used for aching bones.[101] The black gram is also given in rheumatism, nervous and hepatic diseases, as well as in dropsy.

NOTES AND REFERENCES

1. Das, S.R., "Folk Religious Rites: A Study in Origins", *Journal of the Department of Letters,* New Series, Vol. II, Part II, Calcutta, 1958, p. 168.
2. Agrawala, V.S., *Matsya Purāṇa: A Study,* Varanasi, 1963, p. 74; Cf. Gupta, S.M., *Plant—Myths and Tradition in India,* New Delhi, IInd Revised Ed., 1991, p. 8.
3. *Ibid.*
4. Sivaramamurti, C., *Sculpture Inspired by Kalidasa,* Madras, 1942, p. 12.

5. Cowell, E.B. (Tr.), *The Jātaka,* New Delhi, reprinted, 1990, Vol. I, pp. 253, 268; Vol. II, p. 276; Vol. IV, p. 97.
6. Das, S.R., *op.cit.,* pp. 93-97, 116-68.
7. *Ibid.,* p. 168.
8. *Ibid.,* p. 169.
9. *Ibid.,* p. 170.
10. I owe this information to my colleague Ms. Richa Negi.
11. For details, see *ibid.,* p. 172.
12. Marshall, J., *Mohenjo-daro and the Indus Civilization* (Vol. 1), London, 1931, pp. 52-54. 59.
13. *Ibid.,* p. 84.
14. *Ibid.,* p. 90.
15. *Ibid.,* p. 11.
16. *Ibid.,* p. 12.

    Some ring-stones were discovered from Rajghat (Varanasi) showing on the inside head and bust of the Mother-goddess with the upper portion of palm tree. The palm tree is often repeated with the goddess and emphasises its intimate relation with the cult. (Agrawala, 1965: 78-81).
17. *Ibid.*
18. Cf. Dalmia, Y., *The Painted World of the Warlis,* New Delhi, 1988, p. 183.
19. *Ibid.*

    Like Alampur image (Fig. 11) discussed already, there are many such headless goddesses from Nāgarjunakonda (Andhra Pradesh), Siddankote (Karnataka), Sangameshwar and Vyageshwari and Vadgaon (Maharashtra) in stone; and Nevase, Ter, Mahurjhari, Bhokardan (Maharashtra), Bhita and Kausambi in terracotta. R.C. Dhere (1978:182) has dated these images approximately to 3000 BC. Some scholars believe that these nude images are not headless. This is their original form just as the *liṅga* is considered self-contained and both are worshipped together. At present, the *liṅga* is adorned and the nude goddesses are neglected. They are lying in corners of many temples in a bad state of preservation. Śiva as *liṅga* is regarded *bija*, point Garbha, and centre aniconic. While discussing the concept of *mukha-liṅga* of Śiva, Stella Kramrisch mentions (1981:181), the vertical *liṅga* conveys not only the retention of the seed once stirred but its upward conduction through the spinal cord to the brain. She confirms this with ancient knowledge and quotes an example from Girnar (Maharashtra) where in the winter season villagers put woollen scarves around their head in order to keep warm their semen that is stored there. Hence, the transmutation of sexual into mental power, a channelling of the procreative into creative faculty is visually seen.

    The representations of the deities in ithyphallic state is one of the features of fertility cults and is seen in many parts of the world. In India, the earliest example seems to be on the famous Indus valley seal of the horned deity surrounded by animals (Desai, 1975:94). Śiva as Lakulīśa with whom the Pāśupata cult is associated is generally portrayed ithyphallic in the historical period. The eastern Indian shrines specially Bhubaneswar, Khiching and Mukhalingam have ithyphallic images of Śiva in his various aspects as Uma-āliganāmurti, Natarāja and Ardhanārīśvara (*ibid*).

The Pāśupatas enshrined liṅgas to commemorate the name of dead teachers and many such liṅgas are preserved in the Bhāratīmaṭha at Bhubaneswar (*ibid.: 95*). Interestingly, the Nāthapanthis, who buried their dead bodies instead of following the common Hindu practice of cremation represents the *yoni-liṅga* on their graves. It is said that the body of the yogi or *sanyāsin* who has attained liberation is identified with Śiva and hence the symbol of the latter is represented on his grave.

20. *Ibid.*
21. *Ibid.*, p. 180.
22. Agrawala, V.S., 'The terracotta of Ahichchhatra," *Ancient India* (4), 1947-48, p. 109.
23. Dalmia, Y., *op.cit.*, pp. 179-80.
24. *Ibid.*
25. The utmost importance given to mithuna as a makāra in Tantrism, either in its actual or symbolic performance, reveals its closeness to the cults of fertility. The tantric worship of a circle (*Cakrapūjā*) and the worship of young girl (*Kumārīpūjā*) perhaps can also be connected to the fertility rites. Besides, the importance of menstrual blood called *Khapuṣpa* in their *Sandhyābhāsā* or mystic language indicates the close connection of Tantrism with fertility cult. It is worth mentioning that in primitive thought, menstrual blood is associated with rejuvenation and human productivity, and is considered the blood of life.
26. Desai, D., *Erotic Sculptures of India*, New Delhi, 1975, p. 19.
27. *Ibid.*, p. 98.
28. Roth, G., "The woman and tree motif," *Journal of the Asiatic Society*, vol. XXIII (I), 1957, pp. 91-116.
29. Williams, M., *A Sanskrit English Dictionary*, Oxford (New print), 1951.
30. Biswas, T.K., "Culakoka Devatā and the related issue of Fertility cult," *Bharati* (New Series), vol. 3, 1985, p. 43.
31. Vogel, J.Ph., "The woman and Tree or Śālabhañjikā in Indian Literature and Art," *Acta Orientalia,* VII, 1929, p. 98.
32. Bloomfield, M, "The Dohada." *Journal of American Oriental Society,* vol. 40 p. 2.
33. Roth G., 1957, "The Woman and tree motif," *op.cit.*, pp. 108-9.
34. Pisharoti, K.R., "Dohada or the woman and tree motif." *Journal of the Indian*

Society of Oriental Arts, vol. III (2), 1935, p. 119.

35. The festival of women gathering the flowers of the *śāla* tree was common in eastern parts of India, where *śāla* grew in abundance and was specially celebrated in cities like Śrāvastī, Vaiśāli and others associated with the life of Gautama Buddha.
36. Biswas, T.K., "*Culakoka* devatā and the related issue of fertility cult," *op.cit.*, p. 44.
37. Biswas, T.K. and P.K. Debnath, "Aśoka (*Saraca Indica Linn*)—A cultural and scientific evaluation," *Indian Journal of History of Science,* vol. 7 (2), 1972, pp. 99-14.
38. Das, S.R., "Folk Religion Rites : A study in Origins," *Journal of the Department of Letters* (New Series), vol. II(2), 1985, p. 169.
39. The nine plants used in Durgā-pūjā are: (i) plantain, (ii) *kachu,* (iii) *haridara,* (iv) *barley,* (v) *bilva,* (vi) *dārimba,* (vii) *aśoka,* (viii) *māna* or mānaka, (ix) paddy.

    The festival of Durgā pūjā takes place during autumn harvest beginning on the first and ending with the tenth day of the light fortnight of *Ashwin* (Oct.-Nov.).

    Lakṣmī-pūjā is reported from Sambalpur in which a plantain tree is draped in cloth (Das, 1958: 180).
40. *Ibid.*, p. 171.
41. *Ibid.*, pp. 171-72.
42. Sengupta, S. (Ed.), *Tree Symbol Worship in India*, Calcutta, 1965, p.2.
43. *Ibid.*, p. 30.
44. Gupta, S.M., *Plants, Myths and Traditions in India*, 2nd revised ed., New Delhi, 1991, p. 9.
45. Desai, D., *op.cit.*, p. 91.
46. *Ibid.*
47. *Ibid.*, p. 103.
48. Cf. Shrava, S., *A Comprehensive History of Vedic Literature (Brāhmaṇa and Āraṇyaka Works),* New Delhi, 1977, p. 224.
49. *Ibid.,* p. 223.
50. *Ibid.,* pp. 225-26.
51. Cf. Morgan, K. (Ed.), *The Religion of Hindus,* New Delhi, 1987 (Reprinted), p. 106.
52. Cf. *Phallic Tree Worship Cults Arborum,* Varanasi, 1971, p. 9.
53. Majumdar, G.P., *Upana-Vinoda (A Sanskrit-Treatise of Arbori-Horticulture),* Calcutta, 1935, p. 2.
54. *Ibid.*
55. Cf. Sinha, B.C., *Tree Worship in Ancient India,* New Delhi, 1979, pp. 13-14.

56. Majumdar, G.P., *op.cit.*, p. 5.
57. Dutt, M.N., *Agni Purāṇa,* 2 Vols., Varanasi, 1967, pp. 250-51 (English Translation).
58. Dange, S.A., *Encyclopaedia of Purāṇic Beliefs and Practices,* New Delhi, 1986, Vol. I, p. 353; also cf. *Matsya Purāṇa*, 59.10.
59. Majumdar, G.P., *op.cit.*, p. 3.
60. *Ibid.*, p. 7; cf. *Bṛhatsaṁhitā,* Ch. 54, *Vṛkṣhāyurveda,* Vol. II, p. 743 (Sanskrit Original).
61. Majumdar, G.P., *op.cit.*, p. 7.
62. *Ibid.*
63. *Ibid.*
64. Dutt, M.N., *op.cit.*, pp. 889-93.
65. Cf. Majumdar, G.P., *op.cit.*, p. 8.
66. *Ibid.*, p. 9.
67. *Ibid.*, p. 8.
68. For details, see *ibid.*, pp. 9-10.
69. Morgan, K. (Ed.), *op.cit.*, p. 107.
70. Mani, V., *Purāṇic Encyclopaedia*, Delhi, Patna, Varanasi, 1975, p. 881.
71. Cf. Sinha, B.C., *ibid.*, p. 32.
72. Shamasatry, R. (Tr.), *Kauṭilya's Arthaśāstra,* Mysore, 1956 (Fifth Ed.), p. 222.
73. *Ibid.*, p. 107.
74. See chapter on *Varuṇārāmpratiṣṭha* in *Varāha-Purāṇa;* cf. Majumdar, G.P., *op.cit.*, p. fn. 5.
75. *Ibid.*, p. 6.
76. Randhawa, M.S., *A History of Indian Agriculture,* Vol. II, New Delhi, 1982, pp. 187-88.
77. Patyal, H.C., "The Significance of the Aegle Marmelos (Bilva) in the Vedas", *Vishveshvaranand Indological Journal*, Vol. XII, nos. I & II, 1974, p. 269; see also Zimmer, H., *Hindu-Medicine*, Baltimore, 1948, p. 2.
78. Sinha, B.C., *op.cit.*, p. 17.
79. *Ibid.*
80. Dange, S.A., *op.cit.*, Vol. I, p.174.
81. *Ibid.*, p. 83.
82. *Ibid.*, p. 272.
83. *Ibid.*, Vol. III, 1987, pp. 1014-18.
84. *Ibid.*
85. *Ibid.*, see also Vol. IV, 1989, p. 1277.
86. Dutt, M.N., *Garuḍa Purāṇa*, Calcutta, 1908, p. 385.
87. Biswas, T.K. and P.K. Debnath, "Aśoka (*Saraca Indica* Linn)—A Cultural and Scientific Evaluation," *op.cit.*, p. 111.
88. Biswas, T.K. and P.K. Debnath, "Aśvattha (Ficus Religiosa Linn)—A Cultural

and Medicinal Observation," *Vishveshvaranand Indological Journal,* Vol. XII, Nos. I & II, 1974, pp. 45-46.

89. *Ibid.*
90. Patyal, H.C., *op.cit.*, p. 263.
91. Sinha, B.C., *op.cit.*, p. 24.
92. Dange, S.A., *op.cit.*, Vol. III, 1987, p. 1013.
93. Gupta, S.M., *op.cit.,* p. 43.
94. *Ibid.,* p. 50.
95. *Ibid.,* p. 49.
96. *Ibid.,* p. 51.
97. *Ibid.,* p. 61.
98. Dange, S.A., *op.cit.*, Vol. I, p. 282.
99. Sinha, B.C., *op.cit.*, p. 28.
100. Gupta, S.M., *op.cit.*, p. 65.
101. Cf. *ibid.,* pp. 40-102.

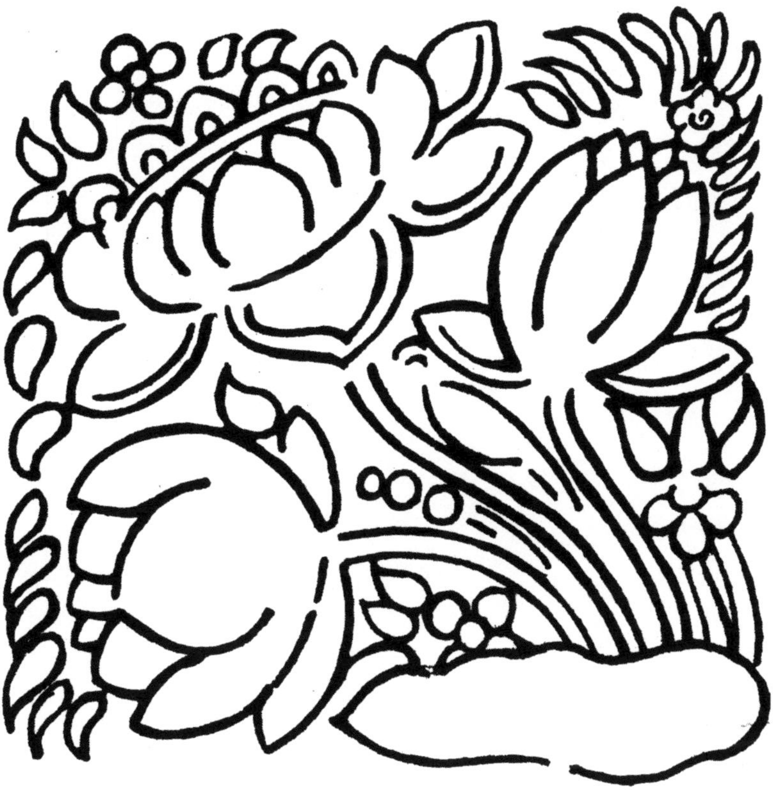

5 TREE MOTIFS IN INDIAN ART

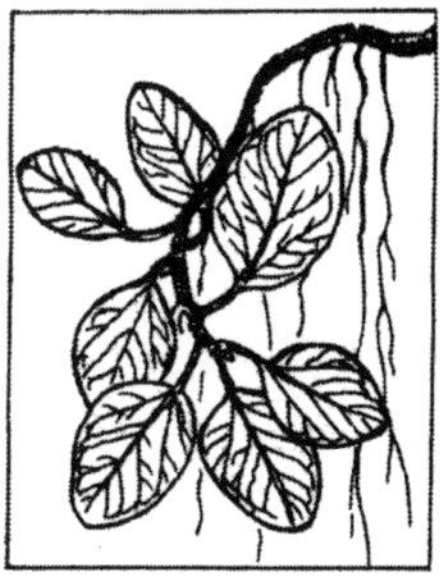

I

TREE IN SCULPTURAL ART

After the decline of the Indus valley civilization and before the rise of the Mauryas, there is not any tangible evidence to prove the continuity of tree worship in ancient India from the archaeological point of view though, there are a number of literary references available in the same period as mentioned in the previous chapters. However, the remains of sculptural art through the ages prove beyond doubt that the concept of tree worship remained in socio-religious practise in this country. Whether the art was influenced by Buddhist, Brahmanical or Jain religious belief, it did not make any difference. The Indian artist used a wide variety of material and technique to depict the known flora artistically, realistically and at times in stylized form also.

Trees in Buddhist Art

During the Buddhist period a very large number of trees were worshipped. A detailed survey of the relief sculptures of the gateways and railings related to the Buddhist stūpas at Bharhut, Bodhgaya, Sanchi and the study of remains of Amaravati and Nāgarjunakonda reveal the depiction of several varieties of trees and creepers. The trees identified from these sites include *aśvattha* or *pipal* (*Ficus religiosa*), banyan tree (*Ficus indica*), *udumbara* (*Ficus glomerata*), *patali* (*Bignonia suavealens*), *śāla* tree (*Shorea robusta*), *śiriṣa* (*Acacia sarisa*), and also *śālabhañjika, aśoka-pushpa-pracāyika, kalpavṛkṣa, kalpalatā,* tree of life (*Śrī-vṛkṣa*) and *caitya-vṛkṣa*. Some of the trees are very realistically executed in relief and quite a few are shown in absolute abstraction.

In one of the medallions from Bharhut, a huge tree is shown relieved with an ornamental pedestal (Pl. 7). This was the period when Buddha was represented in art through certain iconic symbols, the tree within railing being one "*bodhi* tree." In Buddhist texts seven different trees are prescribed for seven *Manusi* Buddhas, and it is stated that under these trees they attained salvation. These trees include *aśvattha, nyagrodha, udumbara, śirīṣa, aśoka, puṇḍarīka* and *śāla* for Śākyamuni (Buddha), Kaśyapa, Kanakamuni, Krakuchhanda, Vipaswi, Sikhi, Viśvabhū, respectively. The medallion under discussion is inscribed at the top and bottom (Pl. 7). The inscription reads that this is the *bodhi* tree of Viśvabhū and the gift of Arya Bhutarakshita. Here four devotees are shown in the attitude of adoration and worship of the *bodhi* tree (*śāla*).

In another medallion from Bharhut, a narrative scene related to the story of a *Jetavana Jātaka* is depicted. The park called Jetavana was purchased from prince Jeta to erect vihāras where Buddha wanted to live for sometime[1] (Pl. 8). On the top left of medallion, three trees represent a grove. Unfortunately, these trees cannot be identified properly. But mango tree within railing down below represents symbolically the presence of Buddha in the scene. The mango tree is commonly depicted on the Buddhist shrines of Sanchi and Bharhut.

In a medallion on a pillar from Bharhut, the adoration and worship by four devotees to a tree within railing are depicted. The inscription on top of it informs that the tree is an *udumbara*, and was prescribed for the *Manusi* Buddha Kanakamuni (Pl. 9).

There is a fragment of a white marble dated 2nd century BC in the Madras Museum. The fragment was collected from Jaggayapetta in the Guntur district of Andhra Pradesh. On this fragment, there is the relief sculpture of the architectural establishments decorated with *caitya* arches. Behind this architecture there is a huge *aśvattha* tree which represents Śākyamuni. Two flying vidyādharas are shown on either side of the tree in the attitude of scattering flowers on the tree (Pl. 10).

A group of elephants are shown worshipping a *bodhi* tree within a railing in a panel on a pillar from Ḅharhut. The panel is now preserved in the Indian Museum, Calcutta. The tree is extremely stylised and it is very difficult to identify which particular tree it would be. Most probably the artist wanted to depict it as an *aśvattha* tree. What is interesting in this panel is that by this depiction the sculptor wanted to show that Buddha had an influence not only on the human beings but had equal influence on the animal kingdom also (Pl. 11).

In yet another medallion from Bharhut, the artist wanted to show the worship of a tree within railing. This inscribed panel helps us to identify the tree as *patali*, which is the *bodhi* tree par excellence of Vipasyin. Coomaraswamy once referred to this *patali* tree as the source for the name of Patliputra.[2] The tree has been very beautifully delineated along with a lump of flowers at various places (Pl. 12).

Nāga king Erapata is shown worshipping a *bodhi* tree, most probably *śiriṣa*, within railing in another inscribed panel from Bharhut. This inscribed panel which shows a beautiful tree full of flowers is the gift of Arya Rishidatta. In the vicinity of this narrative panel, a few more trees are shown which grew at the bank of watery region (Pl. 13).

In the Central Museum, Gwalior, there is a fragment of a sandstone pillar with a group of devotees in two rows worshipping a tree within the railing, which is in the upper part of the pillar. This garlanded flowering tree is not in a position to be identified, but definitely represents a *bodhi* tree (Pl. 14).

In the Government Museum, Mathura, there is an interesting fragment of a red sandstone panel showing a female seated under a stylised tree and playing on a harp. The panel is relieved within a medallion with lotus petals at its edge and huge pericarpa in the middle. It is very difficult to identify this stylised tree. Most probably, the female in question intended to play on her instrument under the shade of a tree (Pl. 19).

There is a fragment of a cross bar from Mathura in the Patna Museum and is dated in the 1st century BC. On this cross bar and within a medallion most probably a *Jātaka* narrative is found to be relieved. Just in the middle of the medallion there is a stylised tree whose leaves are seen adjusted within a definite outline. On the proper right of the tree, a garland is seen hanging. Besides, two persons are shown flanking the tree. The one on the left is standing and has raised his right hand to touch a branch of the tree; and to the right another person is shown in *līlāsana* on a small stool. Below the tree to the right, three logs are shown adjusted to form a stand, the purpose of which is not clear (Pl. 20).

The gateways of Sanchi are generally taken to have been made in the 1st century BC. Of these, a reference is here made to the eastern gate and it is showing western side superstructure. On the topmost architrave of this gateway, there appears seven stylised trees within railing, being worshipped by the devotees. These seven trees within railings may remind us of seven *bodhi* trees, each related to a *Manusi* Buddha. The middle part of the middle architrave in the same gate shows the worship of a *bodhi* tree by different types of animals, serpents and birds. These creatures are shown proceeding towards the *bodhi* tree forgetting their individual enmity, hence signifying the Buddha's influence over them[3] (Pl. 21).

The site Katra Keshav Deo (Mathura) produced an image of seated Buddha, dated in the 1st century AD, and now preserved in the Mathura Government Museum. The image is shown seated on a lion throne and his left hand is placed on his left thigh while the right one displays *abhaya mudrā*. There appears branches of *aśvattha* tree with leaves behind the halo on its either side. This perhaps indicates the same tree under which Gautama the Buddha, attained salvation at Bodhgaya. The branches and the leaves of the tree are very carefully delineated with naturalistic approach (Pl. 23). A common form of depicting the *aśvattha* tree in Buddhist shrines is by showing Gautama Buddha sitting under tree either in *dhyāna mudrā*, *bhūmisparśa mudrā*, or in a pose of giving benediction. In all such panels only a couple of branches of the tree are sculpted behind the head of the Buddha, as if he was sitting under the *aśvattha* tree.

The Indian Museum in Calcutta has in its collection fragment of rail post which was unearthed from Amaravati in the Guntur district of Andhra Pradesh. In the square panel, the middle part is occupied by a *bodhi* tree within the railing, and there is also an empty seat with padded cushions. On either side of the tree, there are two devotees. Each one on both sides of the tree is shown standing in *namaskāra mudrā*. the remaining two devotees hold huge shaft of an umbrella with three discs (*chattravalli*) and shaft of a huge flag (*dhvaja*) on the left and right side of the tree respectively. On the top right and left, two flying vidhyādharas are shown scattering flowers. The stylised tree here represents the attainment of *bodhi* by the Buddha (Pl. 24).

Curiously enough, in the cave no. 90 at Kanheri near Bombay, an image of Buddha is seen in *bhadrāsaṇa* with *dharmacakra pravartana mudrā* on the interior side of the front wall towards its left (Pl. 35). Buddha's two dangling legs are placed on a huge lotus whose abnormally thick stem is being supported by two nāgas. The image is flanked on either side by *cauri*-bearers, who are also shown standing on lotuses. Of these *cauri*-bearers, the one on the left holds in his left hand the huge stalk of a lotus. He may therefore be identified as Padmapāṇi Avalokiteśvara.

In Indian Museum, Calcutta, there is a black basalt image of Buddha, in *bhūmisparśa mudrā* dated in the 9th century AD. The image was collected from Tetrawan in Patna. Just above this head of the Buddha three branches of *aśvattha* tree are very realistically delineated. This is to remind that Buddha attained salvation in Bodhgaya under the shade of an *aśvattha* tree. To commemorate that event, the artist included not only the required *mudrā* in the hands of Buddha but also the tree under which he sat for meditation (Pl. 40).

Trees in Brahmanical Art

The antiquity of tree worship can be traced in the ancient *Indramaha* festival where a tree was stripped of its *leaves* and branches and the *stambha*, i.e. the tree trunk called the *Indradhvaja* or the banner of Indra was worshipped and adored as God Indra himself. The earlier temples were merely trees or a seat of a deity under a tree. Even in present day rural India, such type of temples are frequently found, mostly in the areas with tribal population. In some places, shrines are erected where certain trees are regarded as the abode of the deity and worshipped as such. For example, in Tamil Nadu, mango tree is the *sthalavṛkṣa* of Ekambareshwar temple, Kanchipuram; the *jambu* tree of Jambukeshwar temple, Tiruchirapalli; and the *tillai* tree of Nataraja temple, Chidambaram. Needless to mention, that the Indian art which is handmaiden of religion is based to a great extent on the mythology and beliefs of its people. This art is generally conservative as new ideas are not easily assimilated. From the very early times, the temple rituals, beliefs, folklores and legends have remained almost same, and the scenes and motifs depicted in these temples are based on these legends. The same goes for floral offerings and the depiction of floral motifs on temples. The temple priests even now prefer to accept only those flowers, fruits or even leaves as offerings which are traditionally accepted, depending on the individual character of the temple also. But this does not mean that temple architecture remained static and new ideas were not introduced. Symbolically, the Hindu temple represents the universe in which, everything has a place, whether it is the world of deities, dancers, musicians, beautiful maidens, spirits or celestial beings. It is considered as the house and the body of the universal spirit, the God. In Indian temples there are two main forms of floral depictions. One is purely decorative and the other has religious connotations. But as many of the ancient and medieval temples faced the onslaught of the time, their sculptural art got scattered all-round, even some of these reaching different museums in India and abroad. Many of the are under worship in recently built temples or in open places of worship.

Among the sculptures which have reached different museums, a reference may be made to a fragment of a lintel in red sandstone, dated to the 2nd century AD, in the collection of Mathura Museum, which was acquired from the site of Bhuteśvara (Mathura). This lintel shows a liṅga beneath the tree surrounded by a railing (Pl. 25), and the semi-divine kinnaras are shown approaching liṅga with garlands in their hands to offer it. The tree behind the liṅga should be *vaṭa* or *nyagrodha* as Śiva is also known as Vateśvara.

In the Mathura Museum there is a clay sealing with Brāhmī inscription in its lower half, which reads Achutya-Varma. On the upper half there appears a tree guarded with stylised creeper (Pl. 27). It is rather difficult to identify the tree exactly, but it could be a banyan tree. In that case, the person named below may be named as the follower of Vateśvara Śiva or Padapeśvara Śiva.

A unique though mutilated image of Caturvayuha Viṣṇu was collected from Satasamudri kuan (Mathura), and is now preserved in the Mathura Museum (Pl. 26). This 2nd century AD sculpture in buff sandstone has on its back a huge *aśoka* tree with flowers. The tree is very realistically relieved, and carved with the idea as a sculpture in round. It appears that this tree was particularly associated with the cult of Viṣṇu.

A pillar capital with fan-palm leaves and fruits is preserved in the Central Museum, Gwalior (Pl. 28). Stylistically dated in 4th-5th century AD, this palm leaf capital in all probabilities is associated with Vaiṣṇavite temple at Pawaya in Gwalior. In ancient India, *taladhvaja* was erected in honour of the Samkarṣaṇa, which was the *vyuha* aspect of Viṣṇu.[4]

Incidentally, reference may be made of the lower portion of the eastern pillar to the main entrance on south of the Jethani temple at Tala in Bilaspur (M.P.). It shows a huge pitcher (*ghaṭa*), from the mouth of which are seen issuing out not only two *vyuhalas* but also a huge stylised lotus and its leaves (Pl. 30). The depiction of *ghaṭa pallava* at the bottom of a pillar was very common in early Indian art and represents plenty, affluence and as an auspicious symbol.

The well-known archaeological site at Malhar in Bilaspur (M.P.) produced an interesting panel of buff sandstone. The panel which is dated in c. 4th-5th century AD has a big tree in the middle with flowers (Pl. 31). To its left, a small seated human figure is seen in somewhat dejected manner, while to its right a seated elephant is shown trying to pull down the tree. The exact theme of this narrative panel is yet to be decided, but there is hardly any doubt that the tree plays an important role in the narrative.

The Dasāvatāra temple at Deogarh in the Lalitpur (U.P.) district incorporates within the *ratthikambha* on the eastern *jaṅga* a panel depicting Nara and Nārāyaṇa. The panel is made of red sandstone and is dated in the 6th century AD. The Nārāyaṇa is seen seated under a very stylised tree probably *badari* (Pl. 32). The animals below and the trees above have introduced a typical environment of a hermitage.

In cave no. 3 at Badami (Bijapur), Karnataka, on the central lintel above facade appears a four-handed female figure flanked on either side by two children (Pl. 33). This inscribed panel has been regarded as depicting the mock coronation of child Kṛṣṇa, who is shown on the left. Curiously enough, the four-handed female figure is seen standing beneath a tree, most probably *aśoka* tree with flowers.

In the State Museum, Bhanpura in the Mandasore district of M.P., there is a damaged sculpture of Umā-Maheśvara (Pl. 38). This divine couple is shown seated within a concave *parikara*, the border of which is engraved with certain floral and vegetal designs. Most probably these designs represent stylised lotuses.

In cave no. 32 at Ellora (district Aurangabad), Indra is shown seated in *ardhaparyaṅkāsana* on the back of a couchant elephant on the west wall of the *maṇḍapa* (Pl. 39). Behind the figure of Indra, there is a huge tree, apparently to indicate a *kalpavṛkṣa* with which Indra was associated. The tree may be identified as *nyagrodha*.

There is a damaged image of Gaṇeśa dated to 9th century AD in the Nalanda Museum (Pl. 41). The god here is shown seated in *līlāsana* under a mango tree, and the tree with fruits is partially visible at the top of the back stela.

In the Tanjore Art Gallery there is a 10th century granite image of *Dakṣiṇāmūrti* Śiva (Pl. 44). In this image, the four-handed Śiva is shown in *ardhaparyaṅkāsana*. Behind the seat of the god there appears a huge tree, most probably indicating the tree of knowlege, the *nyagrodha*. In Śaiva temples, plants commonly sculpted are the *nyagrodha* with Śiva sitting under it in his *Dakṣiṇamūrti* aspect; *bilva* and *vaṭa* trees with invariably a Śivaliṅga present under them; sugarcane as a bow in the hands of Kāmadeva, Rati or Devi; and the *arka* plant associated with Śiva. On the Śivarātri day, the liṅga is bathed in milk, decorated and wrapped in the leaves of *bilva* tree. Sati worshipped Śiva on this day with *bilva* fruit and leaves. Its fruit is eaten all over India except in Kerala where the fruit is a symbol of the head of Śiva.

On the north wall of Amriteśvara temple at Amritpur in Chikmagalur district of Karnataka, there is a Kṛṣṇa līlā scene.[5] Made in soapstone, this 12th century sculpture shows child Kṛṣṇa tied to a Yamalārjuna tree. The tree has been very stylistically delineated on the panel. It does not show realistic rendering of the tree and is ornate and visibly decorated (Pl. 47).

In the National Museum, New Delhi, there is a 12th century image of Lakṣmī-Nārāyaṇa seated on Garuḍa in basalt (Pl. 48). The image, hails from Halebid in the Hassan district of Karnataka. Above this image there is a decorative depiction of a stylised tree, apparently a mango tree.

On the eastern wall of *mukhamaṅḍapa* of Īśvara temple at Arsikere in the Hassan district of Karnataka, there is an artistic delineation of Kṛṣṇa as about to punish Kāliyā, the serpent king, when the nāganis or the consorts of Kāliyā appeared and pleaded the Lord to spare the life of Kāliyā. On the left hand side of the composition, there is a huge stylised tree with a child sitting over its top. Possibly the child indicated Kṛṣṇa just before jumping on the spread hood of Kāliyā (Pl. 49).

On the north jaṅghā of the Śiva temple at Deo-Baloda (Durg-M.P.), there is a late 13th century panel showing the *mātṛkās* (Pl. 50). Between two *mātṛkās,* there appears a tree but they are so much stylised that their identity cannot be established.

In the Lakṣmīnarasimha temple at Javagal in Chikmagalur district of Karnataka, there appears an interesting image of Indra on its south-west wall (Pl. 52). The Indra probably with his consort Indrani is seen riding a moving elephant. Indra in his raised right hand holds a *vajra* and by his left hand controls the moving mount. Above this composition there is a meandering creeper, the exact identity of which is very difficult since it is too ornamental. Among the *Vaiṣṇava* themes usually found in Indian temples are scenes from the *Rāmāyaṇa* which include *Saptatala legend*, or young Kṛṣṇa jumping from *kadamba* tree into the river Yamuna to kill Kāliyā Nāga or Kṛṣṇa taking away the clothes of the *gopīs*, the killing of the ass demon, Dhenuka, in the forest of *tala* trees, etc.

Trees in Jain Art

In most Jain temples, figures of Ambika, a Jain deity are found. She is always shown sitting or standing under mango tree, sometimes with a bunch of mangoes in her hand. Ambika is invariably accompanied by a child, usually sitting on her lap or astride her hip. Among the independent sculptures there is a buff sandstone sculpture of yakṣī Ambika, dated in the 6th century AD (Pl. 34) in the Site Museum at Sirpur (district Raipur,

M.P.). Ambika is shown standing here with a child in her left lap under a mango tree, which is full of mangoes. She is also the Yakṣi of Tīrthāṅkara Neminātha of the Jain pantheon. According to the iconographical canons, Ambika had her abode under the mango tree.

A 5th century buff sandstone sculpture from Sahet Mahet in the Gonda district of U.P. shows a couple seated under a stylised tree (Pl. 36). It is very difficult to identify the tree. A couple seated under a tree is a very common type of figure in Jain pantheon. The couple is generally identified as the parents of the Tīrthāṅkara.

On the eastern side of Sonabhandar cave at Rajgir (district Nalanda, Bihar) there appears a badly mutilated and damaged figure of Mahāvira in *dhyāna mudrā* (Pl. 37) under an *aśoka* tree with a number of branches. In Jain tradition, *aśoka* tree is also auspicious because the Jain Tīrthāṅkara Mahāvīra attained omniscience under the *aśoka* tree and his initiation under this tree was attended by the celestials. In some Jain iconographical texts, *caitya vṛkṣa* of Mahāvīra is *śāla* tree. Curiously at Nadia, Sirohi district, Rajasthan, a 7th century temple has a panel with image of Mahāvīra having *śālmalī* flowers sculpted behind.

In the State Museum at Bharatpur (Rajasthan), there is an image of Ādinātha (Pl. 42). Dated in ca. 900 AD, this image of the Tīrthāṅkara was collected from Jaghina in the Bharatpur district. In the sculpture, the Ādinātha is in *kāyotsarga* pose under a *nyagrodha* tree. Unfortunately, the tree at the top has eroded badly.

A reference may be made here of the colossal figure of *Gomateśvara* from *Srāvaṇabelgola* in the Chikamagalur district of Karnataka (Pl. 43). The image made in granite is shown standing in *kāyotsarga* pose and is immersed in meditation. It is said that he meditated in this posture for years, and as a result creepers grew and entwined his body. The artist most probably depicted the figure of Gomateśvara entwined with *aśoka* creepers, because it is believed that *aśoka* removes all sorrows and brings peace to the mind.

In Bharat Kala Bhavan, Varanasi, there is an 11th century *Camukhi* composition of a Tīrthāṅkara (Pārśvanātha) under seven-hooded snake standing in *kāyotsarga* pose (Pl. 45). Unfortunately, the image is in a bad state of preservation. Over the snake hood, there appears a tree.

There is a 13th-14th century black stone image of Ṛsabhadeva in *dhyāna mudrā* in Rajputana Museum at Ajmer (Pl. 53). In the sculpture an umbrella guards the head of Tīrthāṅkara. And above the umbrella there appears a stylised *nyagrodha* tree. This is the tree par excellence under which the said Tīrthāṅkara attained his salvation.

II

KALPAVṚKṢA (WISH-FULFILLING TREES) AND *KALPALATĀ* (WISH-FULFILLING CREEPERS)

Kalpavṛkṣa is said to be a mythological tree and does not find its mention in the Vedic literature. Its conception seems to have been a part of folk cult.[6] In the Hindu mythology, the wishing tree is a jewel which was produced at the time of the churning of the ocean, and later on became the tree *par excellence* of the royal garden of Lord Indra.[7] The *Rāmāyaṇa* (5, 8, 9) recorded that the *kalpavṛkṣa* can only be with Kubera and Indra as their prosperity was the highest concept of wealth. Naturally when Hanumāna is amazed at the wealth and splendour of Rāvaṇa, he compares it to just these two.[8] Incidentally, a reference may be made to Kālidāsa who has described a heavenly cow under the shade of *kalpavṛkṣa* in heaven.[9] The above references indicate that the tree cult of popular religion became associated with Vedic Indra. That the *kalpavṛkṣa* was originally a tree of Uttarakuru is maintained in the *Jātakas, Mahābhārata, Rāmāyaṇa, Divyāvadāna* and *Jain Sūtras*. As per *Mahābhārata* (Bhīṣmaparva), the Siddhas live in the Uttarakuru. There are trees which bear flowers and matured fruits in all seasons, and amongst them there are trees which fulfil all wishes. Some produce streams of milk with the qualities of nectar and flavour of all the six varieties (*rasas*). The branches produce clothes and ornaments and there are also some branches from which maidens of great beauty and youth, and also male and female couples are produced.[10] Similarly, in the *Rāmāyaṇa* (4, 43, 44, 48) it is recorded that Sugrīva sent his monkey heroes in the north to the land of Uttarakuru where grew the *kalpa*-tree that produced in their branches all kinds of apparel jewels decorated with pearls and gems befitting women and men and suitable for all seasons. Such trees produce bedsteads with fine coverlets and garlands that gladden the heart, costly drinks and varieties of food and damsels noted for their excellent character, beauty and youth.[11] To Kālidāsa, the *kalpavṛkṣa* used to supply all the cosmetics desired by the wife of the Yakṣa who was cursed to live in exile by Kubera.[12] The same author further adds in the *Abhijñānaśākuntalam* (4,5) that the gift of jewels by the *Vanadevatās* is made with their own hands peeping through the clumps. The tree has been called by Kālidāsa as *surarāja vṛkṣa*, the tree of the sovereign of the celestials, itself a *vṛkṣarāja*, Lord among noble trees. He compares the *kalpavṛkṣa* with its sister Lakṣmī arising out of the ocean to the Nāga king Kumuda.[13] Mandara is considered to be one of the *kalpavṛkṣas* by the Hindus. There is a belief that this tree was won by Rukmini, and from that time onwards, the tree was associated with Kṛṣṇa. In *Matsya Purāṇa, nyagrodha* is called as *kalpavṛkṣa*, which gives to its worshipper, food and drink, clothes and ornaments, gift of children and even beautiful maidens.[14] In *Mahābhārata*, *jambū* tree that grows south of the Nila and north of the Nishadha is a *kalpavṛkṣa*. In the *Bhāgavata Purāṇa*, *kadamba* is the wish-fulfilling tree.[15] The coconut tree is also regarded as *kalpavṛkṣa* because of its various uses.

In the *Jātakas,* the wish-fulfilling tree has been described as feeding, clothing and in every way most hospitable, attending to the needs of passers-by—seeking its shade, and laden with wealth in pots and bags all arranged near its roots, closely related to *Vanadevatā* concept. The *Mahāvāṇija Jātaka* (4.352) referred to a big banyan tree which was of the nature of *kalpavṛkṣa.* It produced from its eastern branches streams of water, from southern branches food and drinks, from western branches fair damsels and from the northern branches all desired objects.[16] Although *kalpavṛkṣa* is regarded as a symbol of plenty, prosperity, joy and happiness, yet the ascetic religion of Buddha based on renunciation did not agree well with this conception. It is of great interest to see that Buddhists still accord a welcome reception to the theme of *kalpavṛkṣa* in their art.

The happy conception of the *kalpavṛkṣa* must have been quite popular in ancient India. The Vidyādhara emperor Jimūtaketu is said to have given the sovereignty of the Vidyādhara realm and the *kalpavṛkṣa* to his son before he retired to Mount Malaya for penance.[17] According to Agrawala, *kalpavṛkṣa* is the symbol of mind, where *kalpa* signifies "thought" or idea. What one wishes under the *kalpavṛkṣa* tree, one obtains.[18]

The *kalpavalli* (creeper) shows various types of clothes variegated in colour and with different patterns worked on them, different patterns of jewels like earrings, bracelets, anklets, necklaces and so forth. The same creeper produces all these diverse articles of dress and toilet. In *Raghuvaṁśa* (8,47) the creepers are believed to wind themselves around the tree like a damsel embracing her lover.[19]

The Jain texts also speak of *kalpavṛkṣas*. The *Tiloyapannatti* (I.4) has recorded the following list of *kalpa*-trees: *pāṇanga, turiyanga, bhuṣaṇāṅga, vatthaṅga, bhoyaṅga, ālayaṅga, diviyaṅga, bhāyaṇaṅga, mālaṅga* and *tanjaṅga* with excellent drinks, music, ornaments, garments, edibles and ready-made dishes, mansions to live in, lamps, utensils and garlands of flowers respectively, while the last type namely *tanjaṅga*, seems to be self-luminous, serving the purpose of heavenly luminaries. A similar type of list with slight different titles and same type of characteristics is mentioned in the *Paumacariyam* (3.37).[20] *Kalpavṛkṣa* also finds mention in the *Sthānāṅga Sūtra* and *Jivājivābhigama Sūtra*. According to *Samarāṅgaṇa Sūtradhāra* (Ch. 6, V. 15), people in the *Kṛta yuga* used to secure all sorts of enjoyable things from the *kalpa-druma*.[21] Hemachandra reported ten kinds of wish-fulfilling trees in the Uttarakurus. These trees always give to people whatever they desire without effort on their part. Among these trees, the *madyāṅgas* give wine, the *bhṛṅgas* dishes, the *turyaṅgas* choice musical instruments, the *dipa śikhās* and *jyotiṣkas* give wonderful light, the *citrāṅgas* and *maṇyaṅgas* furnish ornaments, the *citrarasas* give food, the *gehakāras* houses and the *anaṅgas* various kinds of divine apparel.[22]

Besides, the wish-fulfilling tree is the symbol of crowns of the Vaimānika gods (*kalpa*-gods) namely Ānanta, Prāṇata, Āraṇa and Acyuta in the *digambara* sect of Jainism.[23]

The popularity of the notion of wish-fulfilling trees and creepers can further be judged by their frequent depiction in Indian art. For example, in one of the medallions of the crossbar in Bharhut railing there is a curious depiction of *padma* and *utpala* creepers, issuing out from the mouth of a Yakṣa (Pl. 3). Similarly, in another medallion from the same railing, the *padma* and *utpala* creepers are shown as issuing out from the navel of a seated Yakṣa (Pl. 4). Lotus was a Buddhist symbol and was specifically related to the event of nativity of the Buddha (*Jati*). In Hindu pantheon, lotus is shown associated with a number of gods and goddesses such as Sūrya, Viṣṇu, Lakṣmī, etc. But these two medallions are referred to for the peculiar origin of these creepers and flowers. Maybe these two male figures represent the personification of water from which the creepers generally grow. Issuing of lotus from the navel was also noticed from the navel of Viṣṇu. But these early depictions had hardly anything to do with the Vaiṣṇavite mythology.

On the coping stones (*usnisa*) of the Bharhut railings, one notices the meandering lotus creepers which have taken the form of wish-fulfilling creeper (*kalpalatā*). The creeper is shown as issuing out from the mouth

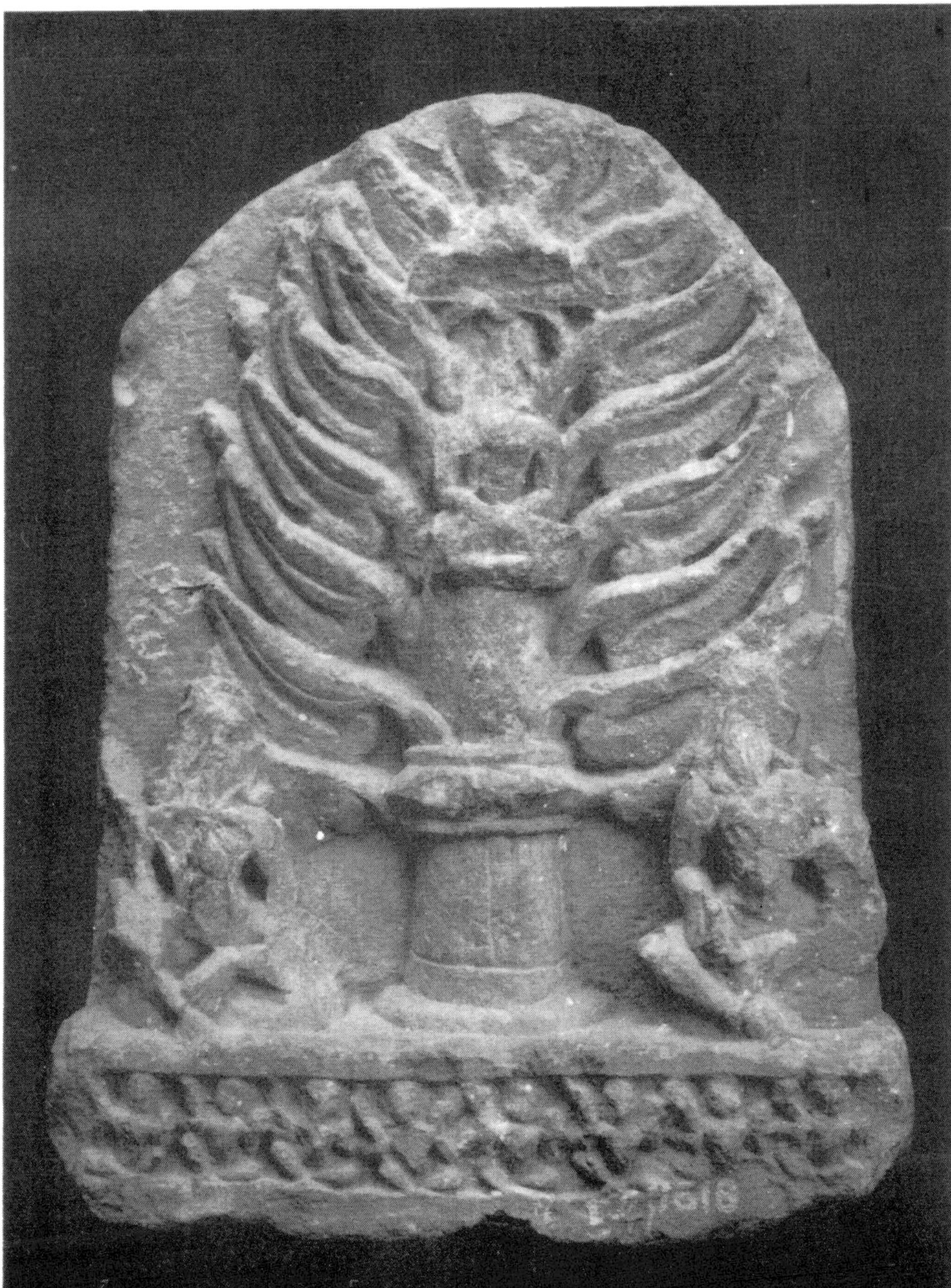

Pl. 46. Kalpavṛkṣa; Modi (Mandasore, M.P.); Sandstone; Central Museum, Indore; 11th century AD.

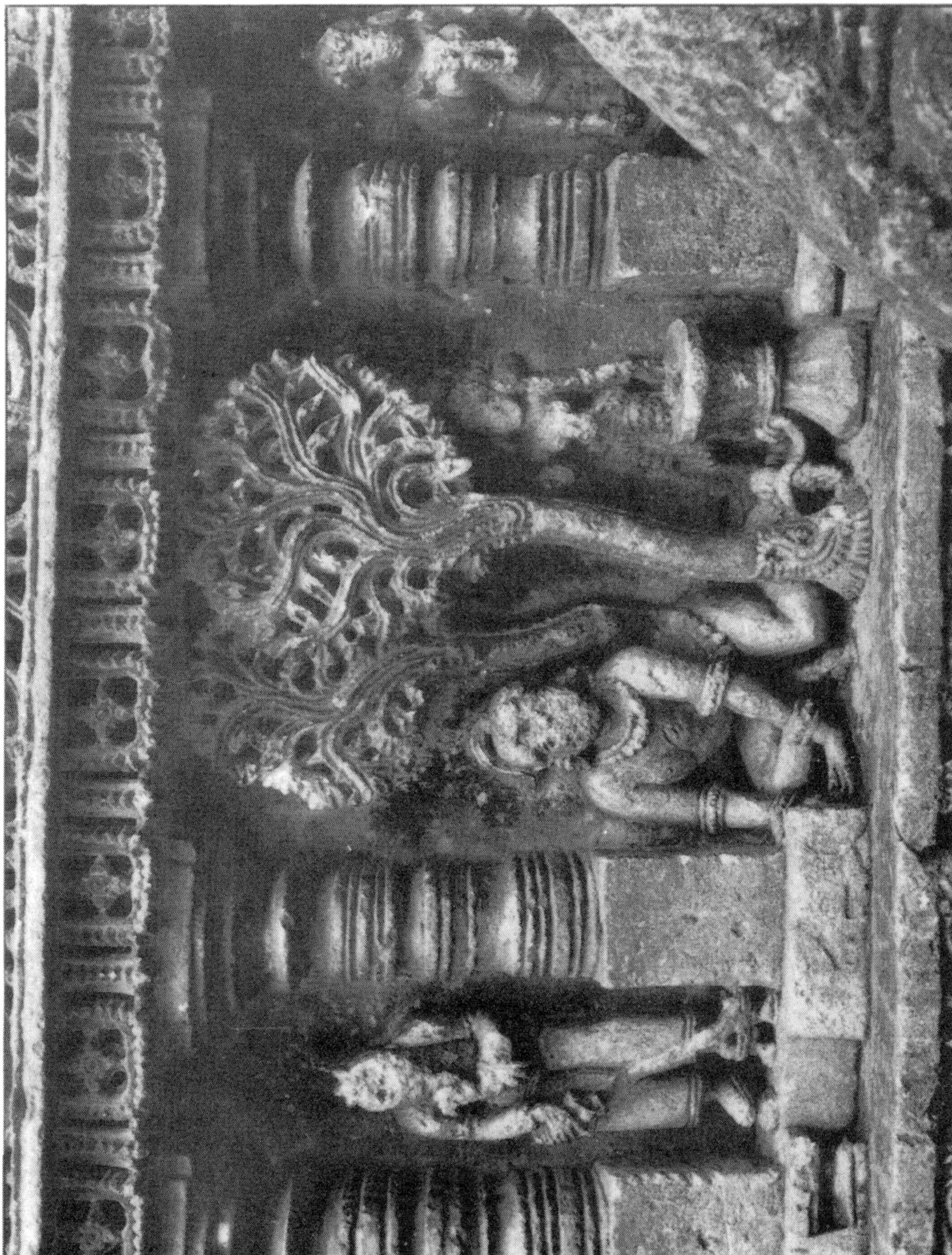

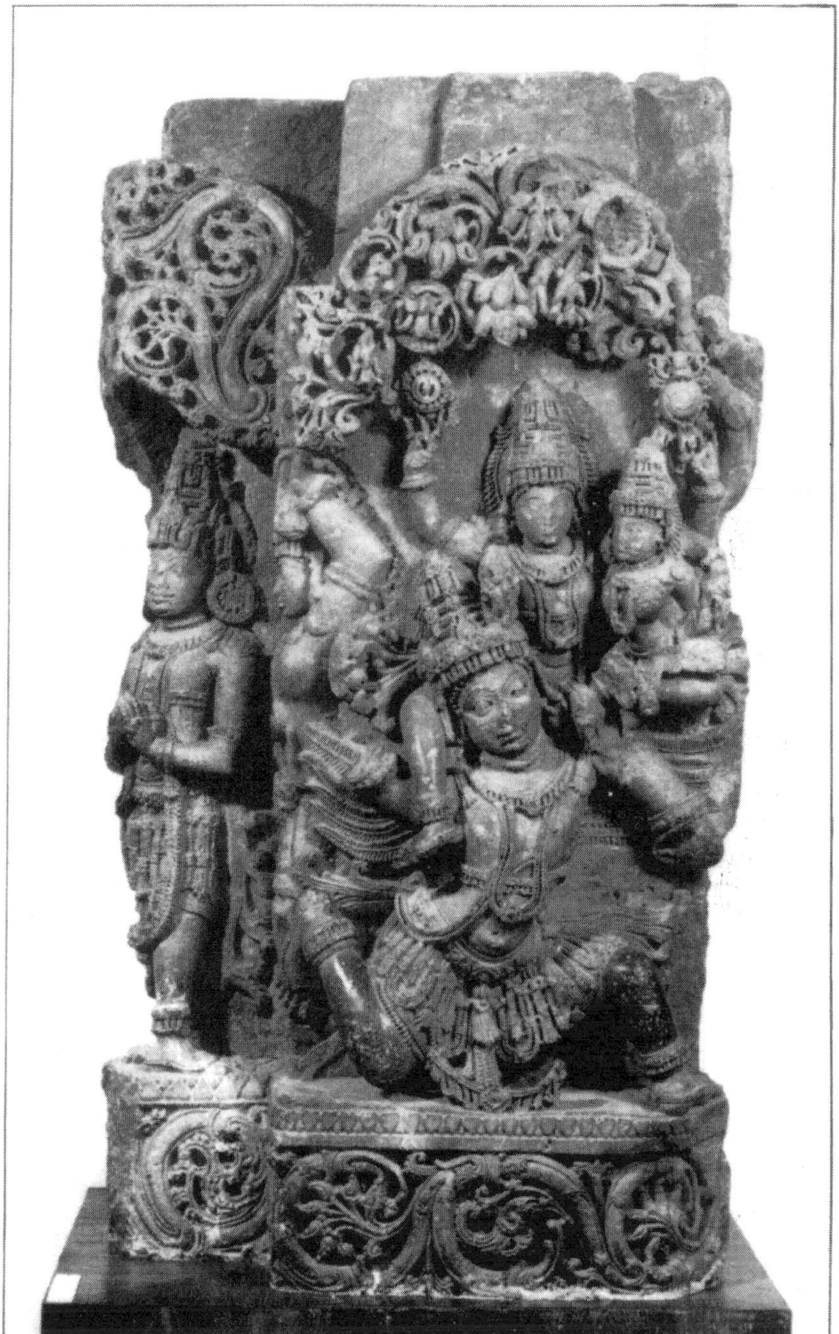

Pl. 48. Lakṣmī-Nārāyaṇa on Garuḍa under a tree; Halebid (Hassan, Karnataka); Basalt; National Museum; 12th century AD.

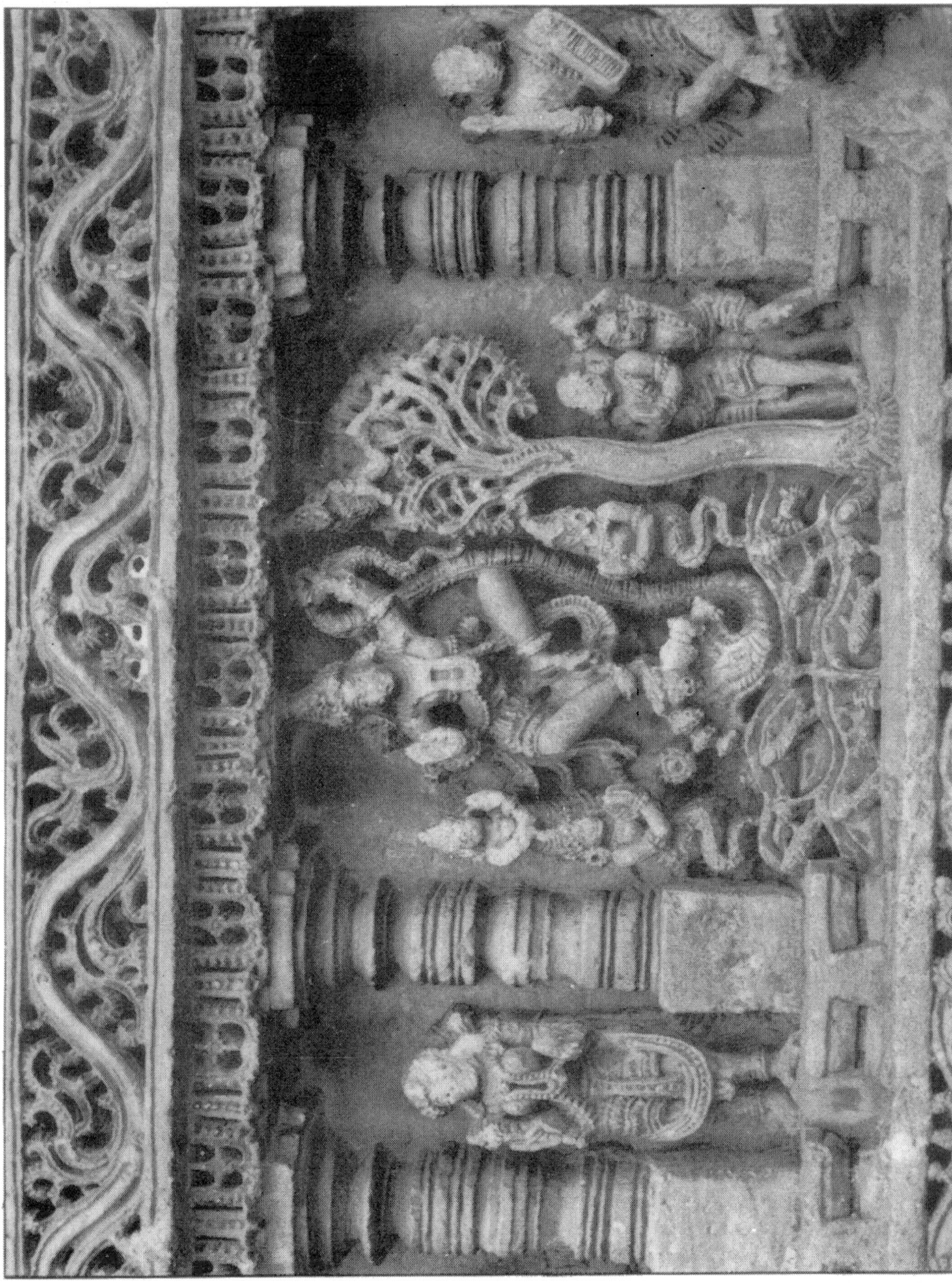

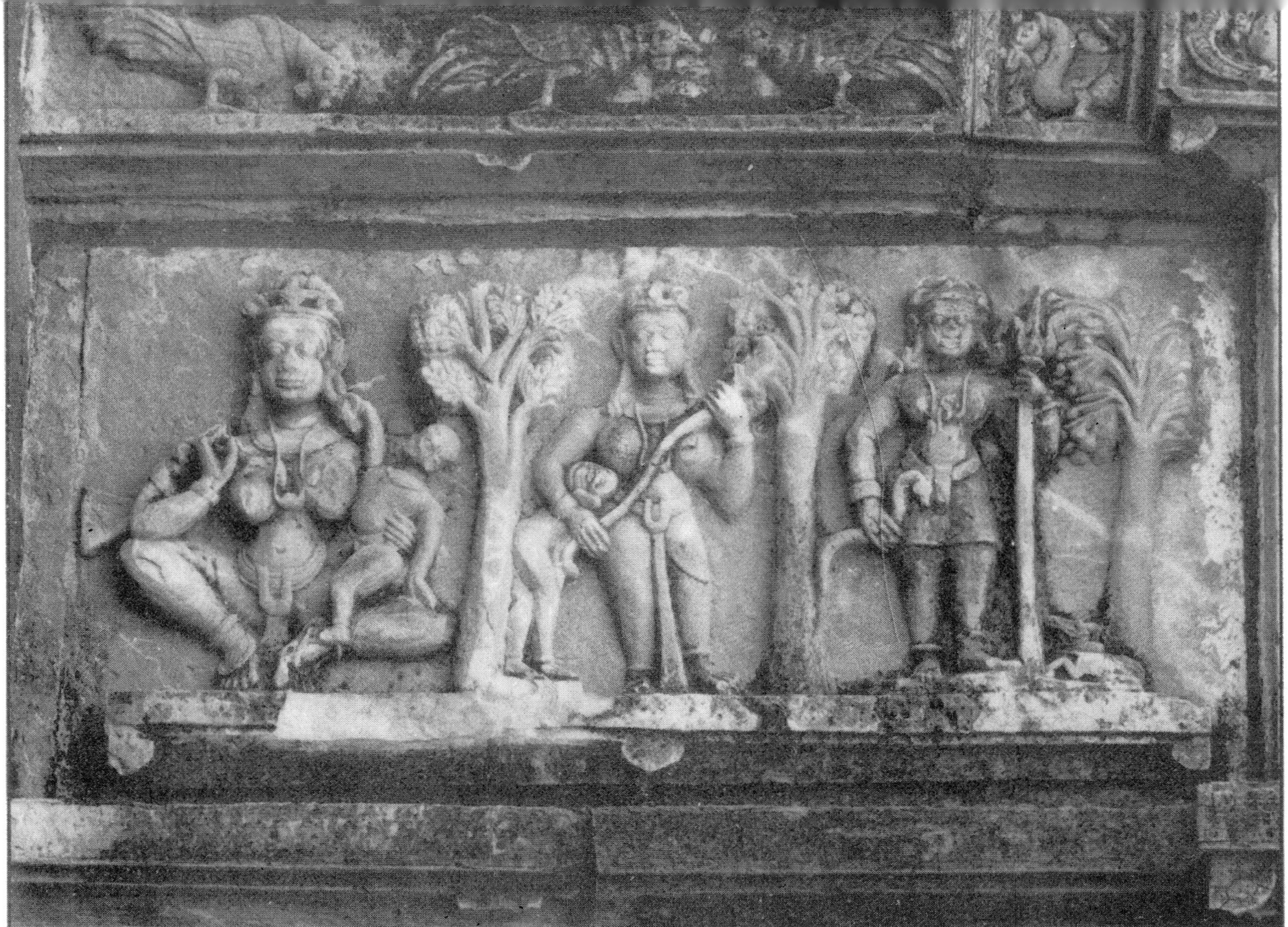

Pl. 50. Panel depicting Mātṛkas with trees; Deo Baloda (Durg, M.P.); Śiva temple; Buff sandstone; late 13th century AD.

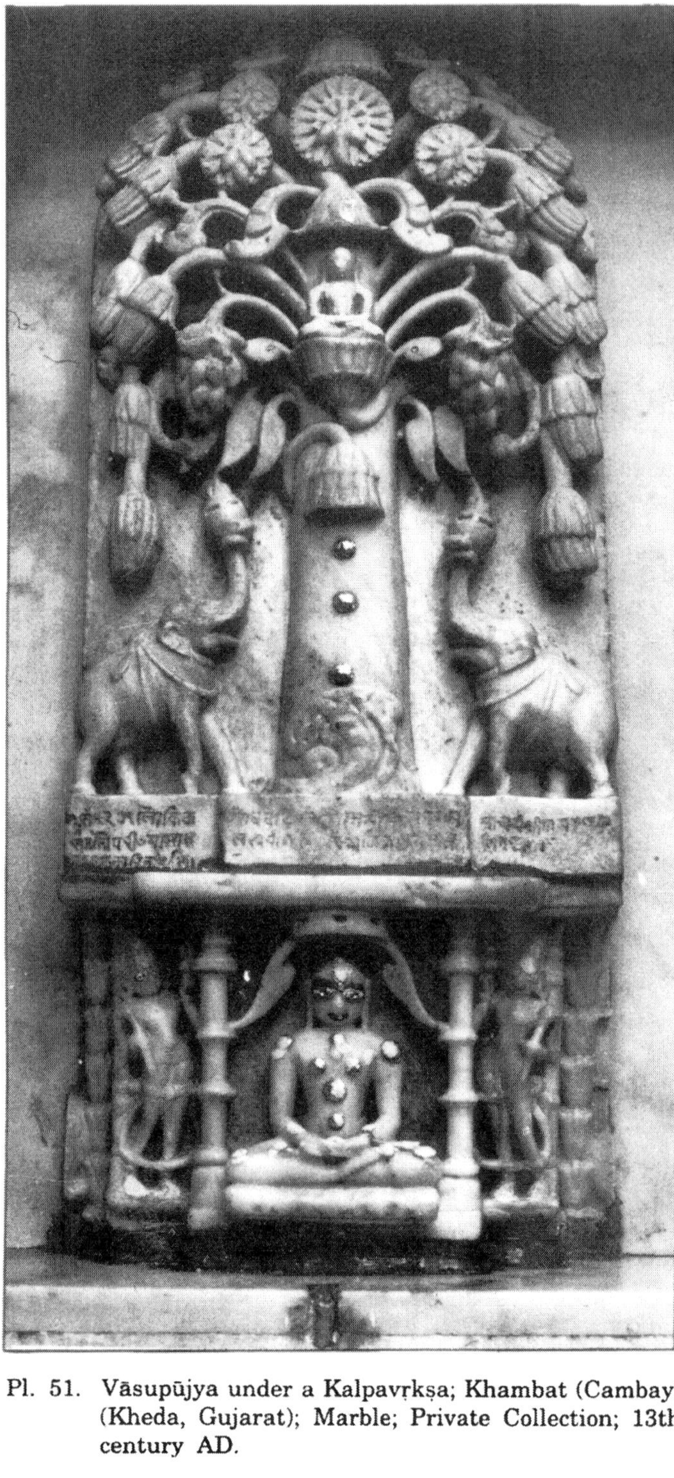

Pl. 51. Vāsupūjya under a Kalpavṛkṣa; Khambat (Cambay) (Kheda, Gujarat); Marble; Private Collection; 13th century AD.

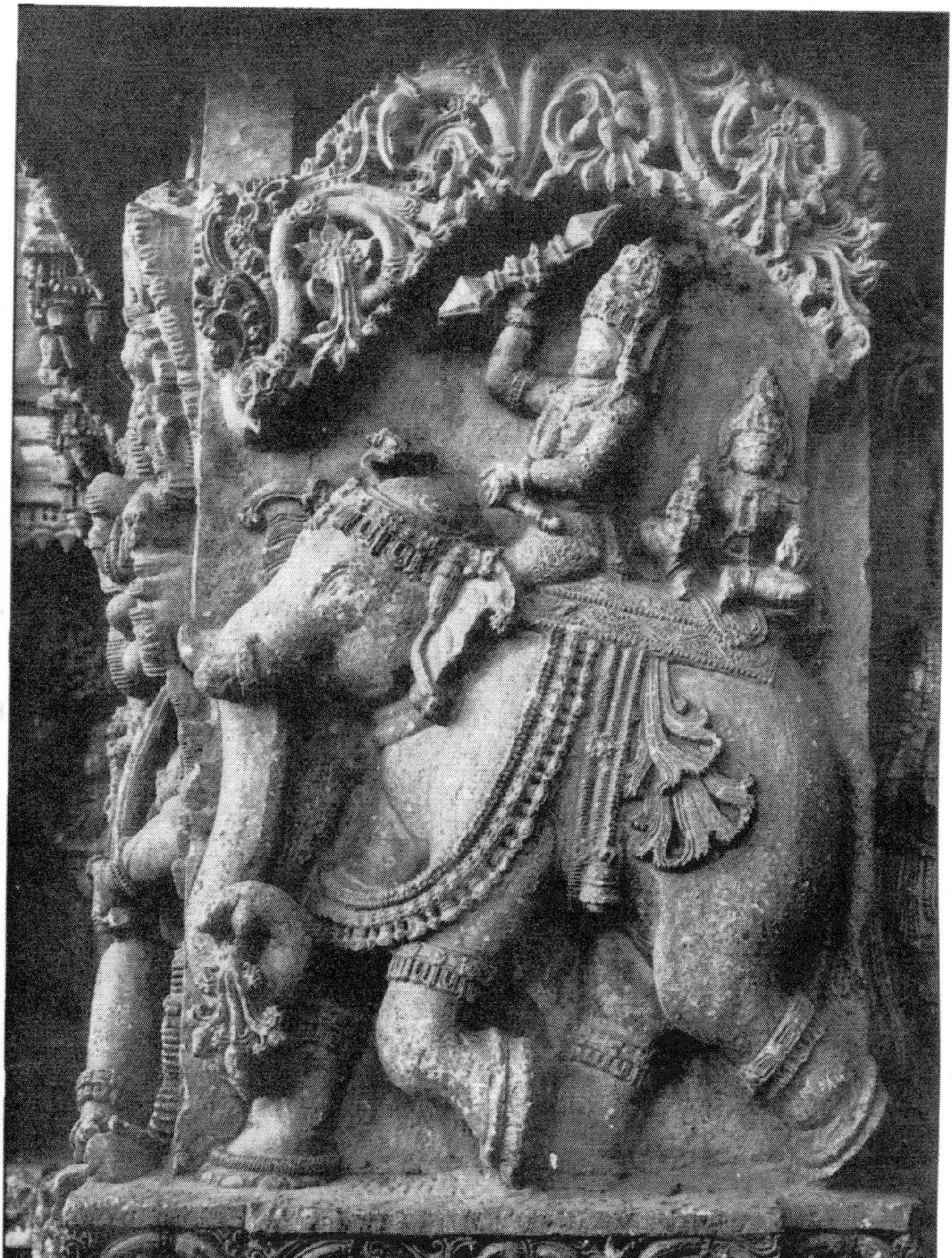

Pl. 52. Indra; Javagal (Chikmagalur, Karnataka); Lakṣmīnarasiṁhā temple, Soapstone; 13th century AD.

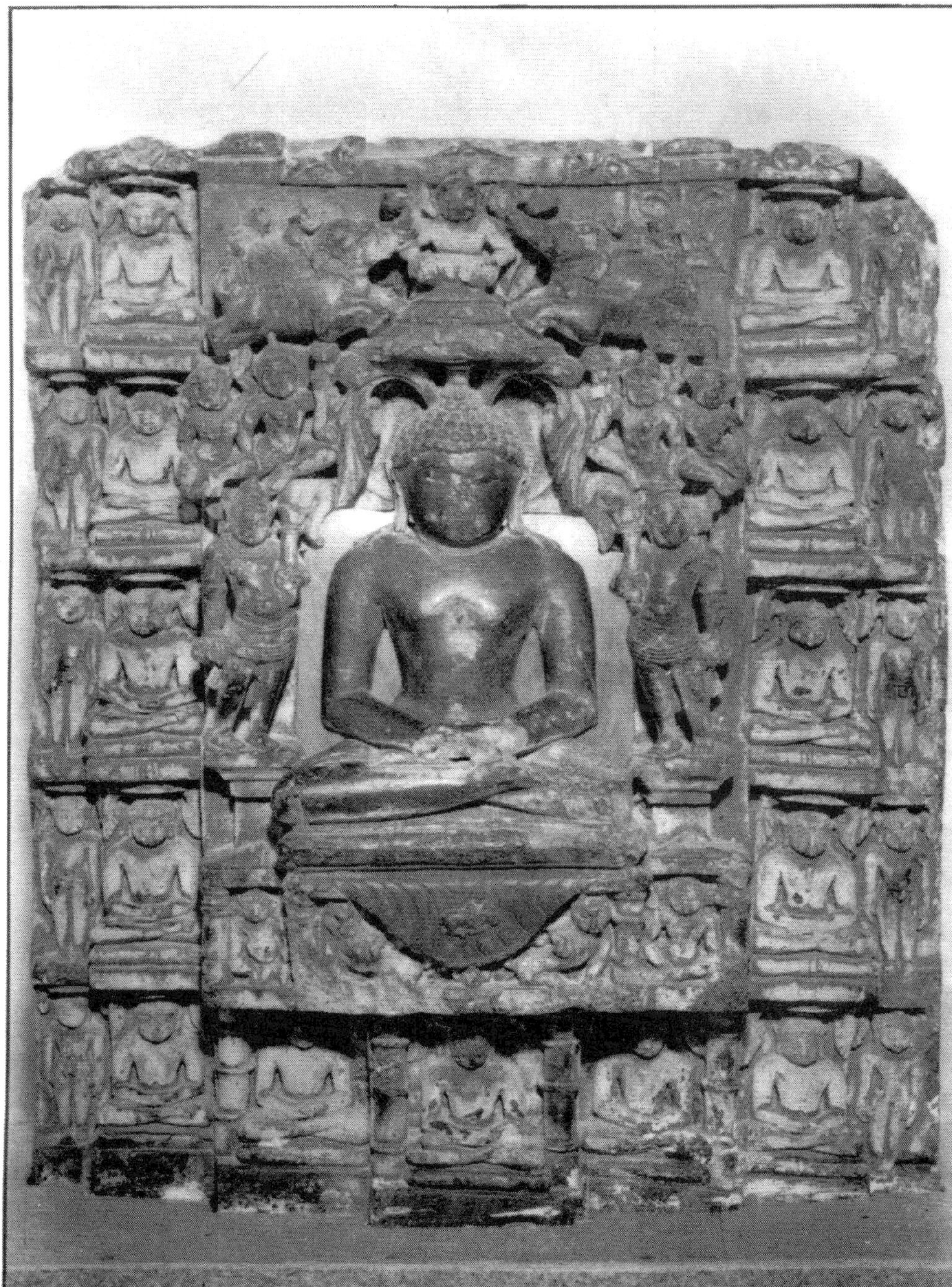

Pl. 53. Ṛsabhadeva seated in dhyāna mudrā under a stylised nyagrodha tree; Tantoti (Ajmer, Rajasthan); Black stone; Rajputana Museum, Ajmer; 13th-14th century AD.

of seated elephant and is bringing out not only lotus flowers but also many other things such as jewellery, religious symbols, etc. (Pl. 5). The elephant in Indian art is related to water cosmology and is also considered as a Nāga. There is a specific relation of water with the elephant. Therefore, creepers issuing out of the mouth of elephant may be explained as creepers issuing out of water.

That the creeper is wish-fulfilling is further proved by another coping stone relief, which is now in the Indian Museum, Calcutta (Pl. 6). The creeper is shown here as issuing from a tree and the tree is nothing but a wish-fulfilling tree (*kalpavṛkṣa*). It is really interesting to note that two human hands are seen coming out from the trunk of the tree, one of which is holding a water pitcher. In front of the tree, a man is shown seated on a small stool, who is seen extending his right hand as if he is going to bring water. It appears that the person is hungry and thirsty and would have approached this wish-fulfilling tree to provide him with food and drinks. Thus, it proves that a tree can provide food and life sustaining sap. In Alakā, the city of Yakṣas, all the needs of the people are supplied by the wish-fulfilling tree (*Meghadūta* II). It is believed to be the same tree in Indra's garden which was coveted by Satyabhāmā.

In Asutosh Museum of Indian Art in the Calcutta University, there is a sculpture of Lokeśvara which has the depiction of *kalpavṛkṣa*. Here in this *kalpavṛkṣa,* one finds not only clothes, ornaments, etc. but also male and female children hang from it (Biswas, 1985 : 45). It seems that the idea that tree offers life led to the coining of word *"Jivana-vṛkṣa,"* the tree of life.

The northern part of the Bangladesh has yielded several Jain sculptures,[24] which depict a seated couple with a child in their lap under a *kalpavṛkṣa* with spreading branches over these figures.

In the Indian Museum collection, there is a stone sculpture (Pl. 15) showing a wish-fulfilling tree within railing. This 2nd century BC wish-fulfilling tree from Besnagar (Vidisa-M.P.) is apparently the part of the railing pillar. It may be identified with a huge banyan tree from which many things are seen hanging. The *nyagrodha* tree is generally associated with the *Manusi* Buddha Kaśyapa.

The bronze hoard which was discovered at Chausa in the Sahabad district of Bihar includes depiction of *kalpavṛkṣa* with a female figure at the top (Pl. 18). This 1st century BC bronze in Patna Museum shows perhaps one of the earliest attempts to depict wish-fulfilling trees in metal in Indian art. The tree has been moulded in a stylised manner with leaves drooping down.

There is a 11th century buff sandstone panel in the Central Museum, Indore, which was acquired from Modi in Mandasore (M.P.). The panel shows a huge but stylised *kalpavṛkṣa* (Pl. 46). At the bottom, a group of figures are shown seated, and two damaged figures are also visible on either side of the tree.

In a private collection, there is an image of Vasupujya which hails from Cambay of Kheda district of Gujarat (Pl. 51). At the top of the image, there appears a *kalpavṛkṣa* very stylistically delineated and in its middle a figure of Tīrthāṅkara in *dhyānāsana* is depicted.

Wooden Sculptures

There are textual references to indicate that sculptures were also made in wood. Unfortunately, many early examples are not available with us as wood is a perishable material. Those wooden sculptures which could survive the onslaught of time include an example of mother and child from Patna (Bihar), dated in the 3rd-2nd century BC, carved in round. This specimen is considered as one of the earliest of its kind and the earliest free-standing sculpture in wood found in India. This sculpture is preserved in the collection of Gopi Krishna Kanodia at Patna.[25] Besides, there are many wooden sculptures of late period preserved in different museums and private collections in India.[26] In certain areas in India, the wooden images are still being made. For making images out of trees, there are certain restrictions in the religious texts. Images for worship by the Brāhmaṇas are made from *deodāra, candan, śamī, madhuka*; for Kshatriyas images are made out of *arishta, aśvattha, khadira, vilva*; for Vaiśyas, *jivika, khadira, sindhuka, syandana*; for Śūdras out of *tinduka, kesara, salya arjuna, āmra* and *śāla*.[27] Perhaps quality and durability of the wood in question were in the mind of religious teachers in ancient India while they were compiling texts on the prescriptions of wooden sculptures.

III

TREE IN COINS

In ancient Indian coins, the trees and flowers do occupy an important place and are frequently found on many coins. In some pre-Mauryan punch-marked coins from Sugh, there are some tree symbols, which included tree within railing.[28] The earliest die-cast coins with a device on one side only are chiefly found at Taxila. Some of these coins bear a *bodhi* tree and are believed to have been issued during the reign of Aśoka.[29] Interestingly, on the coins of Mitra kings found at Ayodhya, a standing cock in front of a palm tree is found. The coins from Kauśāmbī bear a bull on the obverse and tree in railing with the king's name on the reverse.[30] In the coins from Mathura, Lakṣmī is shown standing in between the several symbols and holding lotus in her uplifted right hand.[31] It is noteworthy that the particular trees occur on the coins of the respective regions, such as, palm on Ayodhya coins, *kadamba* on the Mathura coins and the *pipal* on the Vidisa-Eran coins. Further, a conventionalised form of tree is frequently seen on some coins of the Andhra dynasty. After the break of the Mauryan empire, some silver punch-marked coins were issued in the Pāṇḍyan territory and one of the symbols on these coins was depicted as a leafy tree. In many regions of southern and western India, the tree within railing was a favourite theme in ancient period.[32] The coins of Chandragupta II depicts Lakṣmī seated upon a lotus instead of a throne. The same motif was also repeated by Śaśāṅka, the king of Gauda in the first quarter of the seventh century.[33]

Thus, the trees and flowers do occupy an important place in the motifs on ancient Indian coins. Banerjea considers the tree symbol on the coins as *sathalvṛkṣa* and *caitya vṛkṣa*.[34] According to Agrawala,[35] the tree symbol on the coins represents as a *kalpavṛkṣa*, which was churned out as one of the fourteen *ratnās* from the ocean. Similarly, a glimpse at the miniatures of Mughal period gives a clear indication of the importance of trees, plants and foliage that even the Muslim rulers of India gave. While looking into the vastness of the subject it needs a separate study.

NOTES AND REFERENCES

1. For details about the *bodhi* trees in different Jātaka scenes from Bharhut, see Barua, B.M., *Bharhut*, Parts I, II, III, Patna, pp. 1-7.
2. Coomaraswamy, A.K., *History of Indian and Indonesian Art*, New Delhi, 1972, p. 64 fn.
3. For further details about the different trees on Sanchi stūpa, see Agrawala, V.S., *Indian Art*, Varanasi, 1965, pp. 153-68.
4. Banerjea, J.N., *Development of Hindu Iconography*, Calcutta, 1941, p. 14. Banerjea has dated this sculpture in 1st century BC.

5. According to the *Harivaṁśa* (II, 7, 17-19), when Yasoda was tired of the naughty habit of Kṛṣṇa, she tied him to the grinding stone with a rope. Kṛṣṇa dragged himself to the river bank where stood the trees of Yamala and Arjuna. He tried to pass through them and while doing so the trees were hurled down and uprooted by force of the big stone tied to Kṛṣṇa. In *Bhāgavata Purāṇa* (X, 10), these trees are regarded as two yakṣas, who had been cursed to go to the earth in the form of trees till Kṛṣṇa will deliver them (cf. Desai, K.S., *Iconography of Viṣṇu*, New Delhi, 1973, p. 126).
6. Agrawala, V.S., *Ancient Indian Folk Cults*, Varanasi, 1970, p. 118.
7. Sengupta, S. (Ed.), *Tree Symbol Worship in India*, Calcutta, 1965, pp. 2-3. The story of the churning of the ocean appears with slight variations in several *purāṇas*. The *parijāta* tree of the *Matsya Purāṇa* list, of articles which arose from the churning of the milky ocean, is considered as a *kalpavṛkṣa*, the heavenly tree which symbolises mind. It remains with one from birth and one gets whatever one desires, wishing under its shade (see Agrawala, V.S., *Matsya Purāṇa: A Study*, Varanasi, 1963, p. 340).
8. Cf. Sivaramamurti, C., *Approach to Nature in Indian Art and Thought,* New Delhi, 1980, p. 75.
9. *Ibid.*
10. *Mahābhārāta, Bhishmaparva* (7.2-11), reference quoted from Agrawala, V.S. (1970), *op.cit.*, p. 118.
11. *Ibid.*, pp. 118-19.
12. Cf. Sengupta, S. (Ed.), *op.cit.*, p. 3.
13. Cf. Sivaramamurti, C., *op.cit.*, pp. 73-74.
14. Agrawala, V.S., *op.cit.*, p. 188.
15. Cf. Gupta, S.M., *Plant Myths and Traditions in India*, New Delhi, 1991, 2nd Revised Edition, p. 48.
16. *Jātaka*, 4.352, reference quoted from Agrawala, V.S. (1970), *op.cit.*, p. 119.
17. Kshemendra gives precedence to *kalpavṛkṣa* and the empire is mentioned only as an adjunct. (Cf. Sivaramamurti, C., *op.cit.*, p. 74).
18. Agrawala, V.S. (1965), *op.cit.*, p. 53.
19. Cf. Sivaramamurti, C., (1965), *op.cit.*, pp. 73, 77.
20. Cf. Shah, U.P., *Jaina-Rupa Mandana,* New Delhi, 1987, pp. 70-71.
21. Bhattacharyya, T., *Canons of Indian Art or A Study of Vastuvidya*, Calcutta, 1963, p. 5.
22. Ghosh, A., (Ed.), *Jaina Art and Architecture*, Vol. III, New Delhi, 1975, p.487.
23. Shah, U.P. (1965), *op.cit.*, p. 60.
24. Majumdar, R.C. (Ed.), *History of Bengal*, vol. I, Dacca, 1942, p. 465.
25. Dasgupta, K.K., *Wood Carvings of Eastern India*, Calcutta, 1990, p. 81, pl. 20.
26. *Ibid.*, pp. 11-108, pls. 1-50.

27. Cf. Gupta, S.M., *op.cit.*, p. 9.
28. Handa, D., *Studies in Indian Coins and Seals*, Delhi, 1985, pp. 11-12.
29. Sinha, B.C., *Tree Worship in Ancient India*, New Delhi, 1979, p. 79; also see plates.
30. *Ibid.*, p. 80.
31. *Ibid.*
32. *Ibid.*, p. 81.
33. *Ibid.*, p. 82.
34. Banerjea, J.N., *op.cit.*, p. 109.
35. Agrawala, V.S., *op.cit.*, p. 53.

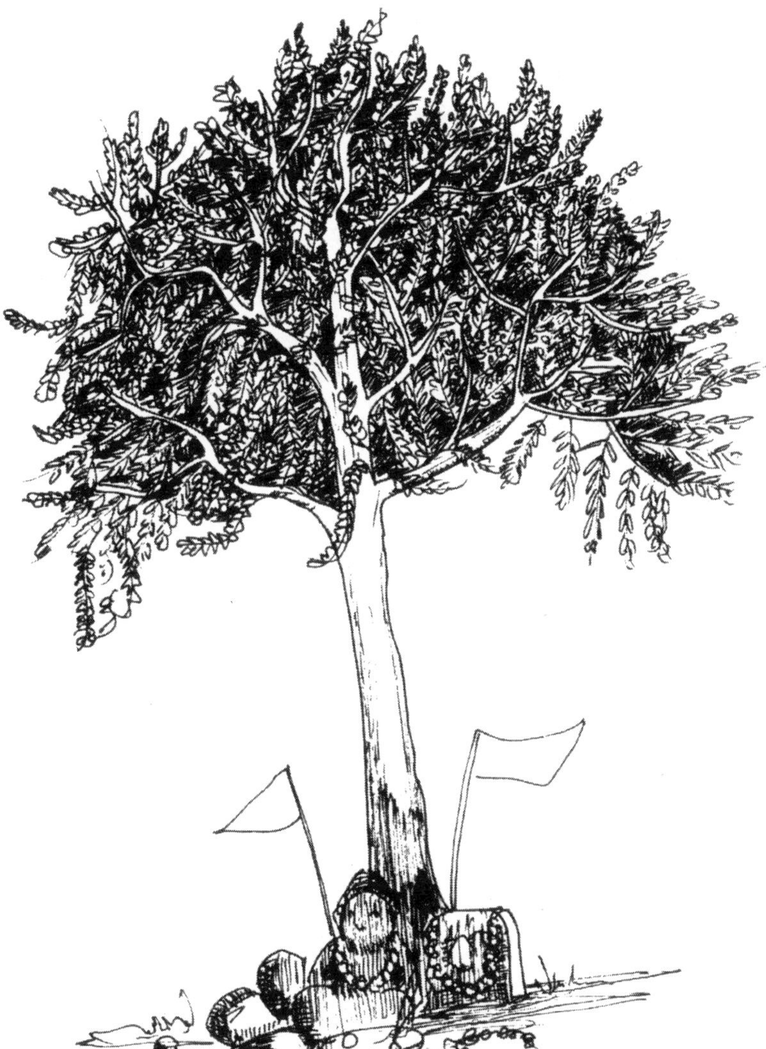

6 ART IS RELIGION, RELIGION ART

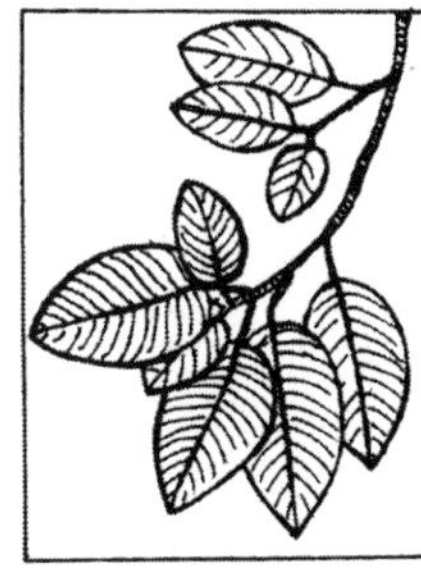

The discussions undertaken in the preceding chapters indicate that the notion of tree worship could be pushed back to the period of Indus valley civilization. A number of seals, sealings, potteries and potsherds were discovered from the Indus valley sites with the depiction of certain trees. These trees include the *pipal,* the *neem,* the acacia, the *śamī* and the date palm, and are depicted in such a way which signifies that the authors of the Indus valley civilization did pay oblations and worshipped at least a few trees. Perhaps it was believed that gods dwell in the trees (*vṛkṣa devatā* or *vṛkṣa devi*), therefore, their divine character was depicted in a befitting manner, sometimes trees as such and sometimes, trees personified. The sacrifices offered to the trees or divine emergence of the trees from the body of a female goddess or the branches of the trees attached to the head gears of the divinities are some of the interesting examples which persuade one to believe that the notion of tree worship was already in the minds of the pre-Vedic people.

After the decline of Indus valley civilization, no tangible archaeological records are available to trace the continuity of tree worship in India till the emergence of Mauryas in the 4th-3rd century BC. However, the hiatus has been filled in by vast literary and textual references. According to the Vedic beliefs and myths, all the plants and trees are sacred as they possess the gifts of immortality, health and general prosperity. The *Ṛgveda* refers to *oṣadhis* as "mothers" and "goddesses", which are invoked chiefly with waters and mountains. It is said in the *Atharvaveda* that the gods of the third heaven are seated under the *aśvattha* and it may also refer to the tree with fair foliage of the *Ṛgveda* (10.135) under which Yama and the blessed ones are said to pass their time. There is also a reference to *caitya-vṛkṣa* in the *Atharvaveda Pariśiṣṭa* (LXXI). The notion of tree worship continued in the later Vedic texts also. In fact, *aśvattha* is regarded as *Brahmā-taru*, the embodiment of knowledge and Great Creator in the later Vedic texts. That is why *aśvattha* is called on certain occasions as 'tree of life' or the 'tree of creation'. In Buddhist religion, the *aśvattha* tree is also regarded as very sacred. According to *Mahapadma-Suttana*, the *bodhi* tree of Buddha was an *aśvattha*. The *Digha Nikāya* (II, 2-8) states that the six previous Buddhas were each enlightened under different species of trees. The *bodhi* tree attained greater importance in Buddhist art, since the Buddha was not represented in its human form in early Buddhist worship and in narrative art. But the Jains were more or less satisfied with recording of the *caitya* trees of different Tīrthāṅkaras and gave them only a secondary importance in art. In both these religions, trees were worshipped, not because they were haunted by spirits, but specially because their patriarchs obtained enlightenment under the shades of such trees. The *aśvattha* is regarded as the *caitya* tree of the fourteenth Tirthāṅkara Anantanātha in both sects of Jainism. In Hindu mythology Śiva is deeply connected with *bilva* tree. It finds its mention in the *Ṛgveda* (V.22.10), *Taittirīya Saṁhitā* (II.1.1-2), *Maitrāyaṇī Saṁhitā* (III.9.3), *Bilopaniṣad* (7; 8; 16; 17; 18), *Śivopaniṣad* (IV.59), and is also considered one of the important sacred trees in the *purāṇas*. Besides, many other trees and plants are held sacred and venerated since Vedic times which include banyan, *śamī, udumbara, khadira, neem, tulsi, palaṣa* and lotus. The tree-spirits have materialized in the *Upaniṣads* as like all other things they are subject to rebirth. If the spirit leaves the tree, the tree withers and dies, but the spirit is immortal (cf. Smith, 1969, p. 7). The tree-spirits play an important role in the *Jātakas,* and are being worshipped with perfumes, flowers and food. These spirits dwell in many kinds of trees but the banyan seems to have been their favourite. The *Jātakas* (nos. 472, 488) even speak of animal and human sacrifice in connection with tree-worship at many places. Indians also developed a notion of *kalpavṛkṣa* and *kalpalatā*, i.e. the wish-fulfilling trees and creepers. This is a mind born aspect. The idea was that if properly cultivated and nourished, a tree has the capacity to fulfil, all the desires of mankind. Detailed discussion about the literary references to tree worship in ancient India is made in Chapter 3.

It appears from the textual references on the depiction of trees in Indian art that there must have been a cult of tree worship in ancient past. Interestingly, only some of the trees were glorified. Perhaps these trees were having some utilitarian qualities and were helpful in various ways for a man; hence they were propitiated. They supplied food, medicine, shelter, shadow and even fuels. The cult of fertility was also associated with the tree. That a tree could fertilize a barren woman and bestow the motherhood have also been indicated in Chapter 4. Likewise, it has also been stated that certain barren trees were fertilized and started flowering and giving fruits when they came in contact with womenfolk. Our ancient Indians were not only concerned about the medicinal qualities of trees but were equally aware about the atmospheric changes, pollution and ecological balances. They, therefore, tried their best to save trees, particularly those which were held useful for the survival of humanity. Just to save these trees from various damaging agencies, trees were identified with gods and goddesses. Thus by showing different kinds of gains, merits, etc., our ancestors encouraged people to protect the trees, to organise pleasure gardens and to save the forests. On the other hand, by prescribing various kinds of punishments, which include a life in hell, attempts were made to protect the trees and forests.

After carefully considering various utilities and usefulness of certain trees, the people in ancient India tried their best to save them from being cut down by the wood-cutters. Each of these trees was, therefore, associated with one or the other god or goddess. The practice was popular in all the three major religions namely Hindu, Buddhist and Jain. The tree worship was equally popular in the indigenous tradition of folk India. When people came to know that a particular tree is the abode of a god or goddess they dared not cut it; in fact, they worshipped it. In order to popularize this notion and in order to create awareness regarding certain trees, the Indian artists carved them in stone, moulded them in terracotta and bronze, and painted them in colour and reflected them in the narrative art of India. Starting from the art of Indus valley and down to the present century, one finds depiction of a number of trees in various ways and in association with various religions. On Mauryan relief sculptures, particularly on the Aśokan Pillar capitals, trees and creepers were very peculiarly depicted. Palmette, acanthus, rosette and honeysuckle are found as alternating motifs on the frieze of the Rampurvā Bull Capital (Pl. 1) of Aśoka. In some ring-stones, the palm tree is often repeated with the Mother-goddess (Pl. 2) emphasising its intimate relation with the cult. A detailed survey of the relief sculptures of the gateways and railings related to the Buddhist stupas of Bharhut, Bodhgaya, Sanchi, Amravati and Nagarjunakonda reveal the depictions of several different trees and creepers. The trees identified from these sites include *aśvattha* or *pipal* (*Ficus religiosa*), banyan tree (*Ficus indica*), *udumbara* (*Ficus glomerata*), *patali* (*Bignonia suavealens*), *śāla* tree (*Shorea robusta*), *śriṣa* (*Acacia sarisa*), and also *śālabhañjikā*, *aśoka-pushpa-pracāyika*, *kalpavṛkṣa*, *kalpalatā*, tree of life (*śrī-vṛkṣa*) and *chaitya-vṛkṣa*. Some of the trees are very realistically executed in relief and quite a few are shown in absolute abstraction. The motif of a woman plucking flowers from a distended bough is met with on the toraṇa of Bharhut and Sanchi in the Śuṅga period and is continued on the railing pillars of the Kuṣāṇa period. It is also found in a limited number of examples in Gandhāra art of the Kuṣāṇa period. In Kuṣāṇa period, interesting motifs of *aśoka-dohada* are shown reported, in which a graceful young woman stands under an *aśoka* tree and bending low its branches with her left hand touches its stems with the left foot.

These studies reveal that the trees and creepers were executed in relief in early Indian sculptures to meet certain religious purposes. Trees were associated with gods and became aniconic symbols of different deities. But judged from the artistic point of view, one finds, that while our ancient artists could realistically render certain trees, they failed to bring on many occasions the naturalism in trees. Some trees have been shown as creepers, while others have been carved within a definite outline and thereby the natural movement of the trees was restricted. In many cases, abstraction is noticed particularly in the formation of leaves while in certain cases, each leaf has been taken with meticulous detail. In many cases, the trees became merely symbols. In the early Buddhist narrative art, by projecting two or three trees, the artist wanted to portray a jungle scene. A row of seven stylised trees at times represented the so-called seven *Manushi* Buddhas. Some trees have been worked out with adequate attention towards their proportion while in certain cases there appears hardly any proportion between trunk, branches and the leaves of the same trees. It appears that artists at this stage were more concerned with the narration, symbol or iconography and were less concerned about the composition, proportion and related aspects of artistic delineation. It is extremely difficult to identify the plants, trees, flowers and fruits in most of the cases. What makes identification baffling is the stylised treatment. However, *aśvattha*, mango, banyan and *śāla* trees are easily identified.

There are textual and archaeological evidences to indicate that sculptures were also made in wood. But most of the wooden sculptures could not bear the onslaught of time, wood being perishable material. For making images out of tree there are certain restrictions in religious texts. Perhaps the quality and durability of wood for making images were in their mind.

Trees are frequently noted on many ancient Indian coins also. In some pre-Mauryan punch-marked coins from Sugh, there are few tree symbols which include 'tree within railing'. Similarly, in many regions of the southern and western India, the tree within railing was a favourite motif on the ancient Indian coins.

The notion of tree worship never ceased to exist and is still being held good among the Indians. Trees appear in rituals in various forms as symbols for the divine. The trees and their meaning may be incorporated into rituals of curing, initiation, marriage and death. Trees used in any of these contents stand for the divine and represent the sacred beliefs being honoured through ritual. To avert the ill luck of a girl, her marriage with a tree is performed. The twig of a mango tree is used in all ritual ceremonies. The leaves of mango and *śiriṣa* trees are hung over the door of the birth chamber of a male child. In all socio-religious observances, the mango twig is put in the *jala-ghaṭa.* In Orissa also, the tree worship is still prevalent. A *tamāla* tree as an incarnation of Kṛṣṇa is worshipped in a temple of Puri district. "In Birbhoom (Bengal), once a year, the whole capital retires to a shrine in the jungle, and makes simple offerings to a ghost who dwells in a *bael* tree." The *jand* tree is worshipped in Punjab and Rajasthan. The same tree is worshipped in west Punjab by women for children. The Semari Bond tribe regards the silk cotton tree as sacred. The Santhals believe that human spirits live in a *bilva* tree. Married women adorn this tree for gaining favour from their husbands. At some places, women worship plantain plant on the 4th day of *Kārtika* for long life of their husbands. In Durgā-pūjā and *Lakṣmī-pūjā,* the plantain dressed as a woman is worshipped.

The *tulsi* plant, which is connected with Viṣṇu, is still grown in the courtyards of many Hindu homes and tended with great care. There are many similar evidences in different parts of India to establish the fact that tree worship is still a living faith in our country. The *bodhi* tree is still worshipped in India as was in the days of Aśoka.

The people of present century are extremely concerned about the merits and demerits of plantation, afforestation and deforestation. The trend of deforestation in the Indian subcontinent is, therefore, causing concern to the environmentalists. Conservation of these forests is necessary not only for development but for our survival too. It was with the sole object of the preservation of trees that *Vana-Mahotsava* was launched in 1950. A countrywide national environmental awareness campaign has been launched on a continuing basis, which seeks to create environmental awareness at the national as well as local levels by involving hundreds of grass-root level voluntary organisations working in remote parts of the country. Besides, there are many other government and private agencies engaged in conserving the soils, watersheds, rare plants and trees. To reduce pressure on forests, for fuel wood, townships in vicinity of forests have been identified for supply of cooking gas and kerosene, and special species are being introduced to provide best and cheaper wood for the livestock. Hence, not only ancient and medieval Indians but the present day Indians are also equally concerned about the usefulness of trees. The concept of *kalpavṛkṣa* (wish-fulfilling tree) and of *kāmadhenu* (wish-fulfilling cow) in Indian culture represents our values towards nature and life in general.

The intermingling of different stages is clearly visible in the worship and use of trees, plants and shrubs. First, we have the stage of animism where trees, plants, etc. are respected because of their aromatic nature, and also because of their natural growth which is apt to inspire awe and fear in primitive minds. In the second stage, the association of spirits with trees, flowers, leaves, etc. is marked. But in the third stage, spirits yielding place to deities, and the worship of these trees, plants, etc. imply, no doubt, worship of respective deities. Finally, most of these trees, plants, leaves, etc. are believed to contain magical properties and powers to scare away evils. The sacred trees may be found along with bushes, shrubs, rocks or even with a temple to make a shrine. Some trees are even taken as symbol of a sacred person because of particular qualities the tree possesses. The trees also served as a vehicle of communication with deities in three ways: through their use in shrines, as the meeting place on earth of a sacred being and mankind; through the relationship between sacred trees and priests, the religious mediators of the divine; and through the use of sacred drinks made from trees that allow a mystical contact with the sacred. Varuṇa obtains *soma,* or *amṛta*, the fruit of immortality, by squeezing the fruit of the celestial tree of life between two stones. The palmyra palm is a symbol of Śiva, yielding an intoxicating and powerful juice. The trees, plants, etc. are also connected with fertility and procreation cult. In course of time when man discovered the usefulness and utilities of trees, he made every effort to save these trees from natural calamities as well as from human vandalism. The introduction of the worship of trees perhaps was one of the important endeavours of mankind in this direction.

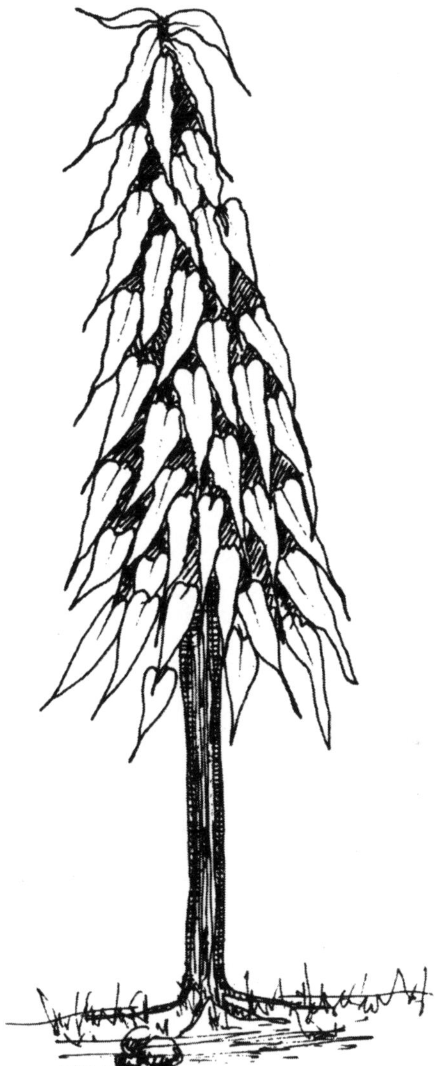

APPENDICES

APPENDIX I

NAMES OF SOME TREES AND PLANTS IN DIFFERENT LANGUAGES

English names	*Latin names*	*Hindi names*	*Sanskrit names*
1	2	3	4
Aśoka	*Saraca ssoca* (Roxb) De Wilde	Aśoka, Aśok	Same as in Hindi
Banyan	*Ficus benghalensis* Linn.	Vaṭa, Vad, Bargad, Ber	Nyagrodha, Vaṭa, Bahupada, Kalpavṛkṣa
Belliric Myrobalam	*Terminalia bellirica* Roxb	Bahira, Vibhitika	Same as in Hindi
Betel	*Pipal* betle Linn.	Paan	Nagavalli, Tāmbūla
Cane Sticks, Great reed, Spanish Cane	*Arundo donax* Linn.	Bari-nari	Nalaka
Child Live tree	Putranjiva roxburghii wall	Jayaputra, Jaiputa	Putranjiva, Jīvaka
Coconut Palm	*Cocos nucifera* Linn.	Nariel	Nārikel
Coral tree	*Erythrina variegata* Linn.	Pharad	Mandara, Pārijata
Cutch tree	*Acacia catechu* Willd	Katha	Khadira
Flame of the Forest, Parrot Tree, Judas Tree	*Butea monosperma,* (Lam), Kuntze syn.	Palāṣ, Dhāk, Teysu	Kiṁśuka, Plakṣa

English names	*Latin names*	*Hindi names*	*Sanskrit names*
1	2	3	4
Gingelly, Sesame	*Sesamum indicum* Linn.	Til	Tili, Tila
Hiptage	*Hiptage benghalensis* Kurz	Mādhavī latā	Same as in Hindi
Immortal fruit	Monstera deliciosa Liebm.	Amarphal	Same as in Hindi
Indian Fig tree	*Ficus religiosa* Linn.	Pipal, Bo tree, Bodhi tree	Aśvattha
Indian Gooseberry	Emblica officinalis	Dhatri, Dhatrica, Amalak, Amlaki, Amla	Same as in Hindi
Indian Jujube, Common Jujube	*Zizyphus mauritiana* Lam.	Ber	Vadari, Badari, Vadara, Kuvala, Madhuraphala
Kadamba	*Anthocephalus cadamba* Miq.	Kadam	Kadama
Krishnascu	*Ficus krishnae* C.D.C.	-	-
Lotus	*Nelumbo nucifera* Gaertn.	Padma, Kamala, Kumuda	Puṇḍarīka
Mango	*Mangifera indica* Linn.	Aaam, Chuta, Kakkola	Āmra
Mimosa	*Prosopis ceneraria* Druce	Jhand, Jand	Śāmī
Plantain, Banana	*Musa paradisiaca* Linn.	Kelā	Rambhā, Kadalī
Rain of Nectar	*Cocculus cordifolius*	Gaduchi, Galuchi, Amrita	Same as in Hindi
Red Silk Cotton Tree	*Bombax ceiba* Linn. Syn.	Simbal	Śalmalī
Sacred Basil	*Ocimum sanctum* Linn.	Tulsi	Tulsi

English names	*Latin names*	*Hindi names*	*Sanskrit names*
1	2	3	4
Screw Pine	*Pandanus odoratissimus* Linn. f.	Keura, Keora	Ketaki
Sour Creeper	*Sarcostemma acidum* Voigt	Somalata	Soma
Tamarind	*Tamarindus indica* Linn.	Imli, Amli	Tintrini
Tree of Sorrow, Night Jasmine	*Nyctanthes arbotristis* Linn.	Harshingar	Pārijāta
Utrasum Bead Tree	*Elacocarpus sphaericus* (Gaertn.) K. Schum	Rudrākṣa	Rudrākṣa
Wood Apple	*Aegle marmelos Gorrea* ex Roxb.	Bel, Bael	Bilva, Vilva
——	*Diospyros peregrina* (Gaertn.) Gurke	Kalatendu	Tinduku
——	*Euphorbia nerifolia* Linn.	Sehund	Snuhi, Manasā tree, Manasasij
——	*Ficus glomerata* Roxb.	Gular	Udumbara
——	*Shorea robusta* Gaestn. f.	Śāl, Shal	Śāla, Shal
——	*Terminalia arjuna* (Roxb) Wight & Arn.	Arjuna	Arjuna

APPENDIX II

BODHI TREES OF SEVEN DHYĀNĪ-BUDDHAS

Śākyamuni or Buddha	*Aśvattha*
Kaśyapa	*Nyagrodha*
Kanakamuni	*Udumbara*
Krakuchhanda	*Śirīṣa*
Vipaswi	*Aśoka*
Sikhi	*Puṅḍarīka*
Viśvabhū	*Śāla*

APPENDIX III

CAITYA–VṚKṢA OF TWENTY–FOUR TĪRTHĀṄKARAS

Tīrthāṅkara	*Śvetāmbara*	*Digambara*
Ṛsabhanātha	*Nyagrodha*	*Nyagrodha*
Ajitanātha	*Saptaparṇa*	*Saptaparṇa*
Sambhavanātha	Śāla	Sarala
Abhinandana	*Piyaka or Priyaka*	*Priyāla*
Sumatinātha	*Priyaṅgu*	*Priyaṅgu*
Padmaprabha	*Caturābha*	*Chatrā*
Supārśvanātha	*Śirīṣa*	*Śirīṣa*
Candraprabha	*Nāga*	*Nāga*
Puṣpadanta (Suvidhinātha)	*Mali*	*Akṣa*
Śitalanātha	*Plakṣa*	*Dhuli*
Śreyāmsanātha	*Tinduga*	*Palaṣa*
Vāsupūjya	*Pāṭala*	*Tenduva*
Vimalanātha	*Jambū*	*Pāṭala-Jambū*
Anantanātha	*Aśvattha*	*Aśvattha*
Dharmanātha	*Dadhiparṇa*	*Dadhiparṇa*
Śantinātha	*Nandi*	*Nandi*
Kunthūnātha	*Tilaka*	*Tilaka*
Aranātha	*Āmra*	*Āmra*
Mallinātha	*Aśoka*	*Aśoka*
Munisuvrata	*Champaka*	*Champaka*
Neminātha	*Bakula*	*Bakula*
Nenunātha	*Vetasa*	*Meṣaśṛṅga*
Pārśunātha	*Dhātaki*	*Dhava*
Mahāvīra	*Śāla*	*Śāla*

APPENDIX IV

TREES ASSOCIATED WITH VYANTARA GODS (JAIN)

Vyantaras	Śvetāmbara	Digambara
Piścācas	*Kadamba*	*Kadamba*
Bhūtas	*Śulasa*	*Śulasa*
Yakṣas	*Vaṭa*	*Vaṭa*
Rākṣasas	*Khaṭvāṅga*	*Badari*
Kinnaras	*Aśoka*	*Aśoka*
Kimpuruṣas	*Champaka*	*Champaka*
Mahoragas	*Nāga*	*Nāga*
Gandharvas	*Tumbaru*	*Tumbaru*

APPENDIX V

KALPAVṚKṢA/KALPA-DRUMA

Hindu	Buddhist	Jain
Banyan	Banyan	Pāṇanga
Jamvu		*Turiyanga*
Mandana		*Bhusaanāṅga*
Pārijāta		Vatthanga
Kadamba		Bhoyanga
		Ālayanga
		Diviyaṅga
		Bhāyaṇanga
		Mālaṅga
		Tenjanga

BIBLIOGRAPHY

Agrawala, V.S., "Kalpavṛkṣa: The Wish-fulfilling Tree", *Journal of the Indian Society of Oriental Art,* Vol. XI, 1943.

——, "The Terracottas of Ahichchhatra", *Ancient India*, vol. 4, 1947-48.

——, *Matsya Purāṇa: A Study,* Varanasi, 1963.

——, *Indian Art,* Varanasi, 1965.

——, *Ancient Indian Folk Cult,* Varanasi, 1970.

Allchin, B. and Allchin, R., *Birth of Indian Civilization, India and Pakistan before 500 BC,* Penguin Books, 1968.

Asher, F.M., *The Art of Eastern India* (300-800 AD), Minnesota, 1980.

Banerjea, J.N., *Development of Hindu Iconography,* Calcutta, 1941.

Banerjee, B.N., *Hindu Culture, Custom and Ceremony,* Delhi, 1979.

Barrett, D., *Sculptures from Amaravati in the British Museum,* London, 1954.

Barua, B.M., *Bharhut,* Books I-III, Patna, 1979.

Beal, S., *The Chinese Accounts of India,* 4 Vols., Calcutta, 1980.

Bhatt, G.P., (Ed.), *Ancient Indian Tradition and Mythology,* Vol. 39, *Padma Purāṇa*, Pt. I, Delhi, 1988, Vol. 40, Pt. II, 1989.

Bhattacharya, P.K., *Iconography of Sculptures,* Darjeeling, 1983.

Bhattacharya, T., *Canons of Indian Art or A Study of Vastuvidya,* Calcutta, 1963.

Bhushan, V., *Cultural History of North India (From 150* BC. *to* AD *350),* Delhi, 1988.

Biswas, K., *Common Medicinal Plants of Darjeeling and Sikkim,* Calcutta, 1956.

Biswas, T.K., "Culakoka Devatā and the Related Issue of Fertility Cult," *Bhāratī,* No. 3, New Series, 1985.

Biswas, T.K. and P.K. Debnath, "Aśoka (*Saraca Indica* Linn): A Cultural and Scientific Evaluation," *Indian Journal of History of Science,* Vol. 7, No. 2, 1972.

——, "Aśvattha (*Ficus Religiosa* Linn): A Cultural and Medicinal Observation", *Vishveshvaranand Indological Journal,* Vol. XII, Nos. I & II, 1974.

Blatter, E. and W.S. Millard, *Some Beautiful Indian Trees,* Bombay, 1937.

Bloomfield, M., "The Dohada", *Journal of American Oriental Society,* Vol. 40.

Chakraberti, K., *Society, Religion and Art of the Kushana India,* Calcutta, New Delhi, 1981.

Chakravarti, M., *The Concept of Rudra Śiva through the Ages,* Delhi, 1986.

Chakravarty, K.K., *The Art of India: Khajuraho,* New Delhi, 1985.

Chandra, A.N., T*he Ṛgvedic Culture and the Indus Civilization,* Calcutta, 1980.

Chandra, P., *The Sculptures of India (300* BC-*1300* AD*),* Washington, 1985.

Chawla, J., *The Ṛgvedic Deities and their Iconic Forms,* Delhi, 1990.

Chowdhury, K.A. and S.S. Ghosh, "Plant Remains from Harappa," *Ancient India,* Vol. 7, 1946.

Colebrooke, H.T., *Essays on Religion and Philosophy*, 1976.

Coomaraswamy, A.K., "Yakṣas", *Smithsonian Miscellaneous Collection,* Vol. 10, No. 6, 1928.

——, "The Tree of Jesse and Indian Parallels or Sources", *The Art Bulletin,* Vol. XI, No. 2, 1929.

——, "The Inverted Tree", *Quarterly Journal of the Mythical Society,* Vol. XXIX, 1938.

——, *History of Indian and Indonesian Art,* New Delhi, 1972.

——, *Elements of Buddhist Iconography,* New Delhi, 1972.

Cowell, E.B., *The Jataka* (Translated from Pali), 6 Vols., (reprinted), New Delhi, 1990.

Crowe, Y., "Some Aspects of the Tree Motif in Medieval Indian Architecture", *Dimensions of Indian Art* (Pupul Jayakar Felicitation Volume), Ed. by L. Chandra and J. Jain, Delhi, 1986.

Cunningham, A., *The Stupa of Bharhut,* 1879.

Czuma, S.J., *Kuṣāṇa Sculpture: Images from Early India,* The Cleveland Museum of Art, 1985.

Dalmia, Y., *The Painted World of the Warlis*, New Delhi, 1988.

Dange, S.A., *Encyclopaedia of Purāṇic Beliefs and Practices,* Vol. I (1986), Vols. II & III (1987), Vol. IV (1989), New Delhi.

Das, A.C., *Ṛgvedic India,* Calcutta, 1927, 2nd Ed. (Revised).

Das, S.R., "Folk Religious Rites: A Study in Origins", *Journal of the Department of Letters*, New Series, Vol. II, Part II, Calcutta, 1958.

Dasgupta, K.K., *Wood Carvings of Eastern India,* Calcutta, 1990.

Desai, D., *Erotic Sculptures of India*, New Delhi, 1975.

Desai, K.S., *Iconography of Viṣṇu (in Northern India, up to the Mediaeval Period)*, New Delhi, 1973.

Desai, N.Y., *Ancient Indian Society, Religion and Mythology as Depicted in the Mārkaṇdeya Purāṇa*, Baroda, 1968.

Deshmukh, P.R., *Indus Civilization, Ṛgveda and Hindu Culture,* Nagpur, 1982.

Dhavalikar, M.K., *Ajanta: A Cultural Study,* Poona, 1973.

Dikshit, K.N., *Prehistoric Civilization of the Indus Valley,* Madras, 1939.

Dikshitar, V.R.R., (Ed.) *Purāṇa Index*, 2 Vols., Madras, 1951.

Donaldson, T.E., *Hindu Temple Art of Orissa,* Vols. I & II (1986); Vol. III (1987), Leiden.

Dubois, J.A., *Hindu Manners, Customs and Ceremonies,* Oxford, 1906.
Dutt, M.N., *Garuda Purāṇa,* Calcutta, 1908.
——, *Agni Purāṇa,* Vol. II, Varanasi, 1967.
Dyke, H.V., *The first Christmas tree*, New York, 1956.
Eliade, Mircea (Ed.), Encyclopaedia of Religions, Vols. 1-16, New York, London, 1987.
Elwin, V., *Tribal Myths of Orissa,* Bombay, 1954.
——, *Encyclopaedia of Religion.*
Fergusson, J., *Tree and Serpent Worship* (reprint), Varanasi, 1971.
Finegan, J., *The Archaeology of World Religions,* London, 1952.
Fischer, E. and J. Jain, *Art and Rituals: 2500 Years of Jainism in India*, New Delhi, 1977.
Frazer, J., *The Golden Bough* (2 vols.), London, 1957.
Ganguli, K.M., *The Mahābhārata,* Vols. I to XII, Calcutta, Revised New Edition, New Delhi, 1976 (English Translation).
Ganguli, M., *Naga Art*, New Delhi, 1993.
Ghosh, A. (Ed.), *Jaina Art and Architecture,* Vol. I, 1974; Vols. II and III, 1975, New Delhi.
——, (Ed.), *Remains of Bharhut Stupa in Indian Museum,* Part I, Calcutta, 1978.
——, (Ed.), *An Encyclopaedia of Indian Archaeology,* New Delhi, 1989.
Goswami, P., *Festivals of Assam*, Guwahati, 1995.
Goyal, S.R., *A Religious History of Ancient India,* Meerut, 1984.
Griswold, H.D., *The Religion of the Rigveda,* London, Edinburg, Glasgow, New York, Toronto, Melbourne, Cape Town, Bombay, 1923.
Gupta, S.M., *Plant Myths and Traditions in India,* New Delhi, 1991, 2nd Ed. (Revised).
——, *Plants in Indian Temple Art,* New Delhi, 1996.
Gupta, S.P., *The Roots of Indian Art,* New Delhi, 1980.
Handa, D., *Studies in Indian Coins and Seals,* Delhi, 1985.
——, *(Ed.) Numismatic Studies,* Vol. I, New Delhi, 1991.
Harle, J.C., *Art and Architecture in Indian Sub-Continent,* London, 1986.
Havell, E.B., *The Art Heritage of India,* Bombay, 1964.
Hazra, R.C., *Studies in the Purāṇic Records on Hindu Rites and Customs,* Dacca, 1940.
——, *Studies in the Upapurāṇas,* 2 Vols., Calcutta, 1958.
Hopkins, E.W., *Epic Mythology,* Strassburg, 1915.
Hora, B. (Ed.), *The Oxford Encyclopaedia of Trees of the World*, 1981.
Huntington, S.L., *The Art of Ancient India—Buddhist, Hindu, Jain,* Tokyo, 1985.
Hutchinson, W. (Ed.), *Customs of the World, A Popular Account of the Manners, Rites and Ceremonies of Men and Women in all Countries,* 2 vols., 1984.
Jain, J. and E. Fischer, *Jaina Iconography*, Parts I & II, Leiden, 1978.
James, E.O., *Tree of Life—An Archaeological Study,* Brill, 1966.

Jayakar, P., *Earthen Drum: An Introduction to the Ritual Arts of Rural India,* New Delhi, 1980.

Kala, S.C., *Sculptures in Allahabad Municipal Museum,* Allahabad, 1946.

Keith, A.B., *Vedic Index of Names and Subjects,* Vols. I & II, Delhi, 1958.

Kramrisch, S., "Śarīravṛkṣa, The Body Tree," *Journal of the Indian Society of Oriental Art,* Vol. IV, Part I, 1971-72.

——, *Indian Sculpture,* Delhi, 1981.

Lall, R.M., *Among the Hindus (A Study of Hindu Festivals),* Cawnpore (U.P.), 1933.

Macdonell, A.A., *Vedic Mythology,* Varanasi, Delhi, 1971.

Macdonell, A.A. and A.B. Keith, *Vedic Index of Names and Subjects,* Vols. I & II, 1958.

Mackay, E.J.H., *Further Excavations at Mohenjo-daro,* Vols. I & II, New Delhi, 1937-38.

Mackenzie, D., *Indian Myth and Legend,* London, 1971.

Maity, P.K., "Folk Cults of West Bengal", *Studies in Orientology* (Essays in Memory of Prof. A.L. Basham), Agra, 1988.

Majumdar, G.P., *Upavana-Vinoda* (A Sanskrit Treatise of Arbori-Horticulture), Calcutta, 1935.

Majumdar, R.C., (Ed.), *History of Bengal,* I, Dacca, 1942.

——, (Ed.), *The Vedic Age,* Vol. I, London, 1957, 3rd Ed.

Malla, B.L., Tree Worship in Ancient India (An ICHR post-doctoral project), 1993.

——, "Trees in Indian Thought and Art", *Vihangama*, Vol. II, No. 3, 1994.

——, "Notion of Tree worship in pre-Vedic Period", *Facets of Indian Civilization* (B.B. Lal Felicitation Volume), edited by J.P. Joshi, New Delhi, 1997.

Mani, V., *Purāṇic Encyclopaedia,* Delhi, Patna, Varanasi, 1975.

Marshall, Sir J.H., *Mohenjo-daro and the Indus Civilization,* London, 1931.

——, *The Monuments of Sanchi,* Vols. 1 & 2, Delhi, 1982, Reprinted.

Mathur, A. (Ed.), *India,* Specially published for the Festival of India in Japan, New Delhi, 1988.

Mathur, R.C., *Systematic Botany,* Allahabad, 1965.

Maury, C., *Folk Origins of Indian Art,* Calcutta, 1969.

Mehta, R.L., *Pre-Buddhist India* (*A Study of Ancient India based on the Jataka stories*), Bombay, 1939.

Miller, J., *The Vision of Cosmic Order in the Vedas*, London, 1985.

Mitra, D., *Buddhist Monuments,* Calcutta, 1971.

Mode, H. and S. Chandra, *Indian Folk Art,* Bombay, 1985.

Mookerji, R.K., *Hindu Civilization,* Bombay, 1977.

Moore, A.C., *Iconography of Religions: An Introduction,* London, 1977.

Morgan, K. (Ed.), *The Religion of the Hindus,* New Delhi, 1987 (Reprinted).

Nath, R., *The Art of Khajuraho,* New Delhi, 1980.

Nautiyal, K.P., *Proto-Historic India*, Delhi, 1989.

Naumayer, E., *Pre-historic Indian Rock Paintings,* New Delhi, 1983.

Nigam, M.L., *Sculptural Art of Andhra,* Delhi, 1980.

Nivedita, S. and A.K. Coomaraswamy, *Myths of the Hindus and Buddhists,* London, 1914.

Pandey, S.K., *Indian Rock Art*, New Delhi, 1993.

Patyal, H.C., "Tree Significance of the Aegle-Mardelos (Bilva) in the Veda", *Vishveshvaranand Indological Journal,* Vol. XII, Nos. I & II, 1974.

Phallic Tree Worship Cults, Arborum, Varanasi, 1971.

Pisharoti, K.R., "Dohada or the Woman and Tree Motifs etc.", *Journal of Indian Society of Oriental Art,* Vol. III, No. 2, 1935.

Prem, Sri Krishna, *The yoga of the Kathopanishad*, Ahmedabad, 1982.

Ragozin, Z.A., *Vedic India,* Delhi, 1961.

Ramakrishnan, P.S. and K.G. Saxena and U.M. Chandrashekara (Ed.), *Conserving the Sacred for Biodiversty Management*, New Delhi, 1998.

Randhawa, M.S., *Beautiful Trees and Gardens,* New Delhi, 1961.

——, *The Cult of Trees and Tree Worship in Buddhist Hindu Sculpture,* New Delhi, 1958.

——, *Evolution of Life,* Chandigarh, 1981.

Ranganathananda, Swami, *The Message of Upaniṣads,* Bombay, 1971 (2nd Ed.).

Rao, Shrimant B.S., *Ajanta: A Handbook of Ajanta Caves Descriptive of the Paintings and Sculptures Therein,* Bombay, 1932.

Rao, T.A. Gopinath, *Elements of Hindu Iconography,* Vols. I & II, Madras, 1914, Reprinted in New York (1968).

Ray, N.R., *Maurya and Post-Maurya Art,* New Delhi, 1975.

Roth, G., "The Woman and Tree Motif", *Journal of the Asiatic Society, Letters and Sciences*, Vol. XXIII, No. 1, 1957.

Roy, U.N., *Śālabhañjikā in Art, Philosophy and Literature,* Allahabad, 1979.

——, "Dohada—A Folk Custom of Ancient India", *History and Culture* (Dr. B.P. Sinha Felicitation Volume, Ed. by Bhagwant Sahai), Delhi, 1987.

Sahai, B., *Iconography of Minor Hindu and Buddhist Deities,* New Delhi, 1975.

Saletore, R., *Encyclopaedia of Indian Culture,* Vol. I (1981); Vol. II (1982); Vol. III (1983); Vol. IV (1984), New Delhi.

Sankalia, H.D., *Prehistory and Protohistory in India and Pakistan,* Bombay, 1963.

——, *Prehistory of India,* New Delhi, 1977.

——, *Prehistoric Art in India,* New Delhi, Bombay, Calcutta, Kanpur, 1978.

Sarasvati, Sri Swamy Hariharanand, "The World Tree," *Journal of the Indian Society of Oriental Art,* Vol. XI, 1943.

Saraswati, B.N. (Ed.), *Cultural Dimension of Ecology*, IGNCA, New Delhi, 1998.

Saraswati, S.K., *Survey of Indian Sculpture,* New Delhi, 1956, 2nd Revised Ed.

Sarkar, H. and S.P. Nainar, *Amaravati,* New Delhi, 1980.

Sastri, K.N., *New Light on the Indus Civilization,* Vol. I, Delhi, 1957.

Sanadeera, K.G., *Buddhist Symbolism of Wish-fulfilment,* Delhi, 1992.

Sengupta, S. (Ed.), *Tree Symbol Worship in India,* Calcutta, 1965.

——, *Sacred Trees: Across Cultures and Nations*, Calcutta, 1980.

Shah, U.P., *Jaina Rupa Mandana,* New Delhi, 1987.

Shah, U.P. and M.A. Dhaky, (Eds.), *Aspects of Jaina Art and Architecture,* Ahmedabad, 1975.

Shamasatry, R., *The Arthasastra of Kautilya,* Mysore, 1956 (Fifth Ed.).

Sharma, B.N., *Iconography of Revanta,* New Delhi, 1975.

Sharma, J.P., *Jaina Yakshas,* Meerut, 1989.

Sharma, P.V. (Ed.), *Sodhal-Nighantu: Namasangraha and Gunasangraha of Vaidhyacarya Sodhala,* Baroda, 1978.

Shrava, S., *A Comprehensive History of Vedic Literature (Brāhmaṇa and Āraṇyaka Works)*, New Delhi, 1977.

Shukla, K.P., "Symbolic Representation of Nature in Ancient Indian Wedding", *History and Art* (Prof. K.D. Bajpai Felicitation Volume, Ed. by K. Deva, L. Gopal and B. Singh), New Delhi, 1989.

Singh, O.P., *Religion and Iconography of Early Indian Coins*, Varanasi, 1978.

Sinha, B.C., *Tree Worship in Ancient India*, New Delhi, 1979.

——, *Hinduism and Symbol Worship*, Delhi, 1983.

Sircar, D.C. (Ed.), *Religious Life in Ancient India*, Calcutta, 1972.

Sivaramamurti, C., *Sculpture Inspired by Kalidasa*, Mysore, 1942.

——, "Amaravati Sculptures in the Madras Government Museum", *Bulletin of the Madras Government Museum,* New Series, Vol. IV, 1942.

——, *Approach to Nature in Indian Art and Thought*, New Delhi, 1980.

Smith, V.A., *The Jaina Stupa and Other Antiquities of Mathura*, Allahabad, 1901.

—, *History of Fine Art in India and Ceylon,* Bombay, 1969 (Reprinted).

Srinivasa, M.N., *Religion and Society among the Coorgs of South India*, London, 1952.

Srinivasan, D.M. (Ed.), *Mathura: The Cultural Heritage*, New Delhi, 1989.

Srivastava, A.L., *Life in Sanchi Sculpture,* New Delhi, 1983.

Srivastava, M.C.P., *Mother Goddess in Indian Art, Archaeology and Literature*, Delhi, 1979.

Sudhi, P., *Symbols of Art, Religion and Philosophy*, New Delhi, 1988.

Thaplyal, K.K., *Studies in Ancient Indian Seals*, Lucknow, 1972.

Tod, J., *Annals and Antiquities of Rajasthan*, Delhi, 1971 (Reprinted).

Trivedi, V.R., *The Heritage of Kashmir*, New Delhi, 1996.

Vats, M.S., *Excavations at Harappa*, 2 Vols., 1975.

Vogel, J. Ph., *Catalogue of the Archaeological Museum at Mathura*, Allahabad, 1910.

——, "The Woman and Tree or Śālabhañjikā in Indian Literature and Art", *Acta Orientalia*, Vol. VII, 1929.

Wakankar, V.S. and Robert R.R., Brooks, *Stone Age Painting in India*, Bombay, 1976.

Ward, Rew W., *The Hindoos* (History, Literature and Religion), New Delhi, 1981 (Reprinted).

Warner, K. (Ed.), *Symbols in Art and Religion*, Delhi, 1991.

Wheeler, R.E.M., *Civilization of Indus Valley and Beyond*, London, 1966.

Wilkins, W.J., *Hindu Mythology*, Calcutta, Allahabad, Bombay, Delhi, 1975 (2nd Ed.).

Williams, M., *A Sanskrit English Dictionary*, Oxford, 1951 (New Print).

——, *Religious Thought and Life in India*, Calcutta, 1978 (Reprinted).

Wilson, H.H., *Viṣṇu Purāṇa*, Calcutta, 1961.

——, *Ṛg-Veda-Saṁhitā: A Collection of Ancient Hindu Hymns*, Vol. I, Poona, 1925.

——, *Analysis of the Purāṇas,* Delhi, 1979.

Witney, W.W., (Ed.), *Atharvaveda Saṁhitā*, Vols. I & II, Delhi, Varanasi, Patna, 1984.

Zimmer, H. (Tr.), "Tree, Huts and Temples", *Journal of the Indian Society of Oriental Art*, Vol. 5, 1937.

——, *Myths and Symbols in Indian Art and Civilization,* New York, 1946.

——, *Hindu Medicine*, Baltimore, 1948.

——, *The Art of Indian Asia*, New York, 1955.

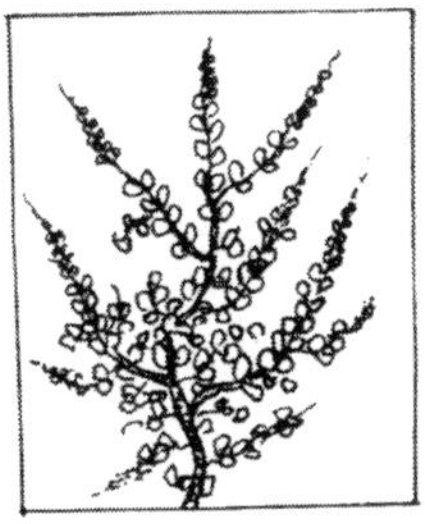

INDEX

Abhijñānaśākuntalam, 104
Abhilaṣitārthacintāmaṇi, 32
Adamgarh, 13
Aditi, 62
Ādityas, 27
Agni, 43
Agni Purāṇa, 39, 46n, 47n, 78, 79, 81, 84, 85, 91n
Agrawala, V.S., 9n, 46n, 47n, 63, 87n, 89n, 190n-111n
Aitareya Brāhmaṇa, 33, 68
Akṣayavaṭa, 33
    vṛkṣa, 33
Alābu, 80
Āmalaka (Dhatrica) tree, 39
Amarakośa, 83
Ambikā, 40
Āmrātakṣa, 80
Amriteśvara temple, 101
Ancient Egypt, 6
    Egyptians, 6
Ancient Mexicans, 8n
Apple, 57
Apricot, 57
Āraṇyāni, 7
Aśoka (tree), 8, 28, 29, 35, 42, 44, 66, 69, 77, 78, 84, 96, 100, 101, 103, 109
Aśokaghṛta, 85
Aśoka pallava, 44
Aśvagandhā, 84
Aśvattha, 4, 6, 28, 29, 36, 37, 52, 53, 59, 68, 69, 76, 79, 95, 96, 98
Aśvattha pata-vrata, 70
Atharvaveda, 7, 26, 27, 40, 43, 46n, 68, 69, 75
Atharvaveda-Pariśiṣṭa, 7
Atharvaveda Saṁhitā, 83
Avadāna Śataka, 66
Avalokiteśvara, 44
Axis Mundi, 3, 5, 7

Baba Amte, 75
Babul tree, 87
Babylonians, 4, 6
Badari tree, 35
Badrinath, 48n
Baine palm, 59
Bāla-Gaṇapati, image of, 32
Baltic religious traditions, 6
Bamboo, 58, 73
    planting of, 53
Banana tree, 56, 58
Banerjea, J.N., 109n, 111n
Banyan (tree), 8, 25, 28, 33, 35, 57, 58, 73, 77, 79, 86, 95, 100, 105, 107
Barua, B.M., 109n
Bela, 8, 53
Betel-nut, 52, 54, 58, 71, 80
Bhaddasala Jātaka, 42
Bhagavadgītā, 4, 27, 45n
Bhāgavata Purāṇa, 34-36, 39, 105, 110n
Bhattacharyya, T., 110n
Bhavabhūti, 33
Bhāvaprakāśa Nighaṇṭu, 85
Bhaviṣya Purāṇa, 44

Bhil goddess, 64
Bible, 29
    Centres, 5
Bilva (tree), 25, 29-32, 52, 53,. 71, 77, 79, 85, 101
Bilvopaniṣad, 30
Biswas, T.K., 45n, 48n, 67, 68, 89n, 90n, 92n
Black kisnaku tree, 4
Bloomfield, M., 66, 89n
Bodhgaya, 29
Bodhisattva, 36, 38, 42, 67
Bodhisattva Padmapāṇi, 43
Bodhi-tree, 29, 51, 95-98, 109
    of Śākyamuni, 28
Brahmā, 27, 33, 31, 35, 37, 40, 85
Brahmā-taru, 16, 27, 51, 68, 69
Brāhmaṇas, 26
Brahmāṇḍa, 37
Brahmāṇi, 34, 38
Brahmavaivarta Purāṇa, 78
Bṛhaddharma Purāṇa, 31, 39
Bṛhatsaṁhitā, 79, 80, 91n
Buddha, 35, 42, 77, 90n, 95, 96, 98, 99, 105
Buddhism, 29
Buddhist art, 43
    belief, 52
    Jātaka stories, 36, 38
    period, 95
    religion, 28, 44
    texts, 28
    world, 28
Buddhists, 38, 40, 44, 51, 57, 68, 95

Campaka, 35
Caraka, 80
    festival, 58
    Saṁhitā, 85
Celestial tree, 5, 6
Chakravarti, M., 45n
Chalcolithic period, 13
Child Live Tree (*Jivaka*), 40
Chillies, 83
Chinese *Chienmu* tree, 3
Chinese mythology, 4
Chipko movement, 75
Christ, 84
Christian era, 62
Christians, 29
Christianty, 25
Coconut, 38, 39
Colebrook, H.T., 26, 45n
Coomaraswamy, A.K., 32, 46n, 65, 96, 109n
Coorgs, 59
    of South India, 59
Cosmic deity, 43
    space, 6
    tree, 3-6
Cowell, E.B., 47n, 88n
Cunningham, A., 28, 45n

Dāḍima, 80
Dalmīa, Y., 88n, 89n
Dange, S.A., 45n-47n, 91n, 92n
Das, A.C., 44n
Das, S.R., 87n, 88n, 90n
Dasāvatāra temple, 100
Dasgupta, K.K., 110n
Dastur, J.F., 83
Date palm, 19, 20
    of the mesopotamians, 3
Debnath, P.K., 45n, 48n, 68, 90n, 92n
Deodar (tree of gods), 56, 108
Desai, D., 89n, 90n
Desai, K.S., 110n
Desai, N.Y., 47n, 63
Dhanvantary Nighaṇṭu, 85
Dhere, R.C., 88n
Digha Nikāya, 28, 35
Dikshit, K.N., 14, 21n
Dikshitar, V.V.R., 48n
Divyāvadāna, 28
Dohada-Śālabhañjikā, 52
Drākṣā, 79

Dravyābhidhāna, 83
Dubois, J.A., 45n
Durgā, 32, 34, 51
Durgā-Pūjā, 32, 71
Dūrvā, 56, 84
Dutt, M.N., 45n, 47n, 91n, 92n

Edicts of Aśoka, 28
Egyptions, 5
Ekambareshwar temple, 99
Eliade, Mircea, 8n, 9n
Elwin, V., 27, 45n
Emperor Aśoka, 77
Eternal Cosmic tree, 4

Fig tree, 27-29, 33, 79, 84
    in India, 3
Finegan, J., 45n

Gaduchi plant, 86
Gandhāra art, 69
Gaṇeśa, 101
Gaṅgā, 42
Ganguli, K.M., 45n-47n
Garuḍa Purāṇa, 31, 35, 38, 45n, 84, 85
Gaurī temple, 72
Gautama Buddha, 28
Genealogical tree, 5
Ghosh, A., 20n, 110n
Gītā, 33
Gobhila's *Gṛhya Sūtra*, 27, 80
Gogal dhup, 56
Golden Temple Complex, 42
Gopinath Rao, 39
Goswami, 53
Goyal, S.R., 45n
Grisworld, H.D., 9n
Gupta, S.M., 45n-47n, 90n, 92n, 110n, 111n

Hajong Tribals, 73
Handa, D., 111n
Harappa, 13, 19, 63
Harappans, 19
Harda, 8
Haripriyā, 42
Harivaṁśa Purāṇa, 110n
Hazara, H.C., 47n
Hebraic teachings, 6
Hewitt, Mariamma, 21n
Himalayan Cedar, 56
    region, 75
Hindu iconography, 38
    mythology, 6, 30, 37
Hindus, 26, 37, 40, 43, 57, 78
    of Bengal, 59
Hiuen Tsang, 28, 29
Hoppins, E.W., 48n

Ind parab, 54
    worship, 53
Indian flora, 75
Indian mimosa tree, 57
Indra, 42, 99, 101, 102, 104
Indus Civilization, 52
    religion, 21n
    valley, 13, 14, 16, 18, 19, 61
Indus valley civilization, 95
Indus valley seal, 19, 63, 89n
Islam, 25
Islamic traditions, 6
Īśvara temple, 102

Jaiminīya Brāhmaṇa, 75
Jain mythology, 35, 42
Jainism, 29, 37, 43
Jains, 29, 38, 49, 51
jala ghaṭa, 71
Jambu, 36, 99
Jambuka, 80
Jambukeshwar temple, 99
Japanese stories, 6
Jātaka stories, 52
Jayakar, P., 14, 21n
Jethani temple, 100
Jewish tradition, 6

Jīvana-vṛkṣa, 51
Jñāna-vṛkṣa, 51
Jujube tree, 42

Kacharis, 58
Kadali, 80
Kadamba tree, 35-37, 47, 78, 102
Kadamba-vana-vāsinī, 37
Kailāsh, 42
Kalam, 53
Kālī, 38
Kālidāsa, 67
Kālikā Purāṇa, 68
Kalmī, 52
Kalpalatā, 68, 95
Kalpavṛkṣa, 6, 13, 34, 58, 68, 83, 95, 101, 104-105
Kāmadhenu, 83
Kapiṣthala Kāṭha Saṁhitā, 76
Karabilva, 80
Karam parab, 55
Karkati, 80
Kārttikeya, 32, 66
Kashmiri Pandits, 56
Kathopaniṣad, 4
Kaumudīmahotsava, 72, 73
Kauṭilya's *Arthaśāstra*, 81
Keith, A.B., 46n, 47n
Ketaki, 79
Kevala-vṛkṣa, 51
of Tīrthāṅkara Ṛṣabhanātha, 35

Khadira, 25, 36
Kharjjura, 80
Kharwai, 13
Khasiyas of eastern India, 59
Khaṭvāṅga, 35
Kikar (acacia), 19, 20, 57
Kṛṣṇa, 34, 36, 38, 102, 105, 110n
Kumārī, 34
Kūrma Purāṇa, 84
Kuṣāṇa period, 69
Kūṣmāṇḍa, 80

Lakṣmī, 27, 32, 35, 39, 41, 42, 71, 105, 106
Lakṣmīnarasimha temple, 102
Lalitā, 37, 40
Leaf of nyagrodha, 34
Liṅga Purāṇa, 58
Liṅgarāja temple, 72
Lothal, 19
Lotus, 25, 43

Macdonell, A.A., 44n, 46n-48n
Mackay, E.J.M., 14, 15, 21n
Madanamahotsava, 72, 73
Mādhavī latā, 39
Mahābhārata, 27, 34, 36, 42, 43, 68, 76, 84, 104, 105
lore, 56
Mahāvana, 8
Mahāvīra, 43
Maitrāyaṇī Saṁhitā, 29, 76
Maity, P.K., 46n
Majumdar, G.P., 90n, 91n
Majumdar, R.C., 1, 10n
Manasā tree, 86
Mandāra, 34
Mango tree, 36, 40, 42, 52, 57, 59, 66, 71, 78, 79, 96, 99, 101, 102
Mani, V., 91n
Mān-kachu plant, 52
Manu, *77, 82*
Mārkaṇḍeya Purāṇa, 39, 47n, 52
Marriage tree, 72
Marshall, John, 13, 15, 20n, 21n, 69, 88n
Mathur, R.C., 48n
Mātṛkās, 102
Matsya Purāṇa, 34, 78, 79, 81, 91n, 105, 110n
Mauryas, 20, 95
Maya Civilization, 8n
Māyādevī, 67, 68
Maya world, 5
Meghadūta, 107
Mesopotamia, 20n

Miller, J., 44n
Minoan Crete, 21n
Mohenjo-daro, 13, 18
 pottery, 20
 seals, 16, 19
Mother Earth, 72
Muchalinda, 35
Mughal period, 109
Mūla-Prakriti, 5
Murray, M., 62

Nandā Devi, 41, 56
Nārikel, 79
Naṭarāja temple, 99
Nath sect (Kanpath yogis), 58
Navapatrikās, 44, 51
Neem, 14, 18, 20, 21n, 25, 35, 52, 57, 58
Neumayer, E., 20n
Nimba, 78
Niṣpanna yogāvalī, 44
Nyagrodha, 96, 100, 101, 107
 leaf of, 34

Oak, 55
 of the Celts and the Gauls, 3
 of Zeus, 3
Old world, 4
Oran tribe of Bengal, 72
Oṣadhi or *virudha* 'plants', 7

Paddy, 58
Padma Purāṇa, 27, 37, 38, 41, 45n, 78
Padmapāṇi Avalokiteśvara, 98
Painnyā, 56
Pālaghaṭa, 62-64
Palāṣa, 25, 27, 42
Palm tree, 109
Pāñcacūda, 63
Pāṇḍav nṛtya, 56
Parabrahman, 5
Pārijāta, 34, 86
Pārvatī, 27, 37, 39-41, 44, 78, 79
Pāśupata cult, 89n
Patali, 95, 96
Patyal, H.C., 9n, 91n, 92n
Pavamana, 25
Peech, 57
Pipal, 8, 13, 15, 16, 18-21n, 25, 27, 53, 69, 79,95, 109
Pipal deity, 16
pipala, imperishable, 33
Pippalāda, 27
Pisharoti, K.R., 90n
Plakṣa-devi, 38
 tree, 25, 37, 38, 79, 86
Plantain (*kadali*), 41, 52, 71
Pomegranate, 57, 78
Portugese, 83
Post-vedic litrature, 20
Prajāpati, 25, 30, 40
Prāṇa (breath), 59
Pre-Buddhist literature, 68
Pre-Vedic age, 18
Pre-Vedic India, 13
 people, 20
Puṇḍarīka, 96
Punnage, 78
Pūrṇaghaṭa, 64
Rabhas of Dudhnai, 58
 of Goalpara, 58
Raghuvaṁśa, 67, 105
Ragozin, A.A., 45n
Rāma, 31, 44
Rāmāyaṇa, 31, 33, 42, 77, 81, 83, 104
Randhāwa, M.S., 91n
Rao, T.A. Gopinath, 45n, 46n, 47n
Ṛgveda, 3, 7, 25-27, 30, 35, 72, 77, 83
River worship, 38
Rogī taru, 51
Roth, G., 66, 89n, 90n
Rudra, 27, 37, 43

Sahai, B., 46n
Śaiva, 30
Śaivites, 41

Śākambharī aspect, 61
Śākta cult, 30
Śakti, 21n
Śākyamuni, 28
Śāla (tree), 42, 43, 66, 72, 90n
Śālabhañjikā, 68
Saletore, R.N., 9n, 47n
Salishan Indians of North America, 5
Śalmali 37, 55
Samabhinat, 75
Samarāṅgeṇa Sūtradhāra, 106
Samavāyaṅga Sūtra, 29
Śamī, 20, 25, 76, 43, 78
Sānchi stūpa, 65
Sankalia, H.D., 19, 21n
Śānkhyāyana Gṛhyasūtra, 77
Santhals, 53, 55
Saora tribe of Orissa, 58, 63
Śārangadhara Sāṁhitā, 85
Saraswati, B.N., 9n
Sastri, K.N., 14-16, 20n, 21n
Saules koks, 6
Scandinavian creation story, 4
Sengupta, S., 44n, 46n, 47n, 90n, 110n
Sesame, 79, 81
Shah, U.P., 45n, 47n, 110n
Shamasatry, R., 91n
Shrava, S., 90n
Siberian birch, 3
Siddha Cakra, 43
Silk Cotton (tree), 37
Śilparatna, 32
Śilpaśāstras, 80
Sinha, B.C., 44n, 45n, 91n, 92n, 111n
Sīriṣa, 71, 95-97
Sītā, 44, 77
Śītalā Mātā, 57
Śiva, 8, 27, 30, 31, 34, 36-44, 47n, 51, 52, 56, 61, 66, 79, 83, 88, 100
Śiva-liṅga, 31, 101
Śiva Purāṇa, 27
Sivaramamurti, C., 87n, 110n
Śivarātri festival, 56
Skanda Purāṇa, 27, 34, 36, 39, 86
Snuhi tree, 39
Soma plant, 33
  Soma or amṛta, 5, 25, 75, 76
Śrī, 65, 66
Sri Krishna, Prem, 9n
Śrī Lakṣmī, 64, 65
Śrī Lankā, 29
Śrīphala tree, 30, 32
Śrī Sūkta, 65
Śrītatvanidhi, 32
Śrīvana, 8
Śrī-vṛkṣa, 31, 95
Stella Kramrisch, 62, 88n
Śukranīti, 80
Śulasa, 35
Sumerian legend, 18
Sumerians, 16
  of Eridu, 5
Sun (*Sūrya*), 2, 7, 29, 51, 72, 106
Śunga period, 63, 69
Suparṇa, 75
Susni, 52
Suśurta, Saṁhitā, 85
Suthānānga Sūtra, 29
Śvetāśvatāra upaṇsad, 8

Taittirīya Brāhmaṇa, 26, 76
Taittirīya Saṁhitā, 3, 4, 29, 46n, 68
Tapovana, 8
Taruṇa Gaṇapati, 32
Tilaka, 78
Tillai tree, 99
Tiloyapannathi, 29, 105
Tree cult, 13
  -goddesses, 36
  woman, 18
  worship, 13, 35, 38
Tree of knowledge, 28
  of life
Tripurasundarī, 56
Tulsi (plant/leaves), 25, 41, 42, 52-54, 58, 86

Tumbaru, 35

Udumbara, 25, 28, 30, 40, 68, 79, 86, 95, 96
Uttānapād, 62

Vadari, 42
Vaiśāli, 28
Vaiśnavite temple, 100
Vaiśnavites, 41
Vakula, 78
Valliphala, 80
Vāmana Purāṇa, 36, 38, 83
Vanadeva, 13
Vana or Vṛkṣa 'trees', 7
Vanaspati, 7
Varāhamihira, 78, 79
Varāha Purāṇa, 47n, 78, 80
Vārtāku, 80
Vasantotsava, 72, 73
Vāstuka, 80
Vasyugam Ostiak (khanty), 5
Vaṭa (tree), 27, 33, 35-37, 51, 79, 80, 101
Vaṭamātaraḥ, 34
Vedas, 37, 42, 62
Vedic Aryans, 16
beliefs, 7
gods, 25
literature, 7, 104
Mahāvrata rites, 72
period, 26
Prajāpati, 18
rites, 3
sacrificial, 26
texts, 26, 27, 29
times, 33
Vihāra, 28
Vilvaḍaṇḍa, 31
Viṣṇu, 27, 36, 37, 39, 40-44, 51, 66, 100, 106
Viṣṇudharmottara Purāṇa, 32
Viṣṇu Purāṇa, 34, 36, 39, 46n
Vogel, J.Ph., 89n
Vṛhat Saṁhitā, 78
Vrindāvana, 36
Vṛkṣa Devi, 20
Devatā, 20
Vyāntara gods, 35

Ward, H.H., 21n
Werner, K., 45n
Williams, M., 46n, 48n, 66, 89n
Wilson, H.H., 46n, 47n
Wood-apple tree (bilva), 52

Yajurveda, 7, 62
Yamalārjuna tree, 102
Yoga Ratnākara, 85
Yoga Taraṅgiṇī, 85
Yoni, 62
Yūpa, 3

Zoroastrianism, 6
Zuni, 5

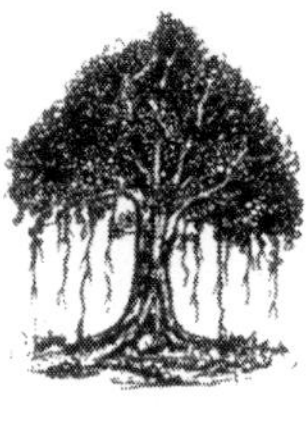

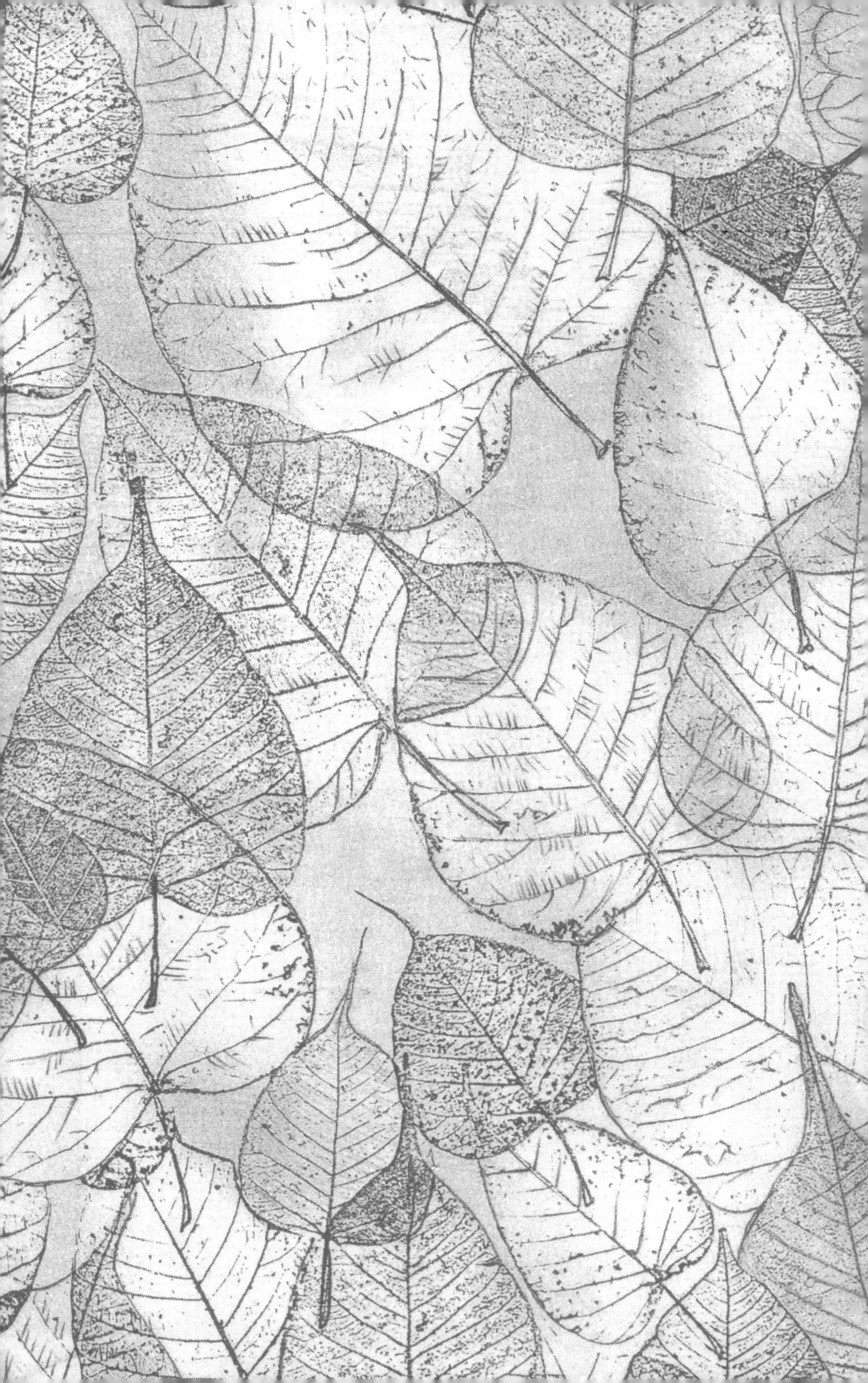